THE LUSITANIA
STORY

Also by Mitch Peeke and Kevin Walsh-Johnson

Lusitania and Beyond:
The Life of Commodore William Thomas Turner

THE LUSITANIA STORY

The Atrocity
That Shocked The World

by

**Mitch Peeke, Kevin Walsh-Johnson
and Steven Jones**

Pen & Sword
MARITIME

First published in Great Britain in 2002 by Leo Cooper
Reprinted in this format in 2015 by
Pen & Sword Maritime
An imprint of
Pen & Sword Books Ltd
47 Church Street
Barnsley
South Yorkshire
S70 2AS

ISBN 978 1 47383 270 1

Printed and bound in England
By CPI Group (UK) Ltd, Croydon, CR0 4YY

Pen & Sword Books Ltd incorporates the Imprints of Pen & Sword
Aviation, Pen & Sword Family History, Pen & Sword Maritime, Pen
& Sword Military, Pen & Sword Discovery, Pen & Sword Politics,
Pen & Sword Atlas, Pen & Sword Archaeology, Wharncliffe Local
History, Wharncliffe True Crime, Wharncliffe Transport, Pen &
Sword Select, Pen & Sword Military Classics, Leo Cooper, The
Praetorian Press, Claymore Press, Remember When, Seaforth
Publishing and Frontline Publishing.

For a complete list of Pen & Sword titles please contact
PEN & SWORD BOOKS LIMITED
47 Church Street, Barnsley, South Yorkshire, S70 2AS, England
E-mail: enquiries@pen-and-sword.co.uk
Website: www.pen-and-sword.co.uk

We would like to dedicate this book to:

The City and People of Liverpool, *Lusitania*'s hometown,
who do so much to keep the memory of her alive.

Jay, my wife who is my 'Sunshine on a rainy day' and whose
love, faith and support have always been to the fore.
(Even though she came *very* close to being
a '*Lusitania* widow' herself at times!)
Mitch

Sonja, my wife with much love and affection.
Kevin

Kim, my wife; also my children Sian and Matthew,
all of whom graciously endured the long hours
I spent on the computer!
Steven

Contents

Addendum 2014

by F Gregg Bemis Jnr. Legal owner of the RMS Lusitania.

In writing this addendum to my original Foreword of thirteen years ago, it seems pertinent to put the subsequent efforts into the record. There are two essential elements to the historical research. One is whether or not she was a legitimate target for the German U-Boat, and the second is the question of what caused the massive second explosion sinking the Lusitania in only 18 minutes with the resulting extraordinary loss of 1,201 lives.

Regarding the first question, several years ago after publication of the first edition of this book, Irish divers located, recovered samples, and subsequently filmed the approximately 3 million rounds of 303 rifle ammunition headed for the front lines. This vast amount of 'war material' under the then rules of war, without a doubt legitimized the Lusitania as a target. The second conundrum concerning the location and cause of the second explosion, following the single torpedo, which sank her unbelievably quickly has been the remaining mystery.

I have been dedicated to the resolution of this historically pertinent matter. Theories abound but proof has been elusive. Government cover-ups of factual history are a curse against civility and humanity. The Lusitania and all of its history except for the second explosion, is well documented and understood. She bears none of the characteristics of an 'archaeological' site and yet a small mindless department of the Irish Government has blocked for 18 years any realistic efforts at proper underwater research into the location and cause of the explosion.

With the 1987 revision of the International "Law of the Seas", she lies in Irish waters, not in international waters. Under the Treaty, Ireland has the right of control over activities in her waters. At a depth of 300 feet (90 meters), very few people will ever get to visit her. As the tragedy which ultimately brought America into WW I with its effect on the outcome of European history, it holds an important role. Blockage of the truth about the sinking is a disgraceful and unjustified misapplication of the rights granted by the Law of the Sea. While the authors of this book have accomplished a great deal with their incredible research and analysis, in situ examination in some degree of thoroughness, would seem desirable, possible, and of vastly greater benefit than the perpetuation of a possible cover-up in which the Irish Government is assisting. Let us hope for enlightenment.

Preface to the Centenary Edition

It has now been 100 years since Friday 7 May 1915; that fateful day during the First World War, when Kapitan-Leutnant Walther Schwieger, commanding the German submarine *U20*, torpedoed and sank the 45,000 ton Cunard liner RMS *Lusitania* with the loss of 1,201 lives. The last survivor of that disaster, a passenger on the *Lusitania* by the name of Audrey Lawson Johnston, died just over four years ago, but the story of the *Lusitania* certainly did not die with her; far from it. In fact, in the thirteen years since this book was first published in England and the United States, our website, *www.lusitania.net* and the interest in it, has grown considerably; worldwide.

Those same thirteen years have seen us being asked to act as historical advisors to several television channels on both sides of the Atlantic, as well as independent filmmakers and even mainstream radio stations. We have also provided images and information to countless magazines, university and college students and other, private individuals. Above all, we have continued to research various aspects of the ship and her people. In December of 2012, we at last acquired a certified copy of the full, 27-page Supplementary Cargo Manifest for her last voyage from President Roosevelt's personal archive. That document has been akin to the Holy Grail in *Lusitania* historical circles ever since she was sunk, and thanks to our dealings with the staff at President Roosevelt's archive, it is now finally and above all, freely; available for public viewing on *www.lusitania.net*. We have also passed free copies to other trusted sites.

At about the same time, we further discovered that the British Naval Intelligence ledger for *U20*'s activities was also available online. Furthermore, an accurate computer simulation of *U20*'s attack on the *Lusitania* has been performed in Germany and an enduring myth concerning one of *U20*'s crew has now finally been examined and an irrefutable conclusion reached. Details of all these new developments can be found in this updated centenary edition.

We are by no means the only ones to have kept busy since the first edition of this book. Gregg Bemis has had several of the more popular theories as to the cause of the ship's foundering, tested to destruction, literally, in a US Government laboratory. Meanwhile, his dive teams have continued to regularly survey the wreck in fantastic detail over those same thirteen years and we've watched in awe as they brought up their first and subsequent finds of the ammunition that she was known to be carrying, from the *Lusitania*'s grave.

The public have been busy, too. We've never ceased to be amazed by the many people who, again over those same thirteen years, have contacted us via the website, with images and stories of relatives who were involved or otherwise connected with the disaster and images of items of memorabilia from the ship (and there was one very notable case when a fairly large artefact was physically sent to us all the way from Australia! We donated it to the Merseyside Maritime Museum in Liverpool). Indeed, the *Memorabilia* page of our website has almost tripled its content since it was first created and has in fact reached its capacity. Public interest in the story of the *Lusitania* truly remains unabated.

It was precisely because of this interest that a centenary edition of this book was planned. As a result of our further researches, there are important new appendices to the original 2002 edition and there are also more photographs. The main text of the book however, remains largely unchanged. This is because even after thirteen more years of research, deliberation and debate, we still believe that this was pretty much the way it happened. So far, nothing has come to light to even remotely suggest otherwise, and what has come to light only seems to confirm what we originally wrote. Other *Lusitania* books, both in 2002 and since, have come and gone; but this book steadfastly remains where it always was, as indeed does our website. We sincerely hope you enjoy this centenary edition of a truly remarkable story. A story that has certainly withstood the test of time: **The Lusitania Story**.

Mitch Peeke and Steve Jones.

Acknowledgements

We would particularly like to acknowledge the tremendous help and information given to us by the following institutions:

National Maritime Museum, London, Merseyside Maritime Museum, Liverpool, New York Public Library, The Museum of the City of New York, University of Liverpool (Cunard archives), Public Record Office, London, Archives department of Hill, Dickinson & Co. (Cunard's lawyers).

On a much more personal level we would like to thank:

Stephen Rodgers of GE Power Systems, Clydebank, (Formerly John Brown Engineering Ltd), Helmut Doeringhoff of the Bundesmilitärarchiv in Freiburg, Germany, Mrs Margaret Phillips of Kent County Library Services, Don Blows, for his computer work, Peter Engberg-Klarstrom, of the Scandinavian *Titanic* Society, Chief Engineer David Garstin RN (retired) who was a font of knowledge regarding the *Lusitania*'s turbine engines, Dr John Bullen, Maritime Curator of the Imperial War Museum, London, Stan Walter, former curator of the Royal Artillery Museum, London, Colonel J. M. Phillips, BA MsocSC and his staff, of the Royal Artillery Historical Trust, Frederick Peeke, a former gunner with the Royal Artillery, Geoff Whitfield, Honorary Secretary of the British *Titanic* Society, whose invaluable research has made the passenger and crew list the comprehensive document that it now is and Peter Boyd-Smith of Cobwebs, Southampton, for allowing us to photograph the Lusitania artefacts in his possession and to use those photographs in this book. Lastly, though by no means least our sincere thanks and everlasting gratitude to F. Gregg Bemis Jr. for his continued support, for writing the foreword to this book and for his much-valued cooperation with the chapter 'The wreck of the *Lusitania*'.

A very special thank you to Richard Heier, Bernd Langensiepen of *Der Marine Nachrichten Blatt* and Ralf Bartzke. Also Tom, at *www.uboataces.com*. Cuxhaven U-Boat Archive, Germany. *The New York Times* Archive. Strandings Museum, Thorsminde, Denmark. Kinsale Museum, Ireland. NARA. Megan Halsband at the US Library of Congress. William Baehr at the Franklin D. Roosevelt Presidential Archive and Library. US Customs Archives. Mr Ray Brooks, MD of Intrada Ships Management, at Chatham Maritime, Kent. The late Sally Wells, (who was a relative of Captain Turner), and her family. George Cogswell. Kevin Roach. David Grew. (G'Day, Mate!)

Introduction

RMS *Lusitania*. The very mention of her name summons a vision of disaster. Ask anyone what they know of the *Lusitania* and the vague reply will invariably be something like, 'Wasn't that the big liner the Germans sank? First World War, wasn't it?' Others may even go so far as to confuse the *Lusitania* with the ill-fated *Titanic*, or they may tell you that it was the sinking of the *Lusitania* that brought America into the war. Or was that Pearl Harbour? Can't remember now.

Prior to 1915 however, the mention of RMS *Lusitania* to anyone then living would not have brought any vague reply. Everyone knew of her, for she and her sister ship, RMS *Mauretania*, were the pride of the Cunard Line and supreme proof, if proof were needed, that Britannia, through her Royal and Merchant fleets, did indeed rule the waves.

But it was so long ago now, beyond living memory almost. And yet there remains a marked degree of mystique surrounding the *Lusitania*. With the *Titanic* story now patently suffering from overkill, media and public interest is rapidly turning toward the largely forgotten *Lusitania*. Sadly though, few will bother to look beyond the disaster of Friday, 7 May 1915. Hardly anyone will take the time to look at the *Lusitania*'s real story, which actually starts in 1902. The events of that fateful Friday have completely blocked the view of her previous life and career, of her great achievements and the groundbreaking advances in the technology of her day that she represented.

Is this the mystique of the *Lusitania*? Undoubtedly for some it is, whilst for others, there is all the allure of a great sunken ship and the many rumours that will always surround such a vessel, such as the popular myth that like almost any lost ship, she was supposedly carrying an absolute fortune in gold bullion. Could it perhaps be all the 'If only's' that attend the story of her final voyage? If only Captain Turner or *Kapitänleutnant* Schwieger had taken different courses of action. If only the torpedo had hit her elsewhere. If only the Admiralty had provided an effective escort for her. If only she hadn't been carrying munitions.

The sinking of the *Lusitania*, unlike that of the *Titanic*, was a totally man-made disaster, a deliberate act and therefore a much bigger event in world history. The *Titanic* disaster held far-reaching consequences for the hitherto complacent sphere of maritime safety regulations. The *Lusitania* disaster held far-reaching consequences for the complacency of human nature, as well as world history.

Yet for all this, her story, like the ship herself, seems to have been largely forgotten for some strange reason and for us at least, this is the ultimate mystique of the *Lusitania*. This is what made us want to write this book.

Until now, if one had wanted to read her complete story, one would have to study at least six different books, all of which will throw differing opinions at the reader. One would then have to make a determined attempt to sort the wheat from the chaff, in order just to begin building a picture of this truly fascinating ship for oneself.

Unlike the story of the *Titanic*, no blockbuster movie has ever been made about the *Lusitania*, even though her loss was the much bigger event. Of the few television documentaries that have been made, most, if not all, stop short of telling anything like her full story for fear of the controversy that still surrounds her loss.

In the *Lusitania* story, one has all the classic ingredients of an enduring tale: a good sea story, a remarkable technical achievement, a study of the social history of her era, shipwreck on a grand scale and an epic 'whodunit?' complete with high-level cover-up. Her story is all the more fascinating for being fact rather than fiction.

In this book, we have tried to bring the best of these ingredients together for the first time into a single volume, to tell the truly absorbing story of a long-forgotten ship and her people. We believe this to be a story that the world has been waiting for, perhaps without even realizing that it *has* been waiting. So here then, for the first time, is her complete story from conception to sinking. It is a cradle to the grave account of one of the most remarkable ships ever to have graced the deep ocean. The RMS *Lusitania*.

Forces of Creation

The start of the twentieth century heralded many new inventions and many new ideas. It was a time of wonder; a time when what often seemed impossible on one day, became a reality the next. The motor car, powered flight, electric light, the gramophone, the telephone, all were perfect examples of this 'great age of miracles'; a time of man's seemingly unstoppable progress in technology.

Britain was then at the forefront of world affairs and her shipbuilding, railway and heavy engineering industries were unrivalled anywhere. The British Empire was at the zenith of its influence during this period, which also saw sharp social contrasts at home. The rich were quite secure in their affluence and the poor were largely content to watch and wonder at them with reverence. The middle class sat where their name suggested, comfortably watching both extremes; aspiring to one, yet reviling the other. In this pre-Hollywood era, the rich and titled served as all the celebrity value that the working classes required. People who had wealth had never had it so good, and they took a great delight in their public display of it.

But 'the Gilded Age' as it became known, also signalled the end of many long-held beliefs, one of these being that as Britannia firmly ruled the waves and would do so for the foreseeable future, no other nation would even contemplate building a navy as strong or stronger than Britain's.

Ever since the Battle of Trafalgar in 1805, the British had considered that having the strongest navy in the world was of the utmost importance for trade, as well as being a matter of extreme national pride. There were few men in the British Admiralty who could see that things were changing, and that unless Britain did something quickly, she would be overtaken by new 'upstart' seafaring nations such as Germany.

1

Kaiser Wilhelm II's Germany was growing in world stature day by day. As Queen Victoria's grandson, Wilhelm felt that Germany should not live in the shadow of the British Empire but take what he deemed to be her rightful place in world affairs. He felt that with German industry also booming, it was only fitting that Germany should possess an Empire of her own.

Kaiser Wilhelm knew that the lynchpin of his grandmother's Empire was the Royal Navy, 'the police force of the Empire', guarding British trade and foreign interests. The Royal Navy had an envied worldwide reputation for its invincibility, and Kaiser Wilhelm knew that for any major power with colonial interests, sea power was the all-important factor. He therefore wanted an 'invincible' navy too. In the forthcoming years, Germany embarked upon an ambitious naval shipbuilding programme in an attempt to reach parity with the Royal Navy.

In the meantime, Germany's two great shipping lines, the Norddeutscher-Lloyd Line and the Hamburg-Amerika Line, constantly vied with each other to build the largest and fastest steamers the world had ever seen. These mighty four-funnelled express liners soon became household names; *Kaiser Wilhelm der Grosse*, *Deutschland*, *Kaiser Wilhelm II*, to name but three, all served to put German prestige foremost. By capturing and holding the Blue Riband for the fastest crossing of the North Atlantic from Britain's Cunard line, the Germans badly dented British national pride. The British were not going to sit back and watch while the German liners dominated the Atlantic and the Kaiser built his 'invincible' Navy.

One feature of all the German express liners was the fact that they were designed for swift conversion into armed merchant cruisers in the event of war. Given the aggressiveness of the Kaiser's new *Weltpolitik* (world policy), this was a distinctly worrying feature for the British Admiralty.

But if the British Admiralty found Kaiser Wilhelm II of Germany a cause for sleepless nights, the actions of an American banker by the name of J.P. Morgan Jr. were about to cause them apoplexy.

By the end of 1902, J.P. Morgan Jr. had successfully taken over the two premier German lines as well as the British-owned White Star Line, Leyland Line and Dominion Line. He already owned the American Line, and he now merged all of these acquisitions into one giant combine called the International Mercantile Marine

Company, with the express intention of monopolizing the North Atlantic trade.

Though it had been a narrow squeak, the Cunard Line had managed to fend off Morgan's takeover bid, but the British Admiralty were perplexed by the thought that almost all of their 'reserve forces' (the Merchant Navy) had now come under foreign control. This situation caused the Admiralty and the board of Cunard to enter into intense negotiations that would secure the futures of both parties.

The Cunard Company had continued to grow, along with the mail subsidies from the Admiralty, ever since Samuel Cunard had formed his company in 1840. This arrangement now culminated in a binding agreement that was finalized in 1903, and would tie the two parties together for the next twenty years. The public copy of the agreement is open to inspection in the Cunard archives at Liverpool University. The conditions placed upon Cunard by this agreement were said to be 'as prolix as they were onerous'. Cunard prepared a lengthy memo at the time, outlining their obligations under the agreement, relevant excerpts of which are reproduced as an appendix at the end of this book.

The agreement left Cunard at the mercy of the British Admiralty in all aspects of their shipbuilding programme, and the Cunard fleet placed at the disposal of the Admiralty in time of war. It also meant a further increase in mail subsidies and a government loan of £2.6 million at the most unusual interest rate of a mere two and three-quarter per cent over the twenty-year span of the agreement. The monies were to enable Cunard to build two new ships. They were to be the *Lusitania* and the *Mauretania*.

So it was that RMS *Lusitania* was conceived, out of the Royal Navy's need and with the British public's money.

Design

One of the earliest projected designs for the *Lusitania* depicted a three-funnelled ship. This was because nobody at that stage had envisaged a quadruple screw arrangement for the proposed new vessels. After careful consideration of all the submitted designs, Cunard decided to proceed with their own design department's vision. Given that the Admiralty's design department laid down the hull specifications to which Cunard would have to adhere, and that the two departments would of necessity be working closely together, the Admiralty had no objection to Cunard's decision.

The design brief handed to Cunard's chief designer, Leonard Peskett, was a formidable one. In essence, his task was to combine the requirements of a naval cruiser and an express Atlantic liner into the one vessel. A floating 'Grand Hotel' for 3,000 passengers and crew, that was also capable of crossing the Atlantic Ocean at an average speed of 24 knots and mounting a battery of twelve 6-inch guns!

Peskett was effectively faced with the task of 'welding' the bottom third of the latest Admiralty design for a heavy cruiser, to the top two-thirds of a super-liner. Therefore, to understand the design aspects of the *Lusitania*, it is essential that we split the ship in the same fashion and look at each separate entity before the two are put together and viewed as a whole.

The first stipulation made by the Admiralty was the minimum average speed of 24 knots. This overriding stipulation in fact governed the design shape of the proposed vessel, which had resulted in a design that would have an overall length of 785 feet and a beam of 78 feet. Calculations had then been made as to the requisite horsepower rating needed for the projected vessel to attain this speed and it had been calculated as being a minimum of 68,000.

After extensive testing of various scale models by Dr R.E. Froude, in the Admiralty's ship experiments tank at Haslar, near Portsmouth, it was found that due to the unusually high freeboard of the proposed design, the first models were extremely unstable and displayed a marked tendency to capsize. This factor resulted in the beam measurement of the full-scale design having to be increased by 10 feet, which proved to be just enough to stabilize the ship.

Dr Froude also found that a quadruple screw model performed best. It was thought that the shafts of a triple screw design might not have been able to withstand the constant loading of the 22,600 or more projected horsepower on each shaft, whereas a quadruple screw arrangement reduced the projected load to 17,000 HP per shaft. The tests had also shown that efficiency was maximized if the outer propellers rotated inwards whilst the inner propellers rotated outwards. Given these factors, the earlier three-funnelled, triple screw prototype was therefore abandoned.

The advent of the marine steam turbine engine, invented by Charles Parsons and so ably demonstrated by him at the Spithead Naval Review of 1897, when he audaciously piloted his tiny craft, *Turbinia*, through the ranks of assembled warships at the astonishing speed of 34 knots, outrunning every fast gunboat the Navy tried to pursue him with, meant that traditional views on the subject of marine propulsion were visibly and most publicly challenged.

However, despite *Turbinia*'s impressive performance, Parsons had only just managed to overcome the enormous problem of how to put the sheer power his turbine engine produced, into the water effectively. Propellers work best when rotated slowly. The optimum speed is in fact less than 100rpm. Parsons' turbine engine produced a shaft speed far in excess of this figure. The answer to this fundamental problem was reduction gearing, but the technology to build such large, and above all reliable, gearboxes wasn't available till 1916. Parsons overcame this problem on *Turbinia* by fitting her with three shafts, each carrying three propellers, but it was a problem that would resurface with the *Lusitania*'s turbine installation.

However, it was fortunate that visionaries like the Admiralty's First Sea Lord, John Fisher, and indeed George Burns, better known as Lord Inverclyde, chairman of the Cunard Line, were quick to realize the amazing potential of Parsons' invention. Fisher revolutionized Naval thinking with the all big gun, turbine-powered HMS *Dreadnought* which was completed in December 1906. Lord Inverclyde revolutionized the board of Cunard's thinking, which resulted in two ships that became known as the 'pretty sisters' entering service with Cunard in 1905.

HMS *Dreadnought* proved to be a resounding success for the Admiralty, once a few 'teething troubles' had been resolved. Therefore in March of 1904, the committee that Cunard and the Admiralty had specially appointed to consider the question of the most suitable propulsion for the two new Cunard ships, decided in favour of utilizing the revolutionary new turbine engines in the *Lusitania* and her sister, *Mauretania*.

In 1905, the 'pretty sisters', *Carmania* and *Caronia*, entered service with Cunard. Both vessels were 676 feet long and both were 20,000 gross registered tons. In *Caronia*, they had specified traditional quadruple expansion reciprocating engines, whilst in *Carmania* the new Parsons' steam turbine engines had been specified. *Carmania* was Cunard's test bed for the new engines.

Carmania soon proved to be the faster under actual service conditions and more economical than *Caronia* to run. The possible short-term reliability problems that Cunard had envisaged with the all-new turbine engines, had largely failed to materialize. Having now taken a firm decision on the question of propulsion, attention was turned toward the actual design of the new vessels.

The Admiralty's design specification for a heavy cruiser required all such vital machinery as engines, boilers, main condensers and steering gear to be located below the waterline, safe from enemy gunfire. The four massive turbine engines that propelled the ship, together with the separate steering engine for turning the equally large rudder, occupied fully one third of the ship's length at the aft end. To supply the turbines with steam at the 195 pounds per square inch pressure needed to drive them, twenty-three double-ended boilers and two single-ended boilers containing a total of 192 furnaces, were arranged in rows across the ship, and the space they occupied was divided into four massive boiler rooms.

Ahead of the forward most boiler room was a huge coalbunker that ran clear across the ship, the height of which was from the keel to the waterline, approximately 30 feet. The next compartment forward was the cargo hold, which in time of war could be converted into the forward magazine if the ship was ever to be used as a cruiser. Next came the chain locker for the huge anchor chains and finally, two trimming tanks for ballasting purposes.

To return to the four massive boiler rooms; each had to be a separate watertight compartment. Here, a problem arose. Each room was far too large to permit buoyancy if flooded, so longitudinal bulkheads were fitted along the outer sides, creating large watertight compartments between the outside of the ship and the boiler rooms. The whole ship was divided into twelve watertight compartments by eleven transverse bulkheads, each with watertight doors, and the watertight compartments flanking the boiler rooms were sub-divided, in accordance with the Admiralty's cruiser specifications. This meant that the *Lusitania* was a 'two-compartment' ship. That is to say, she would stay afloat with any two compartments open to the sea. With more compartments flooded, she would sink.

However, a problem of storage space within the projected bottom now made itself apparent. The coalbunker at the forward end of the ship, though huge, would not be large enough to accommodate the minimum tonnage of coal needed to drive the ship on one single Atlantic crossing. Therefore, another Admiralty measure, and ultimately a fatal one, was adopted. The sixteen watertight compartments flanking the four boiler rooms would be used as the necessary additional bunkers. The Admiralty had adopted this practice in their cruisers some years previously. They were of the considered opinion that filling such compartments with coal gave added protection from enemy gunfire, as well as saving space. However, allowance must be made for the fact that in 1903, the mine or the possibility of a torpedo attack upon the vessel, were not eventualities that were actively considered by the Admiralty.

The fatal flaw in the line of thought about using coal as protection, lay in the fact that filling these watertight spaces with hundreds of tons of coal meant that apertures now had to be cut into the inboard side of each compartment in order to draw the coal. These apertures were then fitted with watertight hatches. However, once opened in order to draw the coal needed to feed the ever-hungry furnaces, these hatches could not be closed again, due to the sheer weight of the coal behind bearing upon them. The system of watertight compartments so carefully designed to keep the *Lusitania* afloat in any emergency, had just been instantly and very effectively bypassed, and nobody had realized the fact. Not Peskett, not even the ever-watchful Admiralty.

Still under Admiralty scrutiny, Peskett's ship design was given a double bottom and then attention was turned to the stern section. Because of the Naval duties envisaged for the ship, the *Lusitania* had to be more manoeuvrable than the average Atlantic liner, so another Naval design feature was adopted to aid this aim. The area at the bottom of the stern forward of the rudder, known in marine architecture as the 'deadwood', was cut away in the shape of an arch. At the aft end of this arch, a rudder of purely Naval design was fitted. These features, combined with a form of 'power steering', meant that not only would the *Lusitania* respond to her helm far more quickly than an ordinary passenger liner of that era could ever hope to, she could also make tighter turns than the ordinary liner. The design for the warship bottom was now regarded as complete and having seemingly satisfied the bulk of the Admiralty's needs, Peskett now turned his attention to those of Cunard.

On top of the Admiralty cruiser's power platform, Peskett had to design a floating five star hotel, and the only way he could go was up. In order to carry a sufficient number of fare paying passengers to make the ship remotely viable, Leonard Peskett raised not the more usual four decks, but six decks, designated A to F, with F deck being the lowest. It was this arrangement that gave the *Lusitania* and her sister their unusually high freeboard.

Cunard had stipulated that the passenger accommodation was to be unrivalled anywhere and was to be unbelievably spacious, whilst setting new standards in comfort and luxury at sea. Following the tiered class system so prevalent in the Edwardian era, most of the first-class accommodation was on the topmost decks, amidships. The second-class accommodation was mainly at the aft end of the ship and at the very bottom, forward, was most of the third-class, or 'steerage', as it was more popularly known. In all classes, the design for the accommodations aboard the *Lusitania* surpassed anything that had previously been seen on the North Atlantic. Third-class on the *Lusitania*, people later said, was as good as first-class on any other ship. The same remark was made later, with the advent of the White Star Line's *Olympic*, and was used yet again to describe the third-class appointments of the *Titanic*. One is left to wonder whether this oft repeated remark came from the press or possibly even the builders' publicity departments. However it originated, one can't help thinking that it is extremely unlikely that this remark ever came from anyone actually travelling in third-class on any of those ships!

Peskett's design plans included electric lifts for passengers, (the first afloat) refrigeration plant, an early form of air conditioning, reading rooms, writing rooms, spacious dining saloons, smoking rooms, an onboard hospital, a children's dining saloon and nursery and grand entrance halls and staircases, the like of which were previously the exclusive preserve of the world's finest hotels.

Continuing the theme of the world's finest hotel afloat, there would be teams of stewards on hand to attend to every need of the travelling public; a battery of domestic staff to keep the staterooms, cabins and public areas clean and a ship's orchestra composed of the finest musicians the Cunard Line could procure. The *Lusitania*, and her sister *Mauretania*, would be the pride of Britain and the envy of the world.

In terms of the external appearance of the two ships, it had earlier been decided that these two revolutionary ships would each have to have four funnels anyway. All the German express liners had four, so Cunard's new flagships could hardly have less. Also, thanks to the German express liners, the travelling public, for some inexplicable reason, had come to regard the number of funnels a ship had as being a good indicator of its speed and safety. As a result of this quirk, the vast majority of first- and second-class passengers therefore preferred to book passage on the four-funnelled liners.

With basic blueprints drawn up, Cunard looked for suitable, reputable builders to bring their dreams to fruition. As it had already been decided to build the two great ships simultaneously, it was thought best to have the ships built in two different yards. The contract to build the *Mauretania* was awarded to the Tyneside yard of Messrs. Swan, Hunter & Wigham, Richardson, whilst John Brown and Co. Ltd. of Clydebank, Scotland, were awarded the contract to build the *Lusitania*. It is to John Brown's yard that our story now turns.

Building the Dream

Founded in 1850, John Brown and Co. Ltd. of Sheffield soon grew into one of the foremost heavy engineering companies in the United Kingdom. In 1899, the company sought to expand its activities into the shipbuilding industry. Prepared to pay a handsome price for a going concern, the search led them to acquire the Clydebank yard of J. & G. Thompson, already renowned as builders of fast, top of the range steamers for the Inman Line as well as Cunard.

By 1905, John Brown's yard had become vastly experienced in the building of warships for several of the world's navies as well as big Atlantic steamers like the pioneering *Carmania*, for Cunard. But the building of the *Lusitania* was an altogether bigger proposition than even Brown's had become accustomed. However, someone at John Brown's was astute enough to realize that the *Lusitania*, landmark that she was going to be, was merely the beginning of the next, and most expensive, phase in a great competition.

Cunard's rival, the White Star Line, would not be content to sit back and watch Cunard steal the thunder. Given their American backers, (J.P. Morgan's great combine, the IMM Company) White Star would undoubtedly embark upon a shipbuilding programme to better Cunard's.

The White Star Line had all their ships built at the Belfast yard of Messrs. Harland and Wolff. Their relationship was quite unique. Harland and Wolff built White Star's ships on a 'cost-plus' basis. That is to say, all the ships were built to White Star's specification regardless of cost, plus whatever Harland and Wolff wanted to charge as a mark-up. White Star never used any other builder and in return, Harland and Wolff would never build a ship for a rival of the White Star Line.

But in 1905, realizing what was about to take place between the two great shipping lines, John Brown's and Harland and Wolff, quietly 'joined forces', though for obvious reasons each company retained its own corporate identity. An equal holding of shares in each company was discreetly transferred to the other, so that neither had a controlling interest. Henceforth, John Brown's held a stake in Harland and Wolff, and vice versa. It was this outstanding joint expertise that would be used to build the *Lusitania*, and later the *Aquitania*, for the Cunard Line, as well as *Olympic*, *Titanic* and *Britannic*, for the White Star Line.

The very first consideration from the builders' point of view was strength, or more accurately, stress. The vast hull, during its construction on the slip, would of course be totally unsupported by water. Due to their collective experience of shipbuilding, they were quite confident that the leviathan would not collapse during building, but the seagoing stress of such a mammoth vessel was quite another matter. With a design length of 785 feet overall, they were concerned that in the turbulent seaway of the North Atlantic Ocean, such a lengthy vessel might well sag in the middle. To that end, a team of stress engineers got to work on the task of calculating the maximum likely stress on the vessel's upper plating in the midship section under the worst possible conditions. As it transpired, their calculations showed that the mild steel plating that they normally used for shipbuilding was more than able to cope with the projected stresses. However, Brown's discovered that there was a new type of high tensile steel that was thirty-six per cent stronger than the usual mild steel they used. If they then reduced the thickness of each plate to seven-eighths of an inch instead of the normal one-inch thickness, a substantial saving in weight was achieved whilst resulting in a plate that was still twenty-six per cent stronger than the usual mild steel plate. To provide added insurance against the projected stress forces, all of the high tensile steel plates would be treble-riveted using hydraulic riveters.

Construction of the hull on the slip was commenced in March of 1905, with Lord Inverclyde ceremoniously hammering the very first rivet home, thereby starting the laying of the keel. The ship's cellular double bottom was then constructed. At the early stages of the ship's construction, the largest weight of any individual component was four tons and to handle this, electric jigger cranes were purchased from W. Arrol and Co. Ltd. Lighter loads were moved in wagons on standard gauge railway track laid beside the slipway and later, on the deck-plating itself. This method of ship construction may strike one as being rather primitive, but it proved to be remarkably efficient as well as extremely cost-effective.

The hull construction progressed at a remarkable pace. The bow section was completed first and then the construction gradually moved aft. This in itself was unusual, as it was the custom to start both ends simultaneously and meet in the middle, but the chief reason for leaving the stern section till last was to give the design team more time to plan the layout of the vast engine rooms.

Everything about the *Lusitania* was big. From the four immense shafts that would drive the incredible 17-feet diameter, three-bladed propellers, each one of which would weigh a staggering 21 tons, to the two 10¼-ton stockless bower anchors, each on a 330 fathom chain that weighed 125 tons. N. Hingley and Sons, Ltd. specially made the anchors and chains. Napier Brothers Ltd. of Glasgow constructed the equally huge steam-driven capstans needed to raise and lower such heavy gear. The ships twenty-five boilers, each of which was 17½ feet in diameter, were under construction in the yard's own engineering unit.

The drums, shafts and spindles for the 25-feet long turbine engines were being constructed at John Brown's Atlas works in Sheffield, whilst the 12-feet diameter turbine rotors were being built at the Clydebank yard. The rotors, and therefore the engines themselves had to be built on such a large-scale in an attempt to keep the shaft speed as low as possible. That fundamental problem of needing a low propeller speed had of course still not been totally solved, and until the advent of reliable reduction gearboxes, it was only ever going to be a compromise, as direct drive was the only option with turbine propulsion at that time.

Brown Brothers Ltd. of Edinburgh, were contracted to manu-facture the steam-powered steering gear. The balanced rudder, which weighed 56 tons when completed, was turned by means of a large steering engine acting upon a worm gear, which in turn operated a friction clutch and spur gear. This arrangement moved a large quadrant-shaped rack that was made of steel. The rack had been cast in three sections and bolted together so that any section showing worn teeth could be easily replaced without involving a major strip-down of the whole assembly. The rack operated connecting rods to the tiller head. With the wheel hard over, the rudder would be able to attain 35 degrees of helm to either the port or starboard hand. There was also to be a reserve steering engine, which would operate heavy chains to move the rack, in case of any breakdown in the main steering engine.

Fourteen months and three weeks after Lord Inverclyde had ceremoniously hammered the first rivet home on *Lusitania*'s keel the hull, now weighing nearly 16,000 tons, was ready for launching. The launch date was in fact eight weeks later than had been originally planned, due to strike action. Sadly, Lord Inverclyde did not live to see the *Lusitania*. He died on 8 October 1905, just eight months before the launching ceremony took place.

On 19 April 1906, the Cunard Company had formally requested that HRH the Princess Louise should do the company the honour of christening their new steamship '*Lusitania*'. On 7 May 1906, Captain Probert, equerry to Princess Louise, wrote to Cunard expressing the princess' great regret and disappointment at being unable to accept Cunard's invitation as she was otherwise engaged. Lord Inverclyde's widow Mary, Lady Inverclyde, would ultimately launch the ship in memory of her late husband, on Thursday, 7 June 1906.

Launch

The launching of such a large vessel had its own attendant problems. The question of the vessel's length of 785 feet had been considered before building was even commenced, as the River Clyde adjacent to John Brown's yard was only 610 feet wide. Therefore, the launching area was sited at the confluence of the Rivers Clyde and Cart. In order to give the *Lusitania* the maximum possible run off the slip, John Brown's had built a new slip for her on the areas previously taken up by two slipways, and had laid this new slip at an approximate angle of 40 degrees to the line of the river. This gave the *Lusitania* a clear run of almost 1,200 feet off the slipway, this last distance being made possible by the Clyde Trust, who cut the corners off the river confluence and carried out deepening and widening work in the channel required.

Another interesting problem that had fortunately been visualized early on was that of the concentrated downward force that would be brought to bear on the slipway as the stern section of the hull became water-borne. This would occur when the hull had travelled approximately 550 feet down the ways. The cradle of oak timbers that bore it would probably protect the hull itself, but at this crucial point of the short journey to the water, it was calculated that a possible twenty per cent increase in load would occur. To avoid the disastrous possibility of the *Lusitania* wrecking the slipway during the launch and possibly even breaking her back in the process, piles were sunk deep into this critical area when the foundations were dug. The piles were then bound with cross ties to distribute the extra loading, however momentary, more evenly.

The whole launching process depended upon the near simultaneous releasing of six trigger mechanisms that were electrically operated. As a precautionary measure, a workman was stationed at each of the triggers armed with a sledgehammer. Should any trigger fail to drop, the workman was to strike the heavy trigger lever with his hammer immediately.

So, on Thursday 7 June 1906, the great ship stood poised in her oaken cradle ready to meet her element for the first time. The hull had been freshly painted in Cunard's colours and the slipway shone in the warm June sun as it had been freshly greased with tons of tallow and soft soap that very morning. The 600 official guests crammed into the yard to witness the great event, while many more than that number lined the riverfront seeking the best view.

Signal flags had been strung between tall poles erected along both sides of the slipway, a Union Jack flew from an improvised flag-pole on the prow of the ship and the Red Ensign flew for the first time at her stern. The blades of the four giant propellers had been fitted with wooden covers to protect them during the launch and 1,000 tons of drag chains lay neatly arranged to arrest the great ship's progress once she was safely in the water. Everything was set.

The dignitaries took their places on the launching platform and as a hush fell over the assembled crowds the new Cunard chairman, Mr William Watson, made a short speech then handed the proceedings over to Lady Inverclyde. At precisely 12.30 hours Lady Inverclyde named the ship 'Lusitania', the old Roman Empire's name for Portugal, and activated the electric trigger circuit, which functioned perfectly as the ceremonial magnum of champagne broke against the ship's bow.

Amid great cheering, the Lusitania started down the ways and into the Clyde. The heavy oak timbers creaked and groaned, the drag chains clanked and rattled and a great roar went up as the 16,000 ton hull entered the water. Heavy rope and wire stays yanked the cradle off the hull and the drag chains, which had previously been used in launching I.K. Brunel's Great Eastern, brought the Lusitania to a halt with her bow only 110 feet out from the end of the slipway. The whole launch had taken exactly eighty-six seconds. Six tugs then took charge and moved the Lusitania to the fitting out berth a few yards up the river, where she would spend the next twelve months, while the 600 official guests sat down to a lavish luncheon in the yard's moulding loft.

After the meal, extensive toasting and speeches of hearty congratulation became the order of the day. The key speech of the afternoon was that given by Sir Charles McLaren, chairman of

John Brown and Co. Ltd. During his speech, Sir Charles told his audience that the *Lusitania* was, 'by far the largest vessel that has ever been put into water' and that her engine power would be sufficient to drive her across the Atlantic, 'at a speed only ever previously accomplished by a torpedo boat destroyer'. He then went on to outline her envisaged naval role, saying, 'This vessel is really the latest addition to the reserves of His Majesty's Navy. With only slight alterations she would become the fastest and most powerful cruiser in the world.' Then referring to the supremacy of the German liners, he finished by saying that, 'There is not a Briton anywhere who ought not to feel proud that this launch has placed Great Britain firmly in the forefront of marine architecture'.

Fitting Out

The fitting out berth at John Brown's yard was a large dock 750 feet long by 320 feet wide and had been designed to accommodate two vessels at any one time. John Brown's had erected two huge cranes each with a lifting capacity of 150 tons, at the open end of the dock, one on each side. Supplementing these two giant cranes was a variety of smaller, mobile cranes of 10- and 20-ton lifting capacities.

The newly launched *Lusitania* was berthed on the east side of the dock, in the shadow of the 150 ton derrick crane supplied by W. Arrol and Co. Ltd. This crane would be needed to lower the mighty turbine engines and the twenty-five boilers into position in their respective rooms before the deck work above was completed.

Once the main machinery had been installed, an army of craftsmen such as electricians, engineers, welders, plumbers, carpenters, joiners, fitters, decorators and plasterers went to work to finish the ship. The superstructure had firstly to be built and only then could work truly begin on the lavish interiors.

As early as 1905, Lord Inverclyde had decided that such magnificent vessels as the *Lusitania* and the *Mauretania* should have their interiors designed by leading architects, despite the fact that traditional ship outfitters such as Waring and Gillow were anxious to secure exclusive contracts for both ships.

Lord Inverclyde saw no necessity to have both ships fitted out identically, so he persuaded the board of Cunard to employ two different architects. The board readily agreed and so Lord Inverclyde chose Harold Peto, famous for his work in leading English country houses, for the *Mauretania* and a young Scottish architect by the name of James Millar for the *Lusitania*.

James Millar was by then very well known and admired as the architect of the 1901 Glasgow Exhibition. He felt both thrilled and honoured to be given the commission and readily signed the contract with Cunard. Once he was in receipt of Peskett's plans he set to work with a passion, unlike Peto who very nearly lost his commission. From the start, Peto took a very high-handed stance by demanding a fee of £8,000. After some very tense negotiations with the board of Cunard, Peto eventually settled for a fee of £4,000 after an angered Lord Inverclyde, who had resolutely withheld the plans for the ship from Peto, told him to take it or leave it.

Both architects opted for the much admired 'period style'. In the *Lusitania*'s first- and second-class sections, Millar went for a mixture of Louis XVI, Queen Anne, William and Mary, Sheraton, Empire, English and Colonial Adamesque and Georgian styles, whilst third-class was in a style that might possibly have been called 'luxuriously utilitarian', if such a label exists!

Although working along similar lines, Millar and Peto actually worked independently of each other. The chief difference between their styles was Millar's extensive use of plasterwork, which ultimately gave the interior of the *Lusitania* a beautifully light and airy feel that proved to be extremely popular with the passengers. Peto on the other hand, had made extensive use of dark wood panelling which, though elegant, gave the interior of the *Mauretania*, a rather dark and slightly oppressive atmosphere.

Millar's masterpiece was undoubtedly the spectacular first-class dining saloon that occupied two decks, though the first-class lounge came an extremely close second.

The lower deck of the first-class dining saloon measured 85 feet in length, 81 feet in width and could accommodate 323 passengers in a single sitting. There was a mahogany sideboard for the cutlery and other tableware, which in itself was 17 feet long.

The upper deck was smaller being 65 feet square, and it too had a mahogany sideboard that was only six inches shorter than its counterpart on the lower deck. The upper deck could seat 147 passengers. The dominating feature of the upper deck saloon was the central well overlooking the deck below. Above the upper deck, this well was capped by a magnificent elliptical plaster dome, which measured 29 feet by 23 feet and contained four oval panels painted in the style of Boucher.

Both levels were decorated in the Louis XVI style with ornately carved mahogany panels, which were white enamelled and then gilded. The floors were of light oak parquet and the upholstery was rose coloured.

The only feature that marred this otherwise splendid suite was the swivel chairs that were bolted to the floor at the tables. This feature was a leftover from Victorian steamers, but Cunard insisted upon retaining it. Unfortunately, this fixed arrangement of the dining saloon furniture meant that some passengers would have to sit too close to the table, whilst others were too distant. Few indeed were the passengers whose personal measurements coincided exactly with Cunard's specifications.

In Millar's other showcase, the first-class lounge, Georgian met Edwardian. The walls of the 68 feet by 55 feet room comprised of inlaid mahogany panels. The sumptuous carpet was jade green in colour with a yellow floral pattern and was supplied by Waring and Gillow, who still retained an interest in working on the two ships.

The room owed much of its pleasantness to the softly diffused lighting effect created by the huge barrel vaulted skylight. In true Millar style, the skylight rose to a height of 20 feet, contained twelve sets of stained glass windows by Oscar Patterson, each depicting a month of the year, and was finished in ornate plaster. At both the fore and aft ends of the lounge, under the ends of the skylight, stood a huge green marble fireplace 14 feet in height, each of which was crowned with enamel panels by Alexander Fisher.

In the first-class writing room and library, located on the boat deck, Millar opted for the eighteenth century style of the Adams brothers. The walls had beautifully carved pilasters and mouldings to space them out, with panels of light grey and cream silk brocade between. The windows all had etched glass and the curtains and valances were of Rose du Barri silk. The specially woven rose coloured carpet was designed to harmonize the surroundings. The chairs and writing tables were all mahogany and the upholstery on the chairs was the same material as the curtains. A large glass-fronted mahogany bookcase completed the picture.

The first-class passenger accommodation featured a choice between standard first-class cabins, or the eighty-seven special en-suite cabins that were appointed in various styles, but for the particularly wealthy, there were the Regal suites.

There were two sets of Regal suites, one on each side of the ship located on the promenade deck, forward. Both were fitted out in the style of Louis XVI, though not identically. These suites comprised of two bedrooms, a dining room, parlour, a small bathroom and an en suite water closet.

The port side Regal suite was based on the Petit Trianon at Versailles and may be used as an example, though to be honest, mere words are hardly likely to do it justice.

The dining room was panelled in walnut with burnished gold mouldings and the dining table and chairs matched the panelling of the walls. There was a marble fireplace and hearth complete with logs. The ceiling comprised white and gold panels, whilst the curtains were of green silk. A sliding glass screen led to the parlour, which was panelled in white with carved gilt mouldings and infilled with painted floral decoration. The curtains were of heliotrope and cream, whilst the mahogany furniture was upholstered in light green. The carpet in both rooms was also green in colour.

The two bedrooms were equally sumptuous, one being decorated in rose coloured silk panels with satinwood furniture inlaid with pale green, whilst the other was decorated in white and gold with Wedgwood cameos. The finishing touch was provided by the blue silk brocade curtains, which were embellished with floral sprays.

The *Lusitania*'s first-class appointments boasted every modern comfort and convenience that Cunard thought the first-class passenger could possibly require. Even such things as internal telephones as well as electric lighting and supplementary radiators were provided. Other comforts included two electric lifts running centrally through the four storey grand staircase and rising to the boat deck, 44 feet above the main deck entrance. At each of the four decks was a spacious hall, 24 feet in length that ran the full width of the ship. The hall on the boat deck was elegantly decorated in white and gold and was well supplied with lounge seats and chairs with rose coloured upholstery. There was even a marble fireplace installed as an added touch. First-class aboard the *Lusitania* was indeed unrivalled anywhere until, of course, the later advent of the White Star Line's *Olympic* and *Titanic*.

The second-class public rooms were really a less opulent version of those in first-class. The second-class lounge was in fact an innovation for Cunard, who did not ordinarily provide such a facility in second-class; but then, *Lusitania* and her sister were not ordinary ships.

The lounge measured 42 feet by 40 feet and was fitted out in mahogany. The furniture comprised comfortable settees, easy chairs and mahogany coffee tables, the whole set off by a rose coloured carpet.

The second-class dining saloon was decorated in the Georgian style. The room was 60 feet long and was the full width of the ship. The white panelled walls with delicate carvings and the white pillars supporting an overhead well, along with the carved balustrade that surrounded this feature, were all very reminiscent of the first-class dining saloon, but on a scale much less grand. At the fore end of the saloon stood an ornately carved mahogany sideboard not dissimilar to the one on the upper level of the first-class dining saloon.

The second-class drawing room, which was in reality the second-class library and writing room, was in fact a smaller and slightly less luxurious copy of its counterpart in first-class.

The Georgian style second-class smoking room was 52 feet in length, 33 feet in width and was mahogany panelled. The ceiling was white and featured a plasterwork dome. The wall at the forward end displayed a handsome mosaic panel by Guthrie and Wells of Glasgow, that depicted a river scene in Brittany. The room also had a slightly unusual feature in that it had sliding internal windows with a milky-blue tint to them. This created a pleasantly unusual diffused lighting effect in daylight.

Overall, the passenger accommodation in second-class was, as we said, simply a scaled down, less opulent version of the standard first-class cabins; the chief difference being that there were obviously no second-class 'special cabins' or Regal suites. Millar himself concentrated on the first-class appointments, but oversaw the workings of John Brown's own architect, Mr Robert Whyte, who dealt with the second-class appointments.

In third-class, or 'steerage', the accommodation was markedly less spartan than had previously been the norm. Steerage passengers were offered the choice of two, four or six berth cabins. No Louis XVI finery in here, but they were at least electrically lit, heated and therefore a good deal more comfortable than steerage cabins used to be. They were though, still extremely basic, consisting of not much more than bunks and a folding washstand. All the bed linen had prominent Cunard logos, to deter theft.

The third-class dining saloon measured 79 feet in length by

60 feet in width and was fitted out in polished pine. The seating arrangement was dormitory style and there was an upright piano at the fore end of the saloon, for passenger use.

Cunard provided two public rooms for steerage passengers, located on either side of the shelter deck, forward. They were the smoking room and the ladies' 'lounge', or ladies' room, to give it its official designation. Both were fitted out in exactly the same style as the third-class dining saloon. The wide space between these two rooms served as the third-class common lounge, being fitted with side seats. It was totally open at the aft end, but it was still a shelter from the elements. At least by the provision of this 'refinement', Cunard could now proudly claim that with the advent of the *Lusitania*, third-class passengers no longer had to confine themselves to their cabins during inclement weather; a vast improvement upon previous liners.

As well as the lavish passenger accommodations, there were several technical applications to be installed too, some for the first time ever. Take for example, the ship's electricity supply. This was generated by four Parson's turbo-generators, which were in fact miniature steam turbines exactly akin to those four massive ones that propelled the ship. Each of the turbo-generators produced 375 kilowatts and was in every respect a forerunner of the much larger power station engines that were to come in later years.

Over 200 miles of electrical cable was fitted to the *Lusitania* to power everything from the giant boiler room ventilation fans, refrigeration plant, kitchen equipment, heaters, Marconi wireless equipment, 6,300 lamps, passenger lifts and various other winches and hoists, to the large deck-mounted cargo cranes.

Another 'first' was the Thermo-tank ventilation system, which was in fact a pioneering form of air-conditioning that could maintain the accommodation areas at a constant 65 degrees Fahrenheit in the coldest weather likely to be encountered on an Atlantic voyage. During the summer months, the action of the Thermo-tank system could be reversed to circulate cold air if desired.

Each Thermo-tank unit consisted of an electrically driven fan that forced air into a tank containing a tube heater. The air was forced to flow over the outside of this heater. Inside the heater's tubes was steam, supplied by the ship's main boilers, at 30lbs per square inch pressure. Surrounding the tube heater was a loop of copper piping with a series of needle-sized holes in it, which added steam to the airflow to humidify it. The fans then fed the heated and humidified air along a ducting system, which connected to the staterooms and cabins. The Thermo-tank system took a mere fifteen minutes to make a cold room habitable. Conventional space heaters took three hours.

The first-class accommodation was connected to twenty-four Thermo-tank units, second-class was connected to nine units, third-class had eleven units whilst the officers and crew's accommodation was connected to five Thermo-tanks. The system was capable of changing the air seven times per hour in all the areas it served. All the Thermo-tanks were interconnected in case one unit failed and twelve very powerful exhaust fans connected by large ducts to the gallies, pantries, bathrooms and lavatories further augmented the whole system. This twelve-fan exhaust system was capable of changing the air fifteen times per hour.

The tanks containing the tube heaters were mainly situated at the base of number two funnel. Even with the system running at capacity, the outside of the Thermo-tank remained cool to the touch. It was an ingenious system, which many subsequent premier liners had fitted to them, including of course, the White Star Line's *Olympic*, *Titanic* and *Britannic*.

In terms of the navigation of the new ship, the design of the *Lusitania*'s bridge had been different from that of any ordinary liner from the outset. For a start, it was fully enclosed and had weatherproof sliding doors on both the port and starboard sides. All the main controls were located on a raised platform underneath the row of windows at the front of the bridge. The heated wheelhouse was located centrally at the back of the bridge and was also enclosed. The *Lusitania*'s bridge had an altogether more naval feel about it than was usual. Indeed, Peskett had intended it to, due once again to the naval duties envisaged for the ship. The bridge layout was therefore designed to be familiar to any Royal Navy captain. All the instruments such as engine telegraphs, repeaters and revolution counters as well as the docking telegraphs, had been ordered from Chadburn's Ship Telegraph Co. Ltd. who normally supplied the Admiralty.

The main bridge telephones that linked to the engine room, steering gear room, aft docking bridge, crows nest and the forecastle, were all of the 'Grahams loudspeaking' type and were pure Royal Navy. Even the ship's triple chime whistles were operated by a control system that was fitted to warships. This was the 'Willet Bruce steamship whistle control system', which allowed the whistles to be sounded by steam, compressed air or electrically. Also to be found on the thoroughly equipped bridge was the controlling gear and indicator board for the thirty-five hydraulically operated Stone-Lloyd watertight doors located in the ship's bulkheads, and the Pearson's Fire and Flood alarm system, with its indicator board.

With features like the longitudinal as well as transverse bulkhead arrangement, the cellular double bottom, the thirty-five hydraulically operated watertight doors and a powerful Marconi wireless set, we can see why the *Lusitania* was, in her day, thought to be just about the safest passenger liner ever to take to the ocean. But one factor that nobody paid any attention to was that the lifeboat regulations from the Board of Trade were hopelessly outdated. This mammoth four-funnelled ship, designed to displace some 45,000 tons and carry nearly 3,000 passengers and crew, was fitted out with only sixteen lifeboats under davits initially. But then, the *Titanic* disaster was still five years away.

Trials and Alterations

The *Lusitania*'s turbines were turned over for the first time in June 1907, while she was still in the fitting out basin. By the end of that month, she was virtually ready.

Her official trials were scheduled for Monday 29 July, but it was decided to stage a special two-day cruise around Ireland to Liverpool, for selected guests of the builders and the Cunard company, commencing on Saturday 27 July. The invitations went out on 1 July, specifying an early reply in order to receive a boarding pass in time.

In order to ensure that everything was ready, the ship underwent preliminary trials in the hands of the builders before being made ready for the all-important two-day cruise. She was then taken to Liverpool and dry-docked in the Gladstone Graving dock for the purposes of hull cleaning. Some modifications to the pitch of her propellers were also made and she then returned to John Brown's yard.

On Saturday 27 July 1907, assisted by six tugs, the *Lusitania* left John Brown's yard with officials of the Admiralty, the Board of Trade, Cunard and the builders aboard. Her initial destination was an anchorage known as 'Tail of the Bank'. Here, she tested her anchors and swung her compass. Next came seven runs over the measured mile course at Skelmorlie, during which she achieved a speed of 25.62 knots with her engines clocking a hitherto unprecedented 194.30 revolutions per minute and producing a very impressive total of 76,000 shaft horsepower. So far, things were looking very promising, but the high speed run also revealed that the new wondership had a rather unpleasant vice.

Later that day, the *Lusitania* anchored off Gourock, and the specially invited guests boarded the ship for the two-day cruise. Their number included such luminaries as Mr William Watson, the

Cunard chairman; Sir Charles McLaren, the chairman of John Brown's; Mr E.H. Cunard, who was Sir Samuel Cunard's grandson; the Honourable Charles Parsons, whose splendid invention was propelling the *Lusitania*; Lord Pirrie, accompanied by the Right Honourable Alexander Carlisle, both of whom were representing Harland and Wolff and Mary, Lady Inverclyde, in her new role as the vessel's sponsor. One invited guest who was unable to attend was Winston Churchill.

The cruise enabled the builders to show off the new ship to the representatives of the Admiralty and Cunard. The select guests were given guided tours of all parts of the ship and were, of course, given a two-day sample of the many delights awaiting those who would travel first-class aboard the new steamer. As the pampered guests enjoyed the lavish hospitality, the engineers made their final adjustments to the ship's engines and boilers, in preparation for the real trials that lay ahead.

During her two-day cruise, the *Lusitania* was run at speeds of 15, 18 and 21 knots for a period of six hours in each case. She was never run at her maximum speed at any time while the special guests were aboard. The vice that she had displayed during the high speed run would doubtlessly have had a most deterrent effect upon them. Due to the high speed at which her propellers revolved, a horrific vibration manifested itself in the stern section. The vibration was so bad that at anything more than three-quarters speed, it rendered most of the second-class section of the ship unusable. The problem of the high shaft speed produced by the turbines, versus the low shaft speed required for optimum propeller efficiency, had now manifested itself physically. It was a very serious problem that the builders would urgently have to address as soon as the trials were over.

Having disembarked the guests off the Mersey Bar on Monday, 29 July, the *Lusitania* headed back to sea to commence her trials proper. Because the Admiralty was paying an annual subsidy of £75,000 in respect of the *Lusitania*, plus her envisaged naval duties, the sea trials were, of necessity, longer and far more comprehensive than was usual for a merchant ship of that era.

The *Lusitania* was run four times over a north–south course between the Corsewall Light on the Wigtownshire coast, Scotland and the Longships Light off Land's End, Cornwall, at speeds of 23 and 25 knots, vibrations not withstanding. The course itself was then changed to a run between Corsewall Light and the Isle of Man, followed by a series of short runs between the Isle of Arran and Ailsa Craig, in the Irish Sea. The mean speed attained over the 1,200 mile course was 25.40 knots, which meant that the Admiralty stipulation of an average speed of 24 knots was surpassed.

The Admiralty and the Board of Trade officials also carefully monitored the stopping and turning trials. For the stopping trial, the *Lusitania* was run toward the measured mile course at Skelmorlie. She entered the mile at a speed of 22.80 knots with her engines clocking 166 rpm. The engines were then put to full astern, and the *Lusitania* came to a complete standstill in three-quarters of a mile, taking three minutes, fifty-five seconds to stop.

The turning tests were carried out at a slightly higher speed. With the ship on a straight course and the engines at 180 rpm, the helm was put hard over in seventeen seconds. The 56-ton rudder went over to 35 degrees in twenty seconds, and the ship completed a full 360 degree turn in five minutes, fifty seconds, cleaving a circle of 1,000 yards diameter in the process. This manoeuvre was carried out to port and starboard, the difference between the two being proved negligible. It was also noted that the vibration problem worsened as the ship turned under helm.

On the plus side, the engine revolutions only dropped by thirty per cent during these manoeuvres, which was deemed to have been a more than satisfactory performance. There was also a short series of reversing manoeuvres, using only the low-pressure turbines, to scribe half-circles. The trials proper lasted three full days and the vibration problem apart, the *Lusitania* exceeded all expectations.

The ship returned to John Brown's on Thursday, 1 August and was reberthed in the fitting out dock. Now began the earnest task of trying to dampen the twofold vibration problems, with time most definitely against them. The first part of the problem was caused by each of the two inner propellers being affected by the turbulent wake of the outer one next to, and forward of it. The second part of the vibration problem was caused by the resonance of the ship's framework with the frequency of her high propeller speed.

In the efforts to alleviate the problems, most of the second-class accommodation was carefully stripped out and then an abundance of heavy steel beams, stiffeners, bracing webs and brackets of every description were fitted to the original structure of the ship. Though this measure greatly improved the resonance-induced vibrations, it was by no means a cure for the whole problem. It also wrought havoc with Millar's decor, which had no place for heavy beams and joists thinly disguised as large ornamental arches and attendant support pillars.

The *Lusitania* spent the whole of August in the fitting out dock, while this all-important work was carried out. Vibration proved to be an ongoing and expensive problem, and one that had to be continually addressed throughout the *Lusitania*'s career.

At the end of August, with the second-class section refitted and the bracing work complete, Cunard formally accepted the *Lusitania*. The date for her historic maiden voyage from Liverpool to New York was set for 7 September 1907.

Lusitania in Service

In the afternoon of Saturday, 7 September, the *Lusitania* was moored at the Sloyne buoy in the River Mersey, until Cunard's former Blue Riband holder, RMS *Lucania*, which was occupying her berth at the landing stage, left for New York via Queenstown, (now Cobh) Ireland, at 16.30 hours. *Lusitania* was then moved to the vacated berth.

All through the day thousands of spectators had been travelling to Liverpool and, by the early evening, a vast crowd of over 200,000 people had gathered, lining every conceivable place on the waterfront to witness the *Lusitania*'s maiden departure. She made a stirring sight as assisted by tugs, she left the Prince's landing stage at a few minutes after 21.00 hours, with the great crowds waving flags and cheering loudly. Under the command of the Cunard Commodore, Captain James B. Watt, she sailed overnight for Queenstown, her first scheduled stop.

Lusitania was anchored off Roche's Point at the entrance to Queenstown harbour at 09.20 hours the next morning, amid a flotilla of pleasure boats all laden with sightseers, awaiting the arrival of the tender. A quarter of an hour later, *Lucania* arrived and dropped anchor there. *Lusitania* had overtaken the older ship during the night, but fog had hampered the progress of both vessels. The little tender brought 776 bags of mail and 120 passengers out to the *Lusitania* and once the tender was clear, the ship weighed anchor and sounded off her whistles in farewell. Once outside of the harbour entrance, Captain Watt rang 'full ahead' on the main engine telegraphs and *Lusitania* quickly gathered speed for what everyone confidently expected would be a record crossing of the North Atlantic.

At 12.10 hours that day, Sunday, 8 September, *Lusitania* passed the Daunt's Rock Lightship. By 15.00 hours she had again over-taken the *Lucania*, which had left Queenstown thirty-five minutes ahead of her.

By noon on Monday, she had covered 561 miles, by noon on Tuesday another 575 miles, by noon on Wednesday, 570 miles; to noon on Thursday 593 miles and finally 493 miles to her arrival at Sandy Hook at 09.05 hours on Friday. Fog had hampered her progress on three of the five days of her Atlantic passage, plus the fact that her engines were not fully run-in. All the same, her time of passage across the North Atlantic had been five days and fifty-four minutes; exactly thirty minutes outside the German held record, and her average speed over the five days had been 23.01 knots. Therefore, the record still belonged, for now at least, to the Germans.

But the Germans knew that they would not long retain the Blue Riband. *Lusitania*'s best day's run of 593 miles, was eleven miles better than *Kaiser Wilhelm II*'s best run and only eight miles behind *Deutschland*'s. Both of the German ships had only recorded their best runs with good weather and fully settled engines.

All week long, the New York press had been speculating about the *Lusitania*'s arrival. No phrase had been left uncoined and no superlatives had been spared in their avid descriptions of the new ship. So much so, that the vast crowds which had gathered in Liverpool to see her off, were as nothing when compared to the immense crowds that gathered in New York to welcome her. The New York Police Department had seen nothing like it before. From Battery Park all the way up to piers 54 and 56 at the end of West 14th Street, hundreds of thousands of eager New Yorkers had lined the banks of the Hudson River.

As the *Lusitania* steamed slowly up river, bedecked with flags and with her 2,320 passengers lining the rails, tugs whistled in salute, a growing entourage of pleasure boats gathered in her wake, ferries abandoned their usual routes to follow her and the people lining the shores all waved and cheered enthusiastically at what the New York press had dubbed 'the eighth wonder of the world'. When she came abreast of piers 54 and 56, both of which were packed dangerously full with spectators, the crowds there were bordering on hysteria.

As the *New York Times* that evening reported, the problem was that at least 5,000 more people had gathered there than could safely be admitted to the piers. They therefore assembled in the street at the pier entrance. As the *Lusitania* was slowly warped into her berth at pier 54, this vast crowd began to jostle, everyone keenly seeking a first glimpse of the new ship. Many people were then caught in the crush as the crowd surged forward, only to be pushed back by the overstretched but determined men of the NYPD. All police reserves had been called out to deal with the situation, which very nearly took on the appearance of a riot, but the police did finally manage to contain the crowd, which was at least good-natured in its intent, and so serious injury was thereby avoided.

At the foot of pier 54, over 100 of New York's four-wheeled, horse-drawn cabs eagerly awaited the *Lusitania*'s passengers. The cab drivers, anticipating a great deal of business, had started queuing that morning long before the ship was due, each driver equally determined not to let the chance of securing a good fare slip past him. Gala occasions of this magnitude were not everyday occurrences, even in a city like New York, so a cab driver certainly had to make the most of it whenever the opportunity presented itself.

From that very first arrival, New Yorkers took the *Lusitania* to their hearts. Even atop the uncompleted Singer building on Lower Broadway, the construction workers there had spelled out the word 'WELCOME' with flags. She may not have taken the Blue Riband on her maiden voyage, but anyone present in New York that Friday would scarcely have noticed. Even the announcement made by Harland and Wolff the previous day, that they were to build three mammoth steamers for the White Star Line, Cunard's rival, could not detract from the sheer spectacle of the *Lusitania*'s maiden arrival.

The ship stayed in New York harbour for a week, which was undoubtedly a gala week in New York. During this time the *Lusitania* was thrown open to the eager sightseers of the American public. There was no doubt about it, the *Lusitania* was the big attraction in New York City that week, as the amount of people who boarded the ship for a guided tour readily testified.

At 15.00 hours on Saturday, 21 September 1907, amid the noisiest of send offs, *Lusitania* duly left New York on her homeward voyage. She reached Queenstown just before 04.00 hours on Friday 27th and arrived in Liverpool twelve hours later. Her first eastbound crossing, (always the longer trip) had taken five days, four hours and nineteen minutes, missing the record again, due to fog. The Germans were delighted.

On Saturday, 5 October 1907, Captain Watt took her out of Liverpool at 19.00 hours, bound for New York via Queenstown, on her second voyage. She left Queenstown at 10.25 hours on Sunday 6th and this time the weather was in her favour. Her engines had now had sufficient time and sea miles to be settled. This time surely, it would be different.

Lusitania reached Sandy Hook at 01.17 hours on 11 October 1907. Her time of passage across the North Atlantic was four days, nineteen hours and fifty-two minutes, at an average speed of 23.99 knots. The Blue Riband was now most definitely hers and what was more, the people of New York City already knew it.

Arriving early, she had been forced to anchor off Sandy Hook until there was sufficient water over the bar to admit her. This gave plenty of time for the news of her record-breaking voyage to reach the city. At 07.12 hours, she was able to proceed up the Ambrose channel and she then anchored again off the quarantine station at Staten Island. One hour later, she steamed triumphantly up the Hudson, the stentorian blast of her whistles returning the general din of the continuous salutes from the tugs, fireboats, pleasure boats and the veritable fleet of small craft that had turned out to welcome her back to her 'second home', New York.

The Germans were not pleased by *Lusitania*'s latest performance, though Gustav Schwabe, of the Norddeutscher-Lloyd Line, did graciously acknowledge Cunard's triumph. Albert Ballin of the Hamburg-Amerika Line, however, remained tacitly silent after his earlier outburst of ill-disguised gloating when *Lusitania*'s maiden voyage had failed to recapture the Blue Riband for Great Britain.

In November 1907, *Lusitania*'s sister, *Mauretania*, entered service. It soon became apparent that *Mauretania* had a distinct edge in performance over her sister. In December 1907, *Mauretania* took the eastbound record. Thereafter, a friendly rivalry developed between the two ships. The British press soon dubbed the Blue Riband an 'inter-Cunard trophy', much to the chagrin of the Germans who had nothing to compare with Cunard's two flagships.

The Cunard Company would never formally acknowledge the Blue Riband trophy. A company spokesman once told reporters, 'ocean racing is not the concern of the Cunard Line'. But what the advent of the *Lusitania* and the *Mauretania* had brought to the North Atlantic ferry was the frequency, punctuality and consistency of service only previously seen on a railway company's timetable. It was exactly the kind of service of which transatlantic business people had hitherto only dreamed. Cunard had now made that dream a reality.

At the end of June 1908, *Lusitania* was dry-docked in Liverpool to have her outer propellers replaced. The replacements were still three-bladed, but of an increased pitch, which it was hoped would not only reduce some of the propeller wake vibration problem, but also improve the efficiency of her two high pressure turbine engines, which in turn would also hopefully improve her performance. Her next westbound crossing was indeed a record passage, but not by the margin hoped for.

In November 1908, Commodore James Bunce Watt retired after thirty-five years with Cunard. Born in 1843, in Montrose, Scotland, his early sailing years had been spent on clipper ships, where he had gained the experience necessary to advance his career. He passed his master's exam in 1866 and was awarded certificate number 25325, joining Cunard in 1873 after commanding sailing ships. The Lloyds list of captains had this noted on his record:

> Captain Watt, commodore of the Cunard fleet, who is retiring after 35 years service, completed his last trip in the *Lusitania* which arrived in Liverpool yesterday. The passengers under the presidency of speaker of the Canadian House of Commons, presented him with an address, in which they said that he and his brother-commanders, who had done so much to promote the comfort and safety of Atlantic travel, were deserving of the deepest gratitude from all ocean voyagers.

On James Watt's recommendation, the board of Cunard appointed Captain W.T. Turner to succeed him as commander of the *Lusitania*. William Thomas Turner was born in Clarence Street, Liverpool, in 1856. At the age of thirteen, he had persuaded his parents to let him leave school and embark upon a life at sea. Like most boys of his age, he wanted to follow in his father's footsteps, in his case by becoming a ship's captain.

In 1886, Turner sat and passed his master's exam and was awarded his master's certificate, No. 02168. After a short spell away from Cunard, to gain experience, he returned to pursue his career. A sea captain of the old school whose shiphandling skills were legendary, Turner was exactly the kind of commander for whom the *Lusitania* had been built.

Under Turner's command, *Lusitania* started to better her own performance records. Turner was also a veritable master of the fast turnaround in port. During his time as *Lusitania*'s captain, Turner forged a close friendship with the ship's chief engineer, the walrus-moustached Archibald Bryce. Where Turner had that certain instinctive 'feel' for the ship, so Bryce had that same quality with her engines. With Captain Turner pacing the bridge and Chief Engineer Bryce heading the engineering department, the *Lusitania* ran like clockwork. She very quickly became every inch the crack British liner she had been built to be.

In January 1909, the ship was dry-docked for her annual over-haul, which took three weeks to complete. She returned to service on 6 February. Then on 8 April, she returned to the Gladstone Graving dock to have all four of her propellers replaced. This time she was given a set of four-bladed propellers of the same type that were fitted to the *Mauretania*. The new propellers were six feet greater in diameter than her old ones and each weighed 23 tons.

On 17 July 1909, she left the dry dock and returned to service. Her new propellers had not only lessened her vibration problem, but had also improved both her engine efficiency and her perfor-mance. To prove it, Captain Turner and the *Lusitania* promptly set a new speed record. However *Mauretania*, under the command of the Cunard Commodore, Captain John Pritchard, swiftly took it back again that same month with a speed of 26.89 knots. Thereafter, *Mauretania* held the Blue Riband continuously until the advent of the German liner *Bremen*, in 1929.

At the end of December 1909, Commodore Pritchard retired and Captain Turner was appointed to command the *Mauretania*. Captain J.T.W. Charles took over command of the *Lusitania* in February 1910, following her annual refit.

James T.W. Charles was born in Winchester in 1866. He

passed his master's exams, gaining certificate No. 015759, in Bombay in 1890, then again in Liverpool, in 1898. He further attained the position of Extra Commander RNR. His career with Cunard started aboard the *Lucania*. His appointment as commander of the *Lusitania* lasted for the next three and a half years.

As of February 1910, *Lusitania* started to make regular calls at Fishguard on her eastbound crossings. This signalled the beginning of the end for the Queenstown stop. Shortly afterwards, Cunard announced that during the winter season, which was November to April, eastbound Cunard ships would no longer call there.

In June 1911, Cunard's rival, the White Star Line, introduced the first of their trio of super-liners, RMS *Olympic*. With a displacement figure of nearly 66,000 tons, she was half as large again as the Cunard flagships. But she had been designed for comfort and luxury, not speed, though in this last respect, she was expected to achieve at least 21 knots.

In December 1911, Captain Charles and the *Lusitania* performed that year's 'Christmas Special'. It was the round voyage from Liverpool to New York and back, in just twelve days. This was a trip for which Captain Turner and the *Mauretania* had set the precedent in 1910. They were set to repeat it, but just two days before *Mauretania*'s scheduled departure she broke free from her mooring at the Sloyne buoy during a gale and ran aground. Consequently, she had to go into the Gladstone dock for repair. Captain Charles and the *Lusitania* therefore stepped into the breach and, thanks to a lightning turnaround in New York, the trip was completed on time.

In April 1912, the second of White Star's trio of super-liners entered service and sailed on her maiden voyage, from Southampton to New York. As her name suggested, RMS *Titanic* was slightly larger than her sister, *Olympic*. The man who had commanded *Olympic* on her maiden voyage ten months previously, Captain Edward John Smith, Commodore of the White Star Line, was to retire after taking *Titanic* on her maiden voyage. Unfortunately, that was not to be. On the fourth night of the voyage, *Titanic* struck an iceberg and sank. One thousand five hundred and three of the 2,207 people on board perished in the disaster, including Captain Smith.

The Board of Trade held an inquiry into the disaster, chaired by

Lord Mersey. One of the most glaringly obvious findings of the inquiry was that the Board of Trade's own lifeboat regulations were hopelessly inadequate. *Titanic* had been granted a certificate, by the Board of Trade, to carry 3,500 passengers and crew. The Board's lifeboat regulations required every British ship of 10,000 tons or over, to carry sixteen lifeboats under davits. The number of persons aboard was not considered relevant. *Titanic* actually carried twenty boats, sixteen of which were suspended in the very latest Wellin double-acting quadrant davits, whilst the remaining four were of the collapsible type, carried flat atop the officers' quarters on the boat deck. Carrying twenty boats meant that the ship actually exceeded the required number by twenty-five per cent, but even if all twenty boats had been filled to capacity on that fateful night, which they certainly were not, there would only have been room in those boats for just over half the maximum number of persons that *Titanic* was certified to carry.

Therefore, as a direct result of the *Titanic* disaster, new lifeboat regulations were immediately, though somewhat belatedly, drawn up. Gone was the old, peculiar formula based upon a ship's tonnage and an odd calculation of cubic space. In its place was a much simpler formula: a place in the boats for every person on board.

For the *Lusitania* and the *Mauretania*, this meant increasing the number of lifeboats to forty-eight and providing some additional life rafts. Boats of the collapsible type were therefore installed beneath those in the davits. But nobody thought it necessary to change the antiquated type of davits fitted to the Cunard flagships. After all, that type of davit had been perfectly adequate on sailing vessels for many, many years. Why change what apparently worked?

1912, it transpired, was not the best of years. Quite apart from the storm caused by the *Titanic* disaster, *Lusitania* too had problems. On 25 June, she limped home to Liverpool with a damaged propeller, which put her out of service for a month while it was replaced. Then on the very last voyage of that year, she suffered the ignominy of incurring major engine damage. Several thousand of the 12 million meticulously machined brass blades in her four turbine engines had buckled, due to an inherent problem with early turbine engines, namely thermal distortion. The extensive engine repairs that were now required would put her out of service from 10 January to 23 August 1913.

The Admiralty decided that this would be a most opportune time to make the initial modifications needed for the ship to take up her possible future role as an armed merchant cruiser. War with Germany looked to be an increasingly likely eventuality within the next twelve months, and as the ship was in for extensive repairs anyway, it would save precious time later if war did come.

The shelter deck was strengthened in the areas designed for the placement of eight of the twelve 6-inch, quick-firing guns. The remaining four guns were to be sited on the forecastle. Once these deck areas were strengthened, the revolving gun rings were installed. All that was then required to mount the armament was to secure each gun to its ring with twelve castellated bolts. The gun mountings that were situated in areas frequented by passengers were sunk into the deck then 'camouflaged' with teak trap doors. The mountings on the forecastle were slightly raised and given metal covers. Situated near to the huge capstans and the mooring bollards, they did not look out of place, as their appearance resembled flattened bitts.

Her engine repairs and refit completed, the *Lusitania* returned to the North Atlantic run on 23 August 1913 under her new commander, Captain Daniel 'Fairweather' Dow. Daniel Dow was born in Castle Bellingham in 1860. Like most captains, Dow finished his schooling early to embark upon a life at sea. He attained his Master's Certificate, No. 011565, in Liverpool in 1887. On the 3 August 1900 he was made a Lieutenant Commander RNR. This appointment lasted until 17 July 1905. His career with Cunard started in 1885 aboard the *Pavonia* and he was known affectionately as 'Fairweather', as he had a tendency to suffer from seasickness! He was therefore deemed to be an expert in the field of smooth Atlantic crossings.

On 25 August 1913, two days after the *Lusitania* returned to service, the board of Cunard announced that henceforth the stop at Queenstown would no longer be on the itinerary of either the *Lusitania* or the *Mauretania*. They would now call at Fishguard instead. *Lusitania* had therefore already made her final scheduled call at Queenstown on 24 August, collecting 179 passengers and nearly 1,100 bags of mail.

In March 1914, *Lusitania* broke her last record, which was one she held already. On a westbound voyage to New York, she recorded a best day's run of 618 miles at an average speed of

26.70 knots. But the clouds of war now loomed ominously on the horizon and as events were to show, *Lusitania* had barely five months of peacetime service left, as the 'Edwardian Summer' drew toward its apocalyptic close. The last peacetime voyage she made was a westbound trip. Her next homeward bound trip actually left New York on the very day that Great Britain declared war on Germany, 4 August 1914.

War!

August 1914. The growing crisis situation in the Balkan states finally came to a head with the assassination in Sarajevo of Archduke Franz Ferdinand, heir to the Austro-Hungarian empire. It had taken barely six weeks since that assassination, for all Kaiser Wilhelm's previous sabre rattling and brinkmanship to come home to roost. The General staff of the German army, who had been preparing for this war for years, now used Germany's treaty obligations to Austria-Hungary as the pretext for railroading their Kaiser into the war that he had so often publicly threatened, but did not in reality want. The 'Gilded Age' was lost forever in the first cannonade, as Europe embarked upon the 'Great War'.

At the time war was declared, it was thought at the British Admiralty that a small force of German light cruisers was somewhere abroad on the North Atlantic. The exact dispositions of SMS *Dresden*, SMS *Karlsruhe* and SMS *Strassburg* were not known, but the Admiralty were convinced that SMS *Dresden* was lurking somewhere off New York and that SMS *Karlsruhe* was heading north from her last known position in the Caribbean, to join *Dresden*. Of the whereabouts of SMS *Strassburg* since she had left her station in the Caribbean, the Admiralty had absolutely no idea, which was all the more worrying to them. The Admiralty's greatest fear was that these three cruisers were forming up as a powerful force of commerce raiders, to prey on the transatlantic shipping lanes.

Unfortunately, the Royal Navy had no vessel in *Lusitania*'s vicinity on 4 August with the turn of speed needed to keep up with the giant Cunarder, let alone to provide her with an effective escort home. The Admiralty duly notified Captain Dow of their fears and warned him of this most profound threat to his ship and of their temporarily powerless position. They had taken the precaution of ordering Admiral Cradock, whose flag was hoisted aboard the armoured cruiser HMS *Suffolk*, to head north with all dispatch from his station near the Bahamas, to deal with SMS *Dresden*. Captain Fanshawe with the cruiser HMS *Bristol* was also ordered towards New York to assist and was in fact slightly ahead of Admiral Cradock. Given this perceived situation, Captain Dow wisely decided against using the usual route home and after the *Lusitania* left New York on 4 August as scheduled, he kept his ship at her maximum speed with the lookouts doubled.

So it is at this point that we come to address one of the great fables in the *Lusitania* story; namely, that she was sighted and pursued by a German cruiser on 6 August, during her first homeward bound crossing of the war, and that she narrowly escaped after a tense chase by virtue of her high speed and a convenient mist.

There are two versions of this incident. One is contained in *The Great War, the standard history of the all-Europe conflict*, a thirteen-volume government inspired publication, which contains a half-page report of this incident in stirring, patriotic tones. Citing SMS *Dresden* as being *Lusitania*'s pursuer, it is perhaps all the more convincing for having been written at the time.

Written much later, the other version is contained in Colin Simpson's widely acclaimed book *Lusitania* and has it as being SMS *Karlsruhe* that was cheated of her prey, albeit at a slightly later date, off the Grand Banks of Newfoundland. So which version gives us the true picture of this exciting episode?

Having been in contact with the Imperial War Museum in London and the *Bundesmilitärarchiv* in Freiburg, Germany, we are now able to study, with absolute certainty, the dispositions of SMS *Dresden*, SMS *Karlsruhe* and SMS *Strassburg* for the days in question.

Under the command of *Fregattenkapitän* Ludecke, SMS *Dresden* was in fact on her way to join Admiral von Spee's forces off the Pacific coast of South America and at the time she was supposedly chasing the *Lusitania*, she was off the mouth of the Amazon, heading south to round Cape Horn. This obviously rules her out.

SMS *Karlsruhe*, under the command of the wily *Fregattenkapitän* Erich Kohler however, was indeed heading north from her last known position in the Caribbean, in the general direction of New York and at flank speed. They had been surprised earlier that morning, whilst transferring guns and ammunition to the Norddeutscher-Lloyd liner *Kronprinz Wilhelm* during a mid-ocean rendezvous 200 miles off the Florida coast, by no less a person than Admiral Cradock in HMS *Suffolk*, on his way to deal with a non-existent *Dresden* off New York. Upon sighting the rapidly advancing *Suffolk*, the two German ships split up and made off in different directions. Cradock wisely decided to chase the greater menace, SMS *Karlsruhe*, which was now speeding away to the north.

The pursuit lasted all day and took *Karlsruhe* 264 miles further north, but Kohler was no fool. He realized that *Karlsruhe* had the edge over *Suffolk* in terms of speed, but he also knew that he could not maintain his present course and speed for much longer. He was waiting for darkness before making a break for it. What he did not know was that he was heading directly toward Fanshawe in HMS *Bristol*. Cradock had ordered Fanshawe to reverse his course as *Suffolk* drove *Karlsruhe* toward the other cruiser. It was a neat trap, but would Kohler fall into it?

In the event, Kohler sighted HMS *Bristol* coming at him off his port bow and even in the fading light, he recognized her for the menace that she was. Turning to starboard, with HMS *Bristol*, he refused to be drawn into Cradock's trap. Now steaming east on parallel courses 6,000 yards apart, the two ships exchanged fire, though neither scored any direct hits upon the other. Kohler managed to cross in front of his opponent as darkness fell. He then fired a broadside at HMS *Bristol* without effect, before running right around her and making off to the south-east at flank speed, passing between both of his pursuers unseen.

This action took place about 150 miles east of the coast of the North American state of Georgia, which was a good 500 miles south of Captain Dow's usual track home. Captain Dow certainly did not steam 500 miles south to avoid the perceived threat to his ship, which means that he could not have sighted or been sighted by SMS *Karlsruhe*. He would in any event have sighted HMS *Bristol* first, which would have warned him off had this been the case.

So we now come to the possibility that it was perhaps SMS *Strassburg*, the cruiser whose whereabouts was totally unknown by the Admiralty, that chased the *Lusitania*. Fortunately for those aboard the *Lusitania*, SMS *Strassburg* was in fact on a direct course home to Germany from the Caribbean. Having been urgently recalled two days before war was declared between Great Britain and Germany, SMS *Strassburg* was almost halfway home at the time of the 'incident'. There were no other surface units of the Imperial German Navy remotely nearby.

The only other possibility therefore, lies in Colin Simpson's assertion that this incident took place at a slightly later date. In his book, Simpson gives the date of the *Lusitania*'s encounter with the *Karlsruhe* as being January 1915.

By January 1915, the Royal Navy had complete command on the surface of the whole North Atlantic, and SMS *Karlsruhe* had been at the bottom of the Atlantic, 200 miles east of Trinidad, since the previous November. After a highly successful three-month period of commerce raiding, and having successfully eluded the determined hunt for him by the Royal Navy, an accidental explosion had finally put paid to Kohler's ship whilst she was on her way home to Germany. Casualties were light and the ship's log was saved. It resides today in the *Bundesmilitärarchiv* and it makes no mention anywhere of any encounter with the *Lusitania*.

One can therefore see that neither version is, in fact, correct and one can only conclude that this rather fanciful British government inspired tale was created purely for home consumption, possibly to bolster public opinion and continue to court public favour for the war, which of course had started rather badly for the British. As a result of our research, we can categorically state that the *Lusitania* was never at any time pursued by any surface ship of the German Navy.

Before the *Lusitania* and for that matter, the *Mauretania*, arrived back in Liverpool after the outbreak of the war, Cunard was told that the ships would be requisitioned by the Admiralty under the terms of the 1903 agreement, for use as cruisers. The regular Cunard officers and crew would not be required. *Lusitania*'s new captain was to have been Captain V.H. Bernard RN. However, Captain Bernard never took up his appointment. The day after the *Lusitania* arrived home, the Admiralty changed its mind and informed Cunard that the ships would not now be required as cruisers. The chief reasons for this decision were the relatively small radius of operation of the two Cunarders, plus their voracious appetites for coal.

But the Admiralty did have other plans for the vessels.

Mauretania was retained as a troopship and the Admiralty paid Cunard to keep the *Lusitania* in Liverpool at its disposal until 12 September 1914. During this time, the *Lusitania* once again went into dry dock for a second Admiralty refit.

The Admiralty's Trade Division had decided to make use of the ship as an express cargo carrier for priority government supplies. During her latest refit the Admiralty gutted most of the third-class accommodation in the lower forward section of the ship and turned that section into additional cargo space, thus considerably enlarging the forward cargo hold. Certain other sections of the ship were now reserved solely for the Admiralty's use and conditions were further imposed on Cunard, who were told that all cargo carried in this new space would be specially insured by the British government. Any unused space on eastbound trips could be utilized by Cunard only with the express permission of the Admiralty. Furthermore, the Senior Naval Officer in New York or Liverpool, prior to every departure, would henceforth give the ship's captain strict navigational instructions from the Admiralty. In other words, Cunard was now under the virtual command of the Admiralty. Thus a much-modified *Lusitania* was handed back to Cunard to resume her duties on the North Atlantic run, but this time, as the Admiralty told Cunard, she had 'a very important job to do'.

The *Lusitania* returned to service still under the command of her regular Cunard captain, Daniel Dow, in October 1914. During October she made two round voyages, completing the second at the beginning of November, when it was noted by Cunard's accounts department that the war, which so far was barely three months old, had already produced a marked drop in passenger demand. It sent a memo to the chairman, Alfred Booth, advising him of this fact and pointing out to him that due to the fall in passenger numbers and a sharp rise in the price of coal, the operation of the *Lusitania* was actually costing the company nearly £2,000 per trip.

With this factor uppermost in their minds, the board of Cunard, faced with a difficult situation, were forced to take a rather contentious decision. The *Lusitania* could not be laid up for the winter; the Admiralty would not allow it. Yet the company certainly could not stand the loss of £2,000 per trip and the Admiralty would not foot the bill either. Therefore, the only option was to reduce the ship's operating costs. The board decided that the best way to achieve this was to reduce her schedule to only one round trip per month and to close the No. 4 boiler room. This last measure would save 1,600 tons of coal per trip, plus the wages of the ninety men normally employed in running the No. 4 boiler room. The combined savings would only just make good the loss, but it also meant that *Lusitania*'s maximum speed had been reduced from 26.7 knots to barely 21 knots, whilst her optimum cruising speed was now only 18 knots. To be fair, even at her reduced maximum speed of 21 knots, she was still faster than any other passenger ship on the North Atlantic, but there were those who held that to handicap so important a vessel as the *Lusitania* in such a way was a most unwise action, and was possibly tempting fate. Be that as it may, Cunard's decision was final and the *Lusitania* commenced her reduced monthly schedule with effect from 21 November, and with boiler room No. 4 closed down.

Outwardly, certainly as far as the travelling public were concerned, the *Lusitania* hadn't changed. Although the number of passengers she carried was fewer, there was still a sufficient sprinkling of rich and famous names to grace her first-class appointments. But below decks forward, something had definitely changed. Where once her cargo had been the passengers' baggage and sundry items of a very general nature, she was now regularly carrying large quantities of government supplies, or to put it more succinctly, war material, home to England.

The British government's need for munitions was great indeed. The war was barely two months old when Lord Kitchener brought to the attention of senior government ministers, the alarming fact that the British armies in France were expending more ammunition each week than Britain's factories produced. Reserve stocks were down to a three-month supply. If a crisis were to be averted, alternative suppliers would have to be found, and found quickly.

As it transpired, the answer lay with one man, American banker John Pierpoint Morgan Junior; the very same man who had caused the Admiralty such consternation back in 1902. In the event, Morgan proved to be entirely pro-Allied in his sympathies. Through him, the British government and the Admiralty set up a complex supply line for the vital American manufactured war supplies that the British so badly needed, despite America's declared policy of strict neutrality. If anyone could be relied upon to drive a bulldozer through all the red tape, it was Morgan.

The British government, by way of the Admiralty's Trade Division, placed their purchase orders with Morgan, who used a complex chain of fictitious companies to secure the necessary items. The International Mercantile Marine's ships and passengers then became the unwitting carriers of this contraband, assisted by any other ships over which the British Admiralty had control, or could otherwise charter.

In order to get the vital munitions aboard the chosen passenger ships, it became standard practice to file a false manifest with the US Collector of Customs in New York, D.F. Malone, who knew exactly what was taking place, but who had been instructed to turn a blind eye. Malone would issue the sailing clearance certificate on the basis of a loading manifest showing only a general cargo.

Despite his declaration of strict neutrality, President Woodrow Wilson also knew what was taking place as did his new Secretary of State, Robert Lansing. Both men however, were prepared to turn a blind eye for, as Senator Calvin Coolidge once said before he became president, 'The business of America is business'. And Americans seldom missed a good business opportunity, especially in the economically recessive times that the European war had suddenly produced, and with a presidential election looming.

Just to keep things nice and 'legal', a supplementary manifest would be filed once each ship cleared New York and was outside of US territorial waters, listing any 'last minute provisions' that had been taken aboard, though any obviously suspect consignments were listed as being machine parts, metallic packages, or possibly furs or extra large quantities of say, cheese or butter. In reality, the cargoes being loaded into the holds of these eastbound passenger liners, including the *Lusitania*, were military goods such as gun cotton, artillery shells, bullets, fuel oil, brass, copper, metallic powders for making ammunition and explosives, fuse mechanisms for shells, vehicle parts, uniforms, motorcycles, aeroplane spares and other such 'sundries'.

By February 1915, it had become obvious to everybody that the war was not going to be of the quick and decisive kind. Lord Kitchener's forecast of a long and drawn out affair had now become a grim reality. Therefore, starting that month, Great Britain declared a naval blockade of Germany and began a long-term strategy aimed at starving Germany of the raw materials she needed.

The Germans responded to this action by declaring the waters around the British Isles to be a war zone and stepping up the operations of their U-boats against British and Allied shipping. Thus measure was followed by countermeasure and the situation quickly escalated. British ships now flew neutral flags and were given strict Admiralty instructions to make a ramming attempt at any U-boat that challenged them.

Up to this point, there had only been one or two isolated cases of ships being attacked without warning. The German U-boats had largely adhered to the 'cruiser rules' when attacking merchant ships. These rules required U-boat commanders to surface, fire a warning shot across a ship's bow then board and search the vessel. If found to be a British vessel or one carrying supplies for the Allies, then sufficient time was duly given for the crew to man the lifeboats and abandon ship. The ship was then torpedoed, or sunk by gunfire.

First Lord of the Admiralty, Winston Churchill, now deliberately used the German U-boat commanders' hitherto largely chivalrous behaviour against them, by his sanctioning of the Q-ship, a seemingly ordinary cargo vessel that was in fact secretly armed and manned by a naval crew and a party of Marines. When stopped by a U-boat, these ships pretended to comply with the cruiser rules. Occasionally, the crew of a Q-ship would even go so far as to feign panic and pretend to abandon their vessel but, as soon as the U-boat's boarding party were on their way over, the concealed 4.1-inch guns were brought into action, the White Ensign was displayed and the now highly vulnerable submarine was sent swiftly to the bottom in a hail of shell and rifle fire.

The Admiralty ordered that any captured U-boat crew were to be treated as 'accused persons' but in reality, prisoners were seldom taken by Q-ships; the Marines saw to that. Not surprisingly, the Germans ordered their submarine commanders to abandon the use of the cruiser rules. The Germans announced that henceforth, all ships encountered by U-boats in the declared war zone were liable to be sunk without warning.

This was in fact exactly the situation that Churchill had striven to achieve. Churchill hoped that he could now successfully goad the U-boat commanders into attacking any ship in British waters.

As First Sea Lord John Fisher had once remarked in a paper on this very subject, 'One flag looks much like another when viewed against the light through a periscope'. Of course, it was Churchill's fervent hope that the U-boats would attack a neutral ship, and ultimately for his purposes, an American one. The following extract from a secret letter he wrote at the time to Walter Runciman, the President of the Board of Trade, outlines his intentions perfectly. He wrote:

My Dear Walter,
. . .It is most important to attract neutral shipping to our shores, in the hope especially of embroiling the U.S. with Germany. The German formal announcement of indiscriminate submarining has been made to the United States to produce a deterrent effect upon traffic. For our part we want the traffic – the more the better, and if some of it gets into trouble, better still.

(signed) W.S. Churchill.

By pursuing a policy deliberately aimed at embroiling America with Germany, Churchill hoped to bring America into the war on the side of the British. But Churchill obviously either did not realize, or perhaps did not care, that America was physically incapable of joining the European war in 1915, even if she desired it. Her standing armies were too small for war on such a scale and would require nearly two years to come up to strength. But of far more importance to the British was the simple fact that if America did declare war in 1915, Britain's supply of much-needed munitions would cease abruptly. The Americans would have to give priority to their own armed forces, having previously maintained only limited stocks.

Fortunately for the British, there were more astute statesmen than the headstrong young Winston Churchill in charge. American neutrality was therefore upheld, the supply of munitions from across the Atlantic was maintained and his political masters kept young Winston in check. But the fact that Churchill could be a dangerous young man, especially when his political frustrations were starting to simmer, was already borne out by his having sired a deadly new strategy, possibly without even realizing it. It was a strategy that was soon to become so abhorrently effective that it would forcibly shake the world out of any complacency it may still have retained. That strategy was called unrestricted submarine warfare and Churchill had steadily driven the Germans to its discovery.

February 1915 also saw the German U-boat *U-21* causing alarm at the Admiralty. On 30 January, still using the cruiser rules, she audaciously sank three ships in Liverpool Bay in broad daylight, right under the nose of the Royal Navy. Having expended her stock of torpedoes, *U-21* then started her voyage home, which brought her into the waters of the Atlantic Ocean off Ireland's south coast. The *Lusitania*, under Captain Dow was also expected off the southern Irish coast at the same time. Having diverted two other Cunarders, the *Transylvania* and the *Ausonia*, into Queenstown harbour, the Admiralty duly informed the *Lusitania* of the U-boat peril. Captain Dow promptly ran up the Stars and Stripes and bolted for Liverpool with all dispatch.

The incident did not pass unnoticed as Colonel Edward House, one of President Wilson's closest advisors, was a passenger aboard the *Lusitania* on that voyage and so there were diplomatic repercussions. However, political oil was poured onto the troubled American waters and no more was said, but it was a measure of the strain Captain Dow was obviously feeling. By the end of the first week in March 1915, the strain finally proved to be too much. Captain Dow had yet to see a German U-boat but his continuing fear of being torpedoed, given that he knew something of the nature of the cargoes his ship was carrying, caused him to worry greatly about the safety of his passengers.

Alfred Booth, the chairman of Cunard, decided that Captain Dow needed a rest. He sent Dow on leave and searched his list of Cunard captains for a suitable replacement master. He stopped looking when his eyes fell upon the name of Turner, William Thomas; the man who had been the *Lusitania*'s second commander and who was now the Commodore of the Cunard Line.

His appointment confirmed, Captain Turner inspected the *Lusitania* thoroughly on 10 March 1915. He found a good deal at fault, but as there was a war on he took the *Lusitania* to New York on 16 March. However, upon completion of the return voyage, which was in fact *Lusitania*'s 200th Atlantic crossing, Captain Turner was both an angry and a worried man. Having consulted with the ship's Chief Engineer, his old friend Archie Bryce, he sat down at his home in Aintree and wrote a scathing report to Alfred Booth, regarding the state of his former ship. He found the turbine engines in need of attention, the standard of the crew's seamanship left much to be desired, some of the lifesaving equipment was defective and he also found that the ship could not be properly ballasted, due to defective trim tanks. He discovered, by way of Archie Bryce, that on Captain Dow's last trip, the 'government people' in New York had managed to fill the *Lusitania*'s double bottom with 100,000 gallons of diesel fuel.

Not content with voicing his concerns to Alfred Booth, Captain Turner also reported the ship's defects to Mr Laslett, the Board of Trade Surveyor in Liverpool and Captain Barrand, the port's Immigration Officer. Captain Turner did not mention the diesel to Captain Barrand, nor to Mr Laslett, but he did tell Alfred Booth that unless the ship's defects were rectified, he would not take the *Lusitania* out again.

A few days later Alfred Booth visited Captain Turner in his spacious day cabin aboard the *Lusitania*, which he noticed was already looking more like her pre-war self, to discuss his report. He had heard of Captain Turner's legendary obstinacy but up till now he'd never encountered it on a personal basis. Dealing with each point in Turner's report, Booth explained that the Royal Navy had taken the best men quite early on in the war. Every effort was being made to provide good men for the *Lusitania*, but it was not always possible, which was why nearly every voyage was made with a scratch crew, and those who signed aboard the ship as stewards had a marked tendency to desert upon the ship's arrival in New York.

Booth went on to explain that due to falling passenger demand and the price of coal, boiler room No.4 had regrettably been shut down to save money, which was why Archie Bryce's engineering department were short of the ninety men required to man the closed boiler room. However, like Captain Dow before him, Captain Turner successfully argued for a full coal supply anyway, which would at least solve the worst of the ballasting problem, even though the ship did not actually need the coal as fuel.

Booth wanted to postpone any work on the turbine engines for as long as he possibly could. Working on the engines invariably caused long delays and he was running to a tight Admiralty schedule, although he did not share that information with Captain

Turner, who was consistently arguing on the grounds of passenger safety, particularly now that there was a war on. It was Cunard's proud claim that they'd never lost a life and Turner was using that very claim to counter all of Booth's objections. He was also using Mr Laslett as an additional lever. Booth found the discussion heavy going and finally conceded, though only the most pressing repairs were to be carried out. The rest would have to wait until *Lusitania*'s scheduled refit. On the question of the lifesaving equipment, the decision of the two Board of Trade officials was final and it resulted in the immediate replacement of three lifeboats.

The only defect that couldn't be remedied to Captain Turner's satisfaction in time, was the one found by Mr Laslett in the engine room. He found what he deemed to be faulty valves in the low pressure turbines and it was his opinion that these valves would probably fail and blow out if 'Full astern' were to be selected under a high steam pressure. Alfred Booth, Captain Turner and Chief Engineer Bryce were therefore duly informed of this.

After a long and arduous discussion, Captain Turner realized that he had in fact got most of what he'd wanted. Booth had an appointment in London and was now pressed for time, so he rose to leave and Captain Turner saw him to the main lift. On the way to the lift, Turner managed to extract one last concession from him. On the grounds of the reduced crew and the fact that he would have to spend most of his time on the bridge due to the submarine threat, the post of Staff Captain was to be reinstated, as it was when he had commanded Cunard's newest flagship, the *Aquitania* on her first three voyages. Captain Turner asked for John Anderson to be his deputy again and Booth granted the request as the lift arrived.

On 17 April 1915, her defects remedied, (apart from the valves on the low pressure turbines) *Lusitania* sailed from Liverpool bound for New York. Staff Captain John Anderson was on the bridge to take her out as Captain Turner, sporting a brand new bowler hat, was up on the forecastle admonishing the bosun for his apparently lethargic windlass crew.

The *Lusitania* completed her 201st Atlantic crossing on the morning of 24 April 1915. Coming off the Atlantic she entered Lower Bay then, keeping Staten Island and Liberty Island (with its famous statue of Liberty) to port, and Battery Park to her starboard side, she entered the Hudson River as she had done 100 times before. *Lusitania* then proceeded slowly up river until she reached a position just past the Cunard piers, where she would turn round in mid-river to be berthed at pier 54.

Turner docked her himself, unaided by tugs, though in nothing like the personal record time of nineteen minutes that he'd set with *Aquitania*. He then left Staff Captain Anderson to see to the formalities and the unloading. Not that there was much unloading to do on this arrival, as they had carried nothing like a full complement of passengers.

The *Lusitania* would spend the next six days in New York, during which time the stage would gradually be set for her 202nd Atlantic crossing; a crossing that should not have been dissimilar to any of her previous voyages. Yet it would be for the final day of this voyage that the *Lusitania* would ultimately be forever remembered.

The Last Departure

At pier 54 in New York harbour at 08.00 hours on the morning of Saturday, 1 May, the *Lusitania* began embarkation. At the head of the gangway stood the ship's purser, the chief steward and some of his staff ready to receive the passengers. With a master-at-arms on each side of the gangway, it must have looked like an official reception committee, except that the Captain wasn't present.

Captain Turner was up on the bridge. Chief Engineer Bryce had reported his section ready for sea. All available boilers were on line, steam pressure was up and smoke gently furled from three of the *Lusitania*'s four immense funnels, all of which were now painted black under Admiralty instructions. This was not in fact done in some vain attempt to disguise her identity; the funnels of every British merchantman under Admiralty charter were always painted black.

Turner walked out onto the bridge wing and looked down at the dockside. There was a bevy of reporters and a newsreel team on the pier. Filling his pipe with his favourite dark tobacco, he carefully tamped it down and lit it, puffing contentedly. Even now, he mused, she still makes the news when she sails. As the black briar pipe warmed in his hand, Turner noticed the figure of Charles Sumner, the Cunard superintendent, making a beeline for the news reporters one of whom was brandishing a newspaper. Well, whatever it was, he thought, Sumner could handle it.

At 08.30 hours, somewhat later than usual as the ship's scheduled departure had been delayed whilst passengers and cargo from another ship were transferred to the *Lusitania*, Captain Turner was enjoying his breakfast in his spacious day cabin. After breakfast he leafed through that morning's copy of *The New York Tribune*. He almost didn't notice it at first, but right next to

Cunard's advertisement for *Lusitania*'s departure was a black-bordered announcement boldly headed, 'NOTICE.' It read as follows:

Travellers intending to embark on the Atlantic voyage are reminded that a state of war exists between Germany and her allies and Great Britain and her allies; that the zone of war includes the waters adjacent to the British Isles; that, in accordance with formal notice given by the Imperial German Government, vessels flying the flag of Great Britain, or any of her allies, are liable to destruction in those waters and that travellers sailing in the war zone on ships of Great Britain or her allies do so at their own risk.

IMPERIAL GERMAN EMBASSY. WASHINGTON D.C.

Was this a direct threat to his ship? He decided to seek out Sumner.

Down on the pier, a picture seller was hawking photographs of the ship, heavily bordered in black. 'Loositaynia's last voyage! Get yer pikchures here!' he shouted in his distinctive New York accent.

By 10.20 hours, mysterious telegrams began to arrive in the ship's Marconi room. The telegrams were addressed to prominent passengers and warned against sailing on the *Lusitania*. The ship's Marconi operator held them back and checked with Captain Turner and Sumner, who retained them, realizing that these telegrams were originated by a newspaper. Sumner then had pier 54 cleared of reporters with the exception of the newsreel team and two members of the Press Association. There were no more telegrams.

At 11.00 hours, Chief Engineer Archie Bryce came back to the bridge to advise Turner that he was beginning to be concerned about the steam pressure. It wasn't critical yet, but if they didn't sail soon, he would have to release some of the pressure, which would mean another delay while it was raised again in order to sail.

Captain Turner had still not received his Admiralty sailing instructions at 11.15 hours. Usually, one of Sir Courtenay Bennett's staff brought them to the ship. Sir Courtenay fulfilled the role of Senior Naval Officer for New York. His office was amongst those of Cunard and at 11.20 hours they finally telephoned a message asking Turner to come at once. Donning his bowler, he made his way off the ship via the third-class gangway and went to Sir

Courtenay's office. On his way, he stopped off at Sumner's office to check on alternative passenger accommodation on other ships. He was now fully expecting the *Lusitania*'s departure to be cancelled or seriously delayed due to the German warnings.

Meanwhile, an air of apprehension prevailed amongst the passengers aboard the *Lusitania*; would she sail? Passengers eyed one another, seeing who, if anyone, would suddenly decide to disembark. Where was the Captain?

At that moment, Turner was just leaving Sir Courtenay Bennett's office. No specific sailing instructions had arrived for him, so Sir Courtenay told him to adopt the same course and instructions as he had used for his last return trip. He was therefore to maintain wireless telegraphy silence, except in the case of an emergency. After clearing Fastnet by at least twelve miles, he was to maintain a minimum distance of ten miles between his ship and the south coast of Ireland. He was given other wireless related instructions, the current naval code and told to use the No.1 edition of the merchant code for transmission, if necessary. He was also handed the details of his naval escort, the cruiser HMS *Juno*, which he was to meet ten miles south and not more than forty miles to the west of Fastnet. Lastly he was handed the British embassy's dispatch bag, which was to be thrown overboard if the ship was attacked. Its lead weights would carry it to the bottom. As an afterthought, Sir Courtenay informed him that a German U-boat in the Irish Sea had just attacked an American ship, the tanker *Gulflight*.

As Turner arrived back at the *Lusitania*, he found that the press, having sensed the mood of the passengers, were badgering some of the more prominent ones for some kind of reaction or quote. They had singled out Alfred G. Vanderbilt, the American millionaire and Charles Frohman, the famous Broadway theatre producer, both of whom were regular passengers of Cunard and known personally to Turner. He walked straight into the little throng and turned to face the reporters. Captain Turner then firmly told the reporters to come back in ten minutes and they would hold a small press conference on the main deck. This gave Vanderbilt and Frohman a chance to recover from the badgering and compose themselves. Ten minutes later, Vanderbilt and Frohman appeared on either side of Cunard Commodore Turner and jocularly answered the reporters' questions. The newsreel team was also present.

During the ten minute interview Turner, Frohman and

Vanderbilt made light of the German warning, emphasizing the *Lusitania*'s speed and the fact that she was a civilian passenger liner. The interview swiftly concluded, Turner went straight to the bridge and rang 'Stand by' on the main engine telegraphs. Archie Bryce breathed a great sigh of relief as he rang the repeaters from the engine room.

Shortly after noon, the gangways were landed and the ropes securing her to pier 54 were cast off. The band played on the quarterdeck and the *Lusitania*, bedecked with flags, was nudged away from the pier by three harbour tugs. As her bow was pointed downstream, the docks reverberated to the stentorian blast of her whistle. The tugs cast her off in midstream and *Lusitania*'s turbines began to churn the Hudson River into foam. She was going home.

With the Statue of Liberty sliding astern, *Lusitania* had one brief stop to make before heading out into the Atlantic. Three miles out, at the limit of US territorial waters, was a small blockading force of Royal Navy cruisers, one of which was a former Cunard passenger liner now fulfilling the role of armed merchant cruiser. Captain Turner recognized her immediately, even though his former command was now HMS *Caronia*.

The reason for the brief stop was to drop off a camera and a short report Turner had penned as the ship left New York. Shortly after the tugs had cast off, the master-at-arms had discovered three un-authorized persons near a pantry. It did not take him long to ascertain that the three men were Germans. Having locked the men in the pantry and confiscated their camera, the master-at-arms reported it to Staff Captain Anderson, who in turn reported it to Captain Turner.

It seems likely that the three men were trying to obtain photo-graphic evidence to support the Germans oft made claim that the *Lusitania* was armed. One of the Admiralty installed gun mount-ings was close to the location where they were discovered. Well, Captain Turner was taking no chances. The camera, plates and his report would be handed to *Caronia* and the three Germans would be given free passage to England in the most comfortable cells on the Atlantic.

As the *Lusitania* neared the *Caronia*, a rowing boat came over to collect the items and to give *Lusitania* the *Caronia*'s crew letters to take back to England. Captain Turner went briefly out onto the port bridge wing to wave to his former shipmates on board the *Caronia*. Then as *Caronia*'s party departed, *Lusitania* hauled down all her flags and set out across the Atlantic for home. Her destiny awaited her.

Meanwhile, in the street just outside the entrance to pier 54, that enterprising picture vendor was trying to sell his last few black-bordered photographs of the ship. He was still calling to the dwindling crowds with his distinctive New York accent, 'Pikchure of the Loositaynia's last departchure. It's yer last chance to buy one folks!'

The 202nd Atlantic Voyage

After the tension and uncertainty that accompanied the *Lusitania*'s New York departure, the normal shipboard routine quickly re-established itself. Deck games were played, people could be seen taking the air as they strolled around the promenade areas, and meal times were eagerly anticipated. The war seemed to be a million miles away to the *Lusitania*'s passengers. That was until Wednesday; day four of the voyage.

Wednesday had started ordinarily enough. In fact Captain Turner had even found time to tie a complicated knot from his days in sail. Having completed a four stranded Turk's head he'd decided to send it, via his messenger, to the officers' wardroom with his compliments and a request for an identical one to be returned to him forthwith.

The ship's Chief Officer, Mr Piper, had taken the Captain's handiwork with more than a feeling of irritation and explained to the other officers that 'the old man' had only done it because he thought the task beyond their capabilities. The task of replicating the knot fell to the ship's newest officer, Junior Third Officer Albert Bestic. He had only joined the ship the previous week in New York and he was not long out of sail. He was also the only one in the wardroom who could identify the knot in the first place. It later amused Captain Turner to discover that it was the new Junior Third, whom he had temporarily christened 'Bisset', rather than the Chief Officer or even First Officer Jones who'd accomplished the task.

But by mid-morning the tension started to creep back in. One passenger, Professor I.B.S. Holborne, a lecturer on classical litera-ture travelling in second-class, was particularly perturbed by what he deemed to be the inexcusable lack of lifebelt and lifeboat drills, given the perceived submarine threat.

Although a daily lifeboat drill was conducted, it did not call for the involvement of passengers. It also centred around one of only two particular lifeboats. Some passengers found it mildly amusing to watch an officer blow his whistle whilst six crewmen, all of whom wore a large badge bearing the lifeboat's number, got into the boat, stood to attention and then got out of it again; but not Professor Holborne. In fact, so persistent was he in voicing his concerns to his fellow passengers that some of the other men in second-class sought him out and told him to keep his concerns to himself. 'You are frightening the ladies, sir,' they told him. Well, that was yesterday. Today, he would speak to the captain about it.

Captain Turner listened intently to Professor Holborne's concerns during an interview conducted in his day cabin, the second such interview with a passenger this trip. At the end of the interview, Captain Turner told Holborne that he would have a word with the Chief Officer about it. Holborne wasn't entirely satisfied with this and decided that the captain was simply a stubborn man who quite obviously resented any helpful suggestions from passengers. As for those other passengers who had told him to keep to himself, he decided to call them 'The Ostrich Club'. However, he said no more on the subject of boat drill for the rest of the voyage.

Much has subsequently been made of Captain Turner's 'failure' to conduct 'proper' boat drills during the *Lusitania*'s final voyage, yet whenever one asks those who raise this point exactly what would have been considered a proper drill, particularly bearing in mind that this was wartime, they seem strangely unable to answer. Let us take a moment to examine the alternatives available to Captain Turner whilst the ship was at sea.

To swing out and fill the boats with passengers, then lower them over the side with the ship making 20 knots on the high seas, would patently have been a dangerous practice. To stop the ship to practice abandoning her, would have presented a sitting target to any German U-boat that may have been in the area. To load the boats with passengers and then unload them again would have been just as pointless as the daily drills already appeared. To swing out empty lifeboats, each weighing five tons, and have them dangling over the side whilst the crew practised lowering them with the ship making 20 knots, would also clearly have been absurd and would probably only have resulted in damage.

The daily boat drills as practiced aboard the *Lusitania* on her final voyage, farcical though they may seem to us at this remove, were merely for the visual reassurance of the passengers. They served no purpose as an exercise of training for the crew, but Captain Turner obviously could not have told his passengers this fact.

Meanwhile, events and circumstances in London, Queenstown and on the Atlantic Ocean that Wednesday, were beginning to assume a shape and form that would ultimately have a bearing on the lives of all those aboard the *Lusitania* quite beyond their belief.

At Admiralty House in Whitehall, London, a briefing was taking place in the map room that Wednesday morning as the First Lord, Winston Churchill, was leaving for France after lunch. The briefing was being held so that the First Sea Lord, John Fisher, and Admiral Oliver, who would deputize for Churchill in his absence, would be up to date with what was known as 'the plot'.

The plot referred to the great map of the world's oceans on which was plotted the latest positions of German U-boats, (obtained by wireless intercepts, sighting reports, reports of sinkings etc.) of units of the Royal Navy and any other important ships, such as those under Admiralty charter or others carrying important war supplies. The positions of each of the vessels on the plot was marked with a brightly coloured pin, colour coded to represent the type of vessel. On the head of each pin, to the scale of the map, was a disc, which represented the field of vision of a lookout on board that vessel. The plot was updated continually as each piece of fresh information came in, and was verified. It was upon the plot that all operational decisions of the Admiralty were made.

The plot that Wednesday morning showed two U-boats on or near the Western approaches. *U-30* was shown north of Ireland and heading roughly north-eastwards round Scotland for home and *U-20* north-west of Fastnet, heading south. Also shown near Fastnet, slightly to the south-west, was the cruiser HMS *Juno*, which was detailed to act as an escort for the approaching *Lusitania*, at the end of her patrol. The largest disc of all represented the *Lusitania*, shown well west of Fastnet but approaching at 20 knots. It did not therefore take a genius to work out that one passenger liner, one warship and one enemy submarine were all converging on the same spot: Fastnet.

The decision was taken to recall HMS *Juno* to Queenstown

immediately, due to her vulnerability to submarine attack. Like the *Lusitania*, she was of the pre-dreadnought type of construction. Unlike the *Lusitania*, she had been built in 1898 and was now showing her age. Despite this, she was the flagship of cruiser force E based at Queenstown.

The two ships' shared construction was similar to the cruisers *Aboukir*, *Hogue* and *Cressy*, which had been sunk in the North Sea in September 1914. These cruisers had been attacked one after the other by just one U-boat, one of Germany's older, paraffin-engined types, the *U-9* commanded by *Kapitänleutnant* Otto Weddigen. The cruisers had all capsized and sank rapidly with appalling loss of life. It had become known as the 'livebait squadron debacle'. Those in charge at the Admiralty that Wednesday morning had no desire for a repeat of the incident. Though the very real danger to both ships was there for all to see, only half of it, the danger to HMS *Juno*, was apparently realized.

Unfortunately, it would seem that the minds of Churchill and Fisher were obviously elsewhere during the briefing. Churchill was off to France that afternoon to take part in a Naval convention, the conclusion of which would bring Italy into the war on the side of the Allies. Then, as a diversion from the stresses and strains of his disastrous Dardanelles campaign, Churchill was off to the Front, to see Sir John French make what would ultimately turn out to be an equally disastrous attack on the Aubers ridge.

Fisher's mind was preoccupied with resentment. There was Churchill off to France on a 'jolly' whilst he was left holding the fort again, at such a critical time too. It was unforgivable as far as Fisher was concerned. Why should it all be left to him?

Admiral Oliver was tired of all the infighting too. Fisher and Churchill differed on so many things recently that it was hard to know exactly what was happening. So now Churchill was off to France for five days and already Fisher was sliding into one of his classic sulks. Where would it all end?

The briefing ended with *Juno*'s immediate recall. She would be ordered to head south-east during the night and clear Fastnet by fifty miles. She was then to make for Queenstown with all speed.

No message was sent to Captain Turner of the *Lusitania* to advise him that his escort had now been withdrawn. Nor was he informed of the now perilous situation he faced, in case the Germans intercepted such a sensitive piece of information.

Churchill met his wife for lunch then hurried to Waterloo station to catch his train. Fisher also went to lunch and then adjourned his activities for his afternoon sleep. Oliver returned to his office and dutifully carried on with his paperwork, in which he was habitually twenty-four hours behind.

Late that afternoon in the Atlantic, U-20 halted and challenged a small schooner off Kinsale. The *Earl of Lathom* wasn't worth a torpedo. Her crew were allowed to abandon ship and then U-20 sank her by placing bombs aboard. A message reached the Admiralty, via Queenstown around 21.30 hours that night. No action was taken other than to update the plot with U-20's newest known position.

By midnight, news had come in that the British steamer *Cayo Romano* had been attacked off Queenstown. Fortunately on this occasion U-20's torpedo had missed its target. Once more, U-20's coloured pin was moved further eastward on the Admiralty's map. This time, action was taken. Admiralty Queenstown broadcast the signal '*SUBMARINES ACTIVE OFF SOUTH COAST OF IRELAND*' albeit twenty hours after the first attack. Given that the Admiralty in London knew to within a few hours the position of U-20, it seems rather a half-hearted measure to have taken.

On the next day, Thursday, 6 May U-20 was in the vicinity of the Conningbeg lightship. This lightship marks the entrance to St George's Channel and the last leg of the voyage to Liverpool. In a position approximately twelve miles east of the lightship, U-20 chased and sank the Harrison Line steamer *Candidate*. She was torpedoed and halted. *Kapitänleutnant* Walther Schwieger's boarding party found her to be armed. U-20 finally sank her by gunfire after allowing her crew to escape. Later that day, *Candidate*'s sister ship, *Centurion*, also defensively armed, was given short shrift by Schwieger when he sank her in roughly the same area. U-20 also attacked, though without success, the outward-bound White Star liner *Arabic*. News of the *Candidate*'s sinking reached the Admiralty in London by 11.00 hours on 6 May, but they in turn did not inform Queenstown until twenty-four hours later. By 03.40 hours on the morning of Friday, 7 May the Admiralty also knew the fate of the *Centurion*.

The early evening of Thursday, 6 May 1915 found Captain Turner in his usual position on the port side of the bridge. His mood could best be described as pensive. So far, the voyage had been relatively normal, passengers concerned about lifeboat practice apart, but a Marconi message delivered to him whilst he was at a small party in Charles Frohman's suite had brought him back to the bridge. The short message was doubly disturbing due to its incompleteness. It simply read, '*SUBMARINES ACTIVE OFF THE SOUTH COAST OF IRELAND*'. Captain Turner had asked for a repeat in case some of the message had been lost in transmission. The reply he received was identical. Perhaps when they met *Juno* in the morning, she might have some definite instructions for him.

In the meantime, Captain Turner gave orders for the lifeboats to be swung out and made ready and for all watertight doors to be closed, except those which it was necessary to have open for the working of the ship. The lookouts were doubled and all bright lights extinguished. The *Lusitania* forged ahead at just over 20 knots, which with one boiler room shut down, was close to her maximum speed.

At present, there was nothing more he could do. He decided to go down to the first-class dining saloon for dinner. This was the one mealtime he would have to spend with his passengers, as custom decreed that he should attend the concert in the first-class smoking room afterwards. More importantly, he would also have to address the passengers.

After the concert, a small lectern was placed at one end of the first-class smoking room and the captain took his place behind it. He decided to dispense with the customary speech and simply hold a question and answer session. He felt that this would be more informative for the passengers and would also save time for him, as he was anxious to return to the bridge.

The passengers had noted that the lifeboats were swung out and ready. This of course had renewed their concerns about boat drill. Captain Turner assured the passengers that it was merely a routine precaution, made necessary by the fact that in the early hours of the next morning they would be entering the so-called war zone. Therefore he had duly ordered a slight reduction in the *Lusitania*'s speed, from 20 knots to 18 knots. He closed the session with a further assurance that upon entering the war zone, a Royal Navy cruiser would be alongside to escort them to Liverpool. 'Tomorrow,' he told them, 'we shall be securely in the hands of the Royal Navy.'

Captain Turner took his leave of the passengers and went straight to the bridge. He arrived just in time to receive another Admiralty message. It read:

TO ALL BRITISH SHIPS 0005:
   TAKE LIVERPOOL PILOT AT BAR AND AVOID HEAD-LANDS. PASS HARBOURS AT FULL SPEED. STEER MID-CHANNEL COURSE. SUBMARINES OFF FASTNET.

Those last three words worried him. How far off Fastnet? He told the Marconi room to acknowledge the signal. He then gave orders to the now doubled lookouts to be especially vigilant and to report anything suspicious, however slight, immediately. Stewards were also reminded to ensure that portholes were securely closed and blacked out and to see that there were no gentlemen smoking cigars out on deck. Having done this, Turner went to his day cabin to consider his options.

The passengers returned to their usual evening shipboard routine. In first-class, the ladies retired whilst the men went to the smoking room or played cards. The tension however, was still there. During the course of one card game, an angry scuffle broke out amongst the group of players. Staff Captain Anderson was called to adjudicate in the dispute, which he settled temporarily by ending the game and confiscating the kitty. He promised to give his ruling and divide the kitty accordingly on the morrow. His decision was final.

Captain Turner meanwhile, sat at his desk in his cabin and lit up his black pipe. He needed to make two plans, a main plan and a bad weather plan. The area he was sailing into was notorious for fog and the barometer reading at that moment was giving every indication that he could expect some. He'd crossed the Atlantic on dead reckoning, as always, but he would need a sighting of some prominent feature on land at some point tomorrow in order to get a precise fix on his position.

He was in possession of his Admiralty sailing instructions from Sir Courtenay Bennett. Those were fixed and he was not permitted to deviate from them unless they were countermanded by specific instructions from either a Royal Navy warship or a Marconi message from the Admiralty. So far, he had received neither.

As things stood at the moment, his orders were to clear Fastnet by at least twelve miles, then maintain a minimum of ten miles between his ship and the south coast of Ireland. One option of course was to divert up the west coast of Ireland then come into Liverpool via the North Channel. He would thereby avoid Fastnet altogether and the submarines that the Admiralty now said were lurking there. Well, perhaps *Juno* would order him to do that at their rendezvous. But at the moment, he had to work on the basis of what he knew.

First and foremost, he decided because of that disturbing Marconi message to clear Fastnet rock, an important landfall, by at least twenty miles. He'd reduced speed to 18 knots so as to pass Fastnet during near darkness, reasoning that if a U-boat was lurking anywhere near there, *Lusitania* would be much further out to sea than perhaps the U-boat captain expected and by extinguishing all bright lights she would be harder to see and harder to identify. He then studied the Admiralty advices to mariners. Possibly there would be something in there that could be of help?

Some of them, it transpired, were of no use at all to man or beast. One said not to steer too far out whilst another warned not to come too close inshore. As neither recommended any specific distances, where did the safest course lie? He discarded those. There was one dated 10 February 1915, which read:

> Vessels navigating in submarine areas should have their boats turned out and fully provisioned. The danger is greatest in the vicinity of ports and off prominent headlands on the coast. Important landfalls in this area should be made after dark whenever possible. So far as is consistent with particular trades and state of tides, vessels should make their ports at dawn.

That seemed like sound advice to Turner, who already had his boats swung out. Another of the advices warned vessels to keep off the usual peacetime trade routes, though in his case it did not matter as the Admiralty had set his route. In any case, the *Lusitania*'s peacetime route was only three miles offshore. Tomorrow's route was to be at least ten miles offshore, if not further.

Another memo, also dated 10 February 1915 recommended steering a serpentine course and making full speed if a U-boat was sighted. In Turner's judgement, these advices made the most sense given his situation. He put these to one side and filed all of the others away.

Turning to his tide tables and his chart, he noted that the best time to arrive in Liverpool was 04.00 hours on Saturday morning with the flood tide. There would be sufficient water over the bar and it would also be in accordance with making his port at dawn. He was cleared to proceed into Liverpool without a pilot, which would save him keeping *Lusitania* outside the bar and presenting a sitting target to any U-boat that might be waiting outside of the port.

Timing his arrival thus, he simply worked backwards from Liverpool to plot his course and speed. In this way, his main plan could be easily modified to suit any unexpected circumstances or adverse weather conditions that may be encountered. That done, he left instructions to be called if anything materialized and then he turned in. He would have to be up very early as he anticipated meeting *Juno* shortly after dawn.

Captain Turner did not get much sleep that Thursday night. He was awakened six times with messages from the Marconi room. Each time it was the same message, a repeat of the earlier signal to all British ships. On the sixth instance, he noted that it was half an hour to dawn so he sent his steward to fetch him some tea while he washed, shaved and dressed. For those aboard the *Lusitania*, 'Fateful Friday' had begun.

As he got up, Captain Turner instinctively looked out of the window. He could see absolutely nothing. Fog had closed in around the *Lusitania*. Gulping down the last of the piping hot tea his steward had brought him, he went straight to the bridge.

The fog could be a godsend Turner thought. Visibility was down to about thirty yards and from the bridge he could only just discern the figures of the two lookouts on the bow. He doubted the chances of success for a U-boat in this weather. But the other problem was that he also had to meet *Juno*.

Upon reaching the bridge, he'd ordered a further reduction in *Lusitania*'s speed, to 15 knots. This was because of the fog. He had no wish to collide with HMS *Juno*, nor did he want to miss meeting her. He also checked that the indicator board showed all watertight doors not essential to the working of the ship were still closed.

Though he did not like to disturb the passengers this early in the morning, there was one more thing he had to do. He gave orders

65

for the ship's foghorn to be sounded, a call for *Juno* to hear, as well as an anti-collision measure. Next he went into the chart room. He didn't know their position exactly, but as near as he could figure it by dead reckoning, they were about seventy miles off Cape Clear. On the table, beside the chart, were the Admiralty advices that he'd selected the night before. He read them again now, because he thought it increasingly likely that he'd miss *Juno* in the fog.

Captain Turner calculated that he still needed a mean speed of 18 knots to arrive at Liverpool at 04.00 hours next morning. He certainly did not want to arrive there any earlier, but he would have some time in hand should the fog continue. He went back to the bridge and occupied the port side corner, as he always did when he was concerned. He was watching for *Juno*. As was usual when the captain was on the bridge, nobody spoke and silence reigned supreme. *Lusitania* glided through the swirling fog at a steady 15 knots on course south 87 east, her foghorn booming out at regular intervals. Captain Turner could do nothing more for the moment. At 07.30 hours, he went down to his day cabin to breakfast.

He was about halfway through his kippers when there was a knock on his door. Turner disliked being disturbed while he was eating but his annoyance vanished when his old friend Chief Engineer Archie Bryce entered the room with his morning report. He motioned him to sit down at the breakfast table and invited him to pour himself a cup of tea. He'd wanted a word with Archie in any case.

Turner quickly outlined the situation. He told Bryce of his overall plan to maintain the maximum cruising speed of 18 knots so as to arrive in Liverpool at 04.00 hours on Saturday, but he wanted the steam pressure kept high just in case he rang down for the absolute full speed of 21 knots in an emergency. Bryce expressed mild alarm and asked Turner if he thought the Germans might try to torpedo them. The captain told him that he doubted it personally. Still, it was best not to take chances.

The captain's breakfast over and the engineer's report delivered, Archie Bryce went back down to the engine room and Turner went back up to the bridge. The foghorn boomed out its monotonous call as he peered forward from the portside corner of his bridge. But where was HMS *Juno*?

At Admiralty House in Queenstown, the man in charge was Vice Admiral Sir Charles Henry Coke. He was responsible for the defence of area 21 which extended from Fastnet rock to Carnsore point. His force was derisively known as the 'Gilbert and Sullivan Navy'. He had a motley collection of ageing torpedo boats which ordinarily were not permitted beyond the confines of the harbour, an armed yacht, some fishing boats and a motorboat with which to 'protect' the 285 miles of Ireland's south coast. The armed yacht had only one gun and the fastest vessel in his 'Navy' was capable of 11 knots.

Also based at Queenstown under Rear Admiral Sir Horace Hood was cruiser Squadron E. This force consisted of five ageing cruisers of which HMS *Juno*, the Eclipse class cruiser of 1898 vintage we mentioned earlier, mounting eleven guns of 6-inch calibre, was the flagship. On a good day this flagship was capable of 16.5 knots. Though totally inadequate for their assigned task, these ships were the best available to Coke at the time. His ships, including cruiser Squadron E, were simply the best of a bad bunch, but something was better than nothing.

Vice Admiral Coke worried greatly about his responsibilities given the woefully inadequate state of his forces. But operationally his hands were just as much tied as Captain Turner's were. The Admiralty laid down strict instructions that had to be adhered to at all times, unless directly countermanded by the appropriate authority. Among those instructions was one that stated that all Marconi messages should be of a general and negative nature as the Germans might intercept the Admiralty's messages.

By the morning of Friday, 7 May Coke must have been pacing his office sick with worry. He knew there was a U-boat off Queenstown. He knew about other attacks and the sinkings off Kinsale and the Conningbeg Lightship. He knew that the *Lusitania* was due and he also knew that her escort, HMS *Juno*, had now been withdrawn.

The Admiralty in London had ordered him to protect the *Lusitania* in the best way that he was able. But how could he protect her without her escort and without telling her where the danger was? It was absurd. '*SUBMARINES ACTIVE OFF THE SOUTH COAST OF IRELAND*' was certainly general and negative in nature. It was the only thing he could think of. But he knew it was not enough.

Meanwhile, out in the Atlantic twenty-five miles south of Cape Clear, the fog still swirled around the *Lusitania*. Though Captain

Turner was practically convinced that he would not find *Juno* if it persisted, he still doubted that any U-boat would find *Lusitania* in it. But he knew that he must establish his position before he even dared to approach St George's Channel. The entrance to the channel was twenty-four miles wide with rocks and shoals on either side. There would also be other shipping using the channel. He could not set an accurate course without a fix.

Just before 11.00 hours, the *Lusitania* broke through the fog into hazy sunshine. To port was an indistinct smudge, which was the Irish coastline. But there was no sign of any other ships and certainly no sign of HMS *Juno*. Captain Turner immediately ordered an increase in speed, back to 18 knots. The foghorn now ceased its booming call.

Barely had he done this when a messenger from the Marconi room brought him a signal. It was twelve words, but Turner did not recognize the cipher. It was from Vice Admiral Coke in Queenstown, relayed through the naval wireless station at Valentia. Because of the high-grade code used to send the signal, Turner would have to take it down to his day cabin to work on it.

At 11.55 hours there was a knock on Turner's cabin door. It was the messenger with another signal from the Admiralty. Turner broke off from his decoding work to read it. It said:

SUBMARINE ACTIVE IN SOUTHERN PART OF IRISH CHANNEL, LAST HEARD OF TWENTY MILES SOUTH OF CONNINGBEG LIGHT VESSEL. MAKE CERTAIN *LUSITANIA* GETS THIS.

This gave Captain Turner another problem. According to this latest message, another U-boat was operating in the very middle of the channel he was aiming for. If this were true, then despite his Admiralty instructions, a mid-channel course was now out of the question. 'Twenty miles South of Conningbeg Light Vessel' WAS the mid-channel point. True, *Lusitania* wouldn't arrive there till later and it would be dark when she did, but it did not make sense to Turner to drive his ship toward a submarine he now knew to be there. More than ever, he now had to determine his exact position, if he was going to have to play a potentially deadly game of cat and mouse with a U-boat in a narrow channel entrance. But first he decided to finish deciphering Coke's earlier message. Perhaps it might contain something concrete upon which he could make a plan.

By 12.10 hours he had finished decoding it completely. What he read galvanized him. He went straight to the bridge. HMS *Juno* didn't matter any more, in fact unbeknown to him she was now entering Queenstown harbour following her urgent recall.

Immediately he entered the bridge he altered the ship's course by twenty degrees to port. Third Officer Lewis was then dispatched to make a fast round of the ship to check that all portholes on the lower decks were closed. The turn to port was so sudden that many passengers momentarily lost their balance. The *Lusitania* was now closing to the land at 18 knots on course north 67 east. Captain Turner needed to fix his position immediately. The clock on the bridge said 12.15 hours, GMT.

Somewhat ahead of the *Lusitania*, in a position roughly twenty-two miles south of Waterford, the German submarine *U-20* blew her tanks and surfaced. The fog, which had been troubling her commander, *Kapitänleutnant* Walther Schwieger, had finally cleared. In many ways, it had been a disappointing patrol, which thankfully was nearly over. The successes of the last two days had improved the morale of the crew, but they were now down to their last three torpedoes and his orders were to save two for the trip home, just in case they encountered an enemy warship and had to fight their way out of it.

Earlier, whilst they had been submerged, the sound of very powerful propellers had been heard passing over them. Coming up to periscope depth, Schwieger saw an old cruiser rapidly disappearing toward Queenstown. It was no use trying to catch her. The cruiser was HMS *Juno*, making all speed and zig-zagging.

Up on the conning tower Schwieger now checked his watch. It was 12.20 hours GMT as the *U-20* headed back toward Fastnet at full speed.

At 12.40 hours, whilst the *Lusitania* was still on course north 67 east, Captain Turner received another Admiralty signal. This one read: '*SUBMARINE FIVE MILES SOUTH OF CAPE CLEAR, PROCEEDING WEST WHEN SIGHTED AT 10 AM.*'

He allowed himself a slight smile. This latest signal meant that the immediate danger was passed. He had been right; the fog had undoubtedly saved them as the submarine off Fastnet had now evidently given up. Cape Clear was many miles astern of *Lusitania*.

The entrance to St George's Channel, and therefore the next notified U-boat threat, would have been four to five hours away if *Lusitania* had maintained her original course. As far as Captain Turner knew, there were now no U-boats in his immediate vicinity.

Yet the most curious thing in all this was that there was no submarine off Cape Clear, there never had been. The 'Fastnet' submarine was obviously a figment of someone's imagination. But the 'Conningbeg' submarine was real enough. Only now of course, it was no longer near Conningbeg.

At 13.20 hours GMT, *U-20* was still running on the surface, heading back toward Fastnet. Schwieger was still up on the conning tower with the lookouts, the air was a lot fresher up there. Suddenly, the starboard lookout saw smoke off the *U-20*'s starboard bow. Schwieger focussed his binoculars on it. He could see the shape of a big ship with one, two, three, four funnels. Only the biggest ships had four. He estimated the distance between them to be twelve to fourteen miles. It would be a long shot but if the ship was heading for Queenstown, it might just be possible. As the diving klaxon screeched out its warning, *U-20* altered course to intercept, and quickly began to submerge.

At 13.40 hours GMT, Captain Turner saw a landmark as familiar to him as his own front door; a long promontory with a lighthouse on top of it, which was painted with black and white horizontal bands. The Old Head of Kinsale. For centuries, the Old Head of Kinsale had been an important landmark for the world's mariners. It was, in a way, like the *Lusitania* herself, impossible to mistake.

Now he knew for certain where he was and ordered *Lusitania*'s course reverted to south 87 east, steady. Turning back to his officers on the bridge, Captain Turner noticed 'Bisset', due to go off watch in about fifteen minutes. 'Ah, Bisset. Do you know how to take a four point bearing?' he asked. Bestic certainly did. He also knew that it took the best part of an hour with the ship's course and speed having to remain rock steady whilst it was done. 'Yes sir,' he replied. 'Good,' said Captain Turner, 'then kindly take one off that lighthouse, will you?' And with that Turner left the bridge and went into the chartroom. He knew what 'Bisset' was thinking, but attention to detail was one of the things that could one day make a good junior officer into a good master.

Bestic needn't have worried. Lewis came back at 14.00 hours and relieved him anyway, knowing what the 'old man' had done. Bestic took the first set of bearing figures to Captain Turner in the chartroom on his way off the bridge. He then went to his small cabin to finish writing up the ship's log.

Using the figures that Bestic had given him, Turner worked out that they were now fourteen miles offshore and west of the Old Head. He needed the full set of bearing figures to be exact, but it was a good start. He now had to plot a safe course through the mine-free channel into Queenstown harbour.

They were not going to Liverpool after all, not yet anyway. The message from Vice Admiral Coke, which was sent in the high-grade naval code, was ordering him to divert *Lusitania* into Queenstown immediately. Exactly as had previously happened to him when he'd brought the *Transylvania* over last February and standard Admiralty practice in situations of grave peril. Obviously, Turner thought, they were not going to allow him to take his ship into the comparatively narrow entrance of St George's Channel knowing that there was a U-boat waiting for him at that very location.

But what Captain Turner didn't know, because the Admiralty hadn't told him, was that the 'U-boat off Conningbeg Lightship' report, far from being current, was already twenty-eight hours old. They hadn't told him that this U-boat had sunk two cargo ships there, attacked a large passenger liner and had, in fact, sunk a sailing ship off Queenstown two days ago. Nor did they tell him that they were certain that this U-boat was now on its way home and at that moment, was off Queenstown; though they had specifically informed Rear Admiral Hood aboard HMS *Juno* of this at 07.45 hours that morning, which is why *Juno* was making all speed and zig-zagging when Schwieger spotted her.

Kapitänleutnant Schwieger was, at that moment, studying the big ship through *U-20*'s attack periscope. Calling to the U-boat's pilot, Schwieger said, 'Four funnels, schooner rig, upwards of 20,000 tons and making about 22 knots.' Lanz, the pilot, checked first in his copy of *Jane's Fighting Ships* and secondly, as confirmation, *Brassey's Naval Annual*. They were two standard British publications that every German U-boat carried to identify potential targets. Lanz called back to Schwieger, 'Either the *Lusitania* or the *Mauretania*. Both listed as armed merchant cruisers and used for trooping.'

U-20 prepared for action. One G-type torpedo was loaded into a forward tube. Wiesbach, the torpedo officer reported the tube ready for firing. Just then, Schwieger noticed the target altering course. He could not believe his luck! He noted later in his logbook 'The ship turns to starboard then takes a course to Queenstown. . .'. Exactly what he had hoped she would do! Involuntarily, *Lusitania* was now closing the distance between them. It would not be a long shot after all.

At a range of about 550 metres (600 yards), Schwieger gave the deadly order, 'Fire One!' The torpedo cleared the tube and streaked towards its target at 38 knots, its running depth set at three metres, about ten feet.

Captain Turner had come out of the chartroom and was standing in his usual place on the port side of the bridge. He was watching Third Officer Lewis working on the four-point bearing. Beyond him, stood a quartermaster right out on the bridge wing acting as a lookout. There was another on the starboard bridge wing. But it was from the crow's nest that the sudden warning came, via the telephone. 'Torpedo coming on the starboard side!'

At that moment, the ship's orchestra was playing Strauss's *The Blue Danube* for the benefit of those passengers who were just finishing lunch. One minute all was the usual picture of tranquillity that was life aboard the *Lusitania*, but in the next moment all hell broke loose.

The Sinking of the *Lusitania*

Captain Turner, responding to the lookout's warning, looked to starboard in shocked disbelief just in time to see the white streak in the water. But before he could even shout a helm order, the torpedo struck the ship with a sound that he later recalled was 'like a heavy door being slammed shut'. Almost instantaneously came a second, much larger explosion, which physically rocked the ship. A tall column of water and debris shot skyward.

At this moment, Junior Third Officer Albert Bestic was in his cabin. The baggage master, Mr Crank, had sent a messenger to him with a request that he come forthwith to the baggage room, to oversee the unloading of the passengers' luggage. Now that they were making an unscheduled stop at Queenstown, Crank thought it prudent to start piling some of the luggage on the foredeck, in order to save time, and possibly passenger complaints, when the ship docked. Bestic was just about to follow the messenger down to the forward hold when he realized that he was still wearing his best uniform. Pausing to change into his working uniform ultimately saved his life, as there were no survivors from the baggage room. They were all killed when the torpedo struck the ship just below the area where they were working.

Up on the bridge, Captain Turner quickly looked at the Pearson's Fire and Flood indicator board. It was going absolutely mad, showing fire and extensive flooding in the whole of the forward section ahead of boiler room No. 1. The tall column of water and debris now cascaded down and wrecked one of the forward starboard lifeboats. A glance at the commutator revealed that the *Lusitania* was already listing five degrees to starboard and was also down by the head. The clock on the bridge said 14.10 hours.

Watching events through his periscope, Schwieger could not

believe that so much havoc could have been wrought by just one torpedo. He noted in his log that, 'an unusually heavy detonation' had taken place and noted that a second explosion had also occurred which he put down to perhaps, 'boilers, coal or powder'. He also noticed that the torpedo had hit the *Lusitania* further forward of where he had aimed it. He therefore revised his estimate of the *Lusitania*'s speed to 'not more than 20 knots'. After allowing Lanz a quick look at the stricken liner, Schwieger brought the periscope down and *U-20* headed back to sea, to begin her voyage home.

On the bridge of the *Lusitania*, the slant of the deck grew steeper by the minute. Captain Turner shouted to Quartermaster Johnston, who was at the helm, to close any watertight doors that remained open and to put the helm over toward land.

Looking forward, Captain Turner suddenly realized that there was no hope of saving his ship. The bows of the liner were dipping toward the sea at an alarming rate. Beaching her was patently out of the question. He knew they were fourteen miles from shore and she was sinking so fast that they'd never make it. He steeled himself and then gave the order to abandon ship. He also instructed Second Officer Hefford to send the ship's carpenter forward to assess the damage. He then went out onto the port bridge wing and looked back along the boat deck.

The first thing he saw was that all the portside lifeboats had swung inboard, which meant that all those on the starboard side had swung outboard. The starboard ones could be launched, though with a little difficulty, but the port side boats would be virtually impossible to launch.

Each of the five-ton wooden lifeboats had a metal chain called a snubbing chain, which held the boats to the deck to steady them when they were swung out. Prior to lowering the boat, a release-pin had to be knocked out using a hammer, otherwise the boat would remain chained to the deck.

Looking forward again, Turner also felt a breeze on his face. The ship was still under way. He had to stop her so that the boats could be safely lowered. Instinctively, he went back inside and rang down to the engine room for, 'full astern'. The engine room dutifully complied and something catastrophic then occurred as the steam pressure was applied to the astern turbines. Probably it was the valve defect in the low pressure turbines that Mr Laslett had reported, or possibly something else equally devastating. Either way, whatever happened down there blew the end cap off a condenser up on the boat deck that nearly took Third Officer Lewis' head off.

Realizing the calamity, the engines were reverted to 'full ahead' to relieve the strain on whatever part of the system had gone disastrously wrong. Unfortunately, the overall steam pressure had now dropped drastically to barely 50psi, having escaped through whatever damage the system had suddenly sustained, so the *Lusitania*'s massive turbines were now virtually out of commission. There was hardly enough steam pressure left to drive them.

Shortly after the torpedo struck, first-class passenger Isaac Lehman went to his cabin to gather up some of his personal belongings. Among the items he put into his jacket pocket was a loaded revolver, just in case.

At 14.11 hours, the *Lusitania* had started sending distress signals from the Marconi room. 'SOS, SOS, SOS. COME AT ONCE. BIG LIST. 10 MILES SOUTH OLD KINSALE. MFA.' The last three letters were the *Lusitania*'s call sign; the distance was a quick guess at their position by Mr Leith, the Marconi operator.

When Vice Admiral Coke received his copy of that distress signal, it must have seemed to him as though his worst nightmare had come true. He had tried in vain all morning to obtain a firm decision from the Admiralty in London. However, Fisher had been 'unavailable' all morning, Churchill was in France and Oliver it seemed, would do nothing off his own bat, or at least not without consulting Fisher, perhaps.

In the end, Coke had been so worried by the obvious danger that he had taken it upon himself to divert the *Lusitania* into Queenstown. Unfortunately, it was all too late. Still, there was one thing he could do. He dashed off a signal to Rear Admiral Hood in *Juno* and sent him to the rescue. Hood cleared Queenstown in a remarkably short time and headed out toward the *Lusitania*'s last known position. Coke then sent a detailed signal to the Admiralty in London, advising them of what had happened and of his actions and the measures he had taken.

On the *Lusitania*, the list indicator had just gone through the 15 degree mark. Captain Turner was back out on the port side wing of the bridge. He had ordered Staff Captain Anderson not to lower any of the boats until the ship had lost a sufficient amount of her momentum to render it safe. In some cases, on the port side, that meant getting the passengers out of the lifeboats in order to lower them to the rail. But the passengers did not want to get out of the boats.

At boat station No.2 on the port side, Junior Third Officer Bestic was in charge. Standing on the after davit, he was trying to keep order and explain that due to the heavy list, the boat could not be lowered. Suddenly, he heard the sound of a hammer striking the release-pin to the snubbing chain. Before the word 'NO!' left his lips, the chain was freed and the five-ton lifeboat laden with over fifty passengers swung inboard and crushed those standing on the boat deck against the superstructure. Unable to take the strain, the men at the davits let go of the falls and No.2 boat, plus the collapsible boat stowed behind it, slid down the deck towing a grisly collection of injured passengers and jammed under the bridge wing, right beneath the spot where Captain Turner was standing.

Bestic, determined to stop the same situation arising at the next boat station, jumped along to No.4 boat, just as somebody knocked out the release-pin. He darted out of the way as No.4 boat slid down the deck maiming and killing countless more people, before crashing into the wreckage of the first two boats.

Bestic then fought his way through the crowd to No.6 boat where Staff Captain Anderson, seeing what had happened, was trying to get the people out of the lifeboat. But as fast as some got out, others got in. Anderson sent Bestic back to the bridge with a request that the port side trim tanks be flooded to counteract the starboard list. They could then lower the port side boats. Having dispatched Bestic, Anderson gave orders for everyone to get out of the boats whilst the crew and some of the male passengers attempted to manhandle the boats over the rail.

By the time Bestic came back to tell him that the generators had failed so there was no power to the trimming system, the shout had gone round that Anderson was preventing women and children from entering the lifeboats. Driven by panic, passengers swarmed into boat Nos. 6, 8 and 10. One after the other they swung inboard and then careered down the deck to join boat Nos. 2 and 4.

Standing on the port bridge wing looking down on the carnage, Captain Turner was horrified by the spectacle. A shout from Quartermaster Johnston telling him that the list had now increased to 20 degrees, cut through his horror. Turning away from the grisly scene he saw that the *Lusitania*'s bows were now completely underwater.

When Isaac Lehman returned to the port side boat deck, he noticed that No.16 boat was gone. It had been smashed to pieces during a futile attempt to slide it down the ship's side laden with passengers, most of whom were now dead or seriously injured in the water. The protruding rivet heads of the ship's hull plating had literally torn the lifeboat to pieces during its descent.

Standing at No.18 boat, Lehman asked one of the seamen, who was holding a fire-axe, why it was filled but not being launched. The seaman told him that the captain had ordered them not to launch any more boats until it was safe. Drawing and cocking his revolver, Lehman levelled the gun at the sailors and said, 'To hell with the captain! Can't you see this ship is sinking! I will shoot to kill, the first man who disobeys my order to launch this boat!'

The frightened crewmen did as Lehman ordered and No.18 boat, laden with fifty to sixty passengers swung inboard as the chain was freed, simultaneously disarming and badly injuring Lehman, then crushing those standing behind it into the smoking room windows, before it too, careered down the deck to join its predecessors.

Meanwhile, in the first-class entrance hall on the boat deck, millionaire Alfred G. Vanderbilt and his valet, Ronald Denyer, were shepherding all the children they could find to the starboard lifeboats. Whilst doing this, they constantly had to ignore the desperate screams of those passengers trapped between decks in the first-class elevators by the power failure.

Though difficult to launch due to the severe list the *Lusitania* had adopted, the crew manning the starboard lifeboats were having marginally more success than their counterparts on the port side, but horrible mistakes were still made.

Because the ship was sinking so fast, some boats were launched in such a hurry that the chains weren't released, so they remained chained to the deck of the sinking liner. Others had the chain freed but were then hastily lowered, landing bow or stern first in the water and spilling the occupants into the sea. One or two were simply dropped into the ocean and smashed to pieces, though some were launched successfully.

Meanwhile, fresh screams from behind him told Captain Turner that yet another of the lifeboats on the port side had added to the carnage below him. The *Lusitania* was set to capsize completely unless her bows struck the bottom first. 'Twenty five degrees to starboard!', shouted Quartermaster Johnston. 'Then save yourself', Turner told him. Johnston needed no second telling. He hurriedly put on a lifebelt and simply stepped into the water, which was rising inexorably up the starboard side of the bridge.

Captain Turner was now alone out on the port wing of the bridge. As the stern rose higher, he gripped the signal halyards and looked aft at the passengers swarming up the boat deck, all desperately seeking the illusion of safety away from the rapidly encroaching water. The *Lusitania*'s four immense black-painted funnels towered overhead at a crazy angle. Just then, the ship's doctor strenuously worked his way 'uphill' to stand with him. Neither man spoke but it was the last Turner saw of him.

Lusitania's forward momentum suddenly ceased. Looking quickly toward the liner's bows, Turner realized that they had in fact struck the bottom. The sea was now swirling over the bridge floor. He went back inside and worked his way into the chartroom, seizing the chart he'd been working on and quickly stuffing it inside his tunic, though he didn't know why. The *Lusitania*'s stern now began to settle back and a surge of water flooded the bridge, sweeping him out of the port side door and off the ship.

As the *Lusitania* sank beneath the waves, that same surge of water swept along the boat deck, carrying Junior Third Officer Bestic, who had witnessed the earlier efforts of Vanderbilt and Denyer, out through the first-class entrance hall and into the ocean. The *Lusitania* was gone. It was 14.28 hours GMT.

Only six lifeboats out of a total of forty-eight were afloat amid the wreckage. Neither Vanderbilt, nor theatre producer Charles Frohman survived, as neither man could swim. The last picture of Charles Frohman that anybody saw was of him standing on the deck with his friends near the first-class entrance hall, the very picture of calm. He was leaning heavily on his 'wife', the walking stick that he had relied upon since developing rheumatoid arthritis, and quoting a line from the play that he himself had made famous, *Peter Pan* by J. M. Barrie. 'Why fear death? To die would be an awfully big adventure!' he said, as they suddenly all joined hands and were engulfed by the water surging up the boat deck.

As those fortunate enough to have survived, whose number included some of Frohman's party as well as Isaac Lehman,

1. RMS *Lusitania.*

(*via Lusitania Online*)

2. Invitation sent to selected guests for the trial cruise of the *Lusitania.*
(*via Lusitania Online*)

The Chairman & Directors of John Brown & Company Limited
and
The Chairman & Directors of The Cunard Steam Ship Company Limited
request the honour of the company of

at the Trial Cruise (round Ireland to Liverpool) of the
Quadruple Screw Turbine Steamer, "Lusitania,"
on ————————— The Steamer will leave the Tail of
the Bank at (about) 7·30 p.m., on arrival at Gourock of 6·30 p.m.
train from Central Station, Glasgow, which connects with 10 a.m.
train from London, (Euston).

Clydebank,
July, 1907.

Vessel will probably reach Liverpool early on Monday.

————

Card of Admission will be sent on receipt of acceptance.

An early reply is requested.
Addressed to Clydebank.

RMS "LUSITANIA"   SUNDAY, SEPTEMBER 13, 1914

Menu

Tortue Verte   Crême Chatrillon

Supreme de Sole—Palace

Mousse de Jambon—Alexandra

Sirloin & Ribs of Beef

Green Peas   Rice   Cauliflower á la Crême
Boiled, Mashed & Chateau Potatoes

Chapon—Chipolata

Salade de Saison

Pouding Saxone

Gâteau Mexicaine   Petits Fours

Bavarois au Chocolat

Ices

Dessert   Café

3. Menu for RMS *Lusitania* on Sunday, 13 September 1914.
(Cunard Archive via Lusitania Online)

4. This silver teaspoon was part of the cutlery aboard the *Lusitania* on her maiden voyage.
(Cobwebs/Lusitania Online)

5. Part of the *Lusitania*'s dinner service. This plate is one of only a few which survived the salvage operation.
(Cobwebs/Lusitania Online)

7. *Lusitania* being docked in the Sandon half-tide basin in Liverpool. The tugs are from the Alexander Towing Company.

(*via Lusitania Online*)

6. *Lusitania* loading at the Prince's landing stage in Liverpool.

(*via Lusitania Online*)

8. *Lusitania* on a foggy winter's day at the Prince's landing stage, Liverpool.

(*via Lusitania Online*)

9. Captain Turner was the Commodore of the Cunard Line. This photo was taken when he was in command of the Cunard flagship *Aquitania* in 1914.

(via Lusitania Online)

10. *Kapitänleutnant* Walther Schwieger, commander of *U-20*.

(Illustration by John Gray)

11. *Lusitania* is struck by *U-20*'s torpedo. *(Illustration by John Gray)*

12. Diagram showing the impact point of Schwieger's torpedo on the *Lusitania*.
(via Lusitania Online)

New York Tribune

First to Last—the Truth: News · Editorials · Advertisements

Vol. LXXV....No. 25,010.

[Copyright, 1915,
By The Tribune Association.]

SATURDAY, MAY 8, 1915.

PRICE ONE CENT In City of New York, Jersey City and Newark. ELSEWHERE TWO CENTS

GUARANTEE
Your Money Back
If You Want It.
See Editorial Page, First Column.

WEATHER
FAIR TO-DAY AND TO-MORROW;
SOUTHWEST TO WEST WINDS.
Yesterday's Temperatures:
High, 61; Low, 56.
Full report on Page 13.

900 Die as Lusitania Goes to Bottom;
400 Americans on Board Torpedoed Ship;
Washington Stirred as When Maine San[k]

CAPITAL AROUSED, SITUATION GRAVEST YET FACED IN WAR

Washington Determined That Germany Shall Not Be Allowed to Shirk Responsibility for Deaths.

GREATLY FEARS LOSS OF AMERICANS

President Shows Nervousness as Bulletins of Disaster Come In—Strongest Protest Yet Made Planned Even if No U. S. Citizens Were Lost

From The Tribune Bureau.]

Washington, May 7.—The news of the heavy loss of life on the Lusitania stirred Washington as it has not been stirred since the sinking of the Maine. The earlier reports that both passengers and crew had been landed safely had quieted apprehensions of an immediate crisis in the relations of the United States and Germany. But when it became clear that Americans—undoubtedly a considerable number of them—were to be counted among the victims of German savagery at sea the full significance of the tragedy of Queenstown struck home.

President Wilson made little effort to conceal his feelings. At 8 o'clock to-night the President received the following dispatch from the United States Consul at Cork:

"Lusitania sank at 2:30 o'clock. Probably many survivors. Rescue work proceeding favorably. Shall I send you list of survivors?"

As soon as he read it he put on his hat and walked out of the White House without the knowledge of the Secret Service men who were guarding him. The President walked up Sixteenth Street to Corcoran Street, crossed over to Fifteenth Street and back to the White House, where he went into his study to await further information and to turn over in his mind the message that it is expected he will send to the German Foreign Office as soon as all the details of the disaster are known.

Cabinet To Be Called Together.

The President will probably call the Cabinet together to-morrow to discuss what action this government may take in reply to the inquiry from Consul Frost, at Queenstown, as to whether he should send a list of survivors, the State Department instructed him to send a list of all Americans dead, injured or missing.

That State Department officials feared the sinking of the Lusitania for some other basis passenger-carrying vessel was indicated a few days ago, when Secretary Bryan issued a statement saying that no passports would be issued to persons going abroad for pleasure.

High officials in the administration declined to-night to discuss the possibility of this country being drawn into the war because of the loss of American lives. They insisted upon taking an optimistic view of the situation and asserted that when the loss of survivors was finally made up few would be found to be missing.

That the situation will be acute when loss of American lives is proved is admitted on all sides. No action will be taken by this government until all the details of the torpedoing of the Lusitania are received. There is no thing certain, however, and that is that Germany will not be allowed to shirk any responsibility for the disaster, should investigation show that the act was performed by a German submarine.

The possibility of the Lusitania being struck a mine was discussed here to-night on the basis of news that the British Admiralty had given assurances that there were no mines in the neighborhood in which the vessel was threatened.

Protest Will Be Vigorous.

Even if an American loss had been lost, the sinking of the Cunard liner by a German torpedo would have been made a part of the most vigorous protest that the American government yet transmitted to the German Foreign Office. This is the belief of officials high in the administration to-night.

The United States has repeatedly protested that it recognizes the right of no nation to wield such wanton rule, and that it would hold the German government to strict accountability for the loss of any American lives through the underseas warfare of the German government.

The United States has no comment over the sinking of the Lusitania itself, but it is gravely concerned over the probable loss of lives of American citizens through the activity of German submarines in the war zone. In the note of the American government to the German Foreign Office the American government declared that this country would take any steps to safeguard American lives and property and to secure American citizens the full enjoyment of

Continued on page 2, column 2

LONDON SEES VITAL QUESTION FOR U. S.

America Is 'Bound to Defend Lives of Its Subjects,' Declares 'Daily News.'

[By Cable to The Tribune.]

London, May 7.—The "Daily Chronicle" says editorially to-day:

"To destroy by deliberate aim one of the great floating towns which ever cross the Atlantic without submerging the 2,000 lives in their keeping, is to attempt in cold blood such a massacre as foam-combatants as even the most ferocious conquerors have seldom perpetrated save in real.

"When, last October, the Germans began to saw floating mines in the Atlantic, a shudder went through the nation in the blow struck at Britain, the 'torch enemy,' through the tampering of the Lusitania.

"This is a masterstroke, which will carry transatlantic travelling and interlade Great Britain more effectively than a whole fleet of super-dreadnoughts could possibly accomplish," said a stalwart captain of cavalry. "It's the dawn of Great Britain."

Toasts to U Sailors.

And then followed the toasts to the Kaiser, to von Tirpitz and to the U boat heroes.

At Luschow's, in Fourteenth Street, the show of patriotism was subdued. The orchestra had been instructed to play only patriotic songs, and those were sung with a vim by the Germans, who packed the premises to suffocation. The women and children they had come to celebrate the "victory."

The goblet and toasts raised often to the Kaiser last night at the Hofbrau Haus, Broadway and Thirteenth Street, and at the Kaiserhof, 24th Broadway. There was little heart as either place, but there was a muffled feeling of good cheer and camaraderie in the news that the Lusitania had been sunk by a German submarine.

A thousand dollars was raised to night, the German custom at the Hofbrau Haus, "The Hyphen," for the sake of hearing the greatest exhibitions of German feeling...

GERMANS TOAST 'VICTORY' AMID 'HOCHS' IN CAFES.

Steins Clink as Celebrators Predict Downfall of Britain's Sea Power.

OFFICERS GAY IN CLUBHOUSE

Restaurants Thronged and Entire Families Out to Cheer Kaiser and His Submarines.

"Deutschland, Deutschland Über Alles" resounded last night wherever Germans met to discuss and to toast "the day" which, in their need, sealed the fate of British world dominion on the seas. In the fashionable German Club, headquarters of the Teutonic élite and camping ground of German military officers unable to join their colors, the sinking of the Lusitania was the principal topic of animated conversation. Everything else was forgotten, in the sinking of the Lusitania.

"An act of barbarity without justification," was the expression of Frederic R. Coudert, of the law firm of Coudert Brothers, in referring to the torpedoing of the Lusitania.

"I make that statement on the supposition that lives of citizens of the United States, a neutral nation, were destroyed by the sinking of the vessel," he added. "Until it is known definitely that the results of the explosion are it is unreasonable to hint at the stand this government may take.

"There is no justification, however, for ruthlessly sinking a merchant ship in the open seas when that vessel is not engaged in any manner as a belligerent vessel and when the lives of non-combatants depend upon its safety.

"Of course, a great deal depends upon whether the Lusitania was armed...

U. S. OWES IT TO SELF-RESPECT TO ACT, SAYS ROOSEVELT; 'PIRACY ON VAST SCALE'

[From a Staff Correspondent of The Tribune.]

Syracuse, May 7.—After the appalling details of the Lusitania disaster had been told to Colonel Roosevelt to-night he said: "It seems inconceivable that we should refrain from taking action on this matter, for we owe it not only to humanity but to our own national self-respect.

"This represents not merely piracy, but piracy on a vaster scale and more than any old-time pirate ever practiced. This is the warfare which destroyed Louvain and Dinant and hundreds of men, women and children in Belgium; warfare to innocent men, women and children travelling on the ocean, to our own fellow country men and country women who are among the sufferers."

ACT OF BARBARITY, SAYS F. R. COUDERT

Lawyer Insists Sinking of Lusitania Is Without Justification.

MANY NOTED NEW YORKERS ON LUSITANIA

Alfred G. Vanderbilt Was on Way to England on Business Trip.

N. J. REPRESENTED ON FIRST CABIN LIST

Charles Frohman, Lindon Bates, Jr., Charles Klein and Justus Miles Forman Aboard.

As usual, a large proportion of the Lusitania's first cabin list was composed of New Yorkers.

Alfred G. Vanderbilt was necessarily a prominent figure among the passengers. His brother, Cornelius, was, like many others, skeptical when he heard the first rumors about the Lusitania's fate. Captain George C. Day and Commander F. L. Sawyer, both United States naval officers, who are working with Mr. Vanderbilt on the plans for the reception of the Atlantic fleet, were incredulous, too. But when Mr. Vanderbilt learned through The Tribune that the news had been confirmed, he asked the newspaper for confirmation bulletins.

His brother Alfred expected to be gone for four or five weeks on a business trip. Had it not been for the war, Mrs. Vanderbilt would have accompanied her husband on the trip.

Major F. Warren Pearl and Mrs. Pearl, who sailed with their children, are well known in New York. Both had intended to do war aid work. Major Pearl, who is a surgeon, was to be attached to a field hospital for the Allies in Belgium, while Mrs. Pearl hoped to assist in relief work for the Belgians. Their four children were a daughter of Mrs. J. F. Duncan and sister of Mrs. Otto Drucker.

Continued on page 2, column 4

FIRST SURVIVORS' NAMES RECEIVED

The first names of survivors of the Lusitania disaster received here are as follows:

Lessinger, General, and son, first cabin.
Brashuran, Mrs., second cabin.
Smith, George A., New York, class merchant.
Smith, Jas. J. T., Braceville, Ohio.

TWO TORPEDOES FIRED, SAYS STEW[ARD]

Attack Made About Eight Miles from Irish C[oast,] Broad Daylight and in Fine Weather—Survivor Tells of Bravery of Cunard Officers

[By Cable to The Tribune.]

London, May 8, 3 a. m.—At least 900 lives were lo[st when] the Lusitania was torpedoed without warning at s[ea] yesterday afternoon by a German submarine, accord[ing to] mates by survivors. The estimate of First Officer Jon[es may] total nearer 1,500.

Of the dead, more than two hundred are suppo[sed to be] Americans, as it is believed that over 400 on boa[rd]

A dispatch from Queenstown sent out at midnight s[aid:]

"Up to the present 520 passengers from the Lus[itania] have been landed here from boats. Ten or eleven b[odies] ashore, and others are expected."

The motor boat Elizabeth has arrived at Kinsale [and says] that at 3:30 p. m. she picked up two lifeboats contain[ing] 16 survivors of the Lusitania, respectively. A Cork tug [also] rescued to Queenstown. They were mostly women and [children.]

The Lusitania could not launch many of her lifeboat[s.]

The tiny hospitals at Kinsale and Clonakilty, and the [sta-] tions at Cork and Queenstown are jammed with survivors [of the] ocean horror, those not actually wounded suffering terr[ible] shock. The giant Cunarder now rests on the bottom of t[he sea] about eight miles off Kinsale Head and twenty miles fro[m en-] trance to Queenstown Harbor.

ADMIRALTY GIVES OUT NEWS.

Telegrams have been filtering into London last n[ight and] early this morning stating that the rescued are being l[anded at] Queenstown by three steamers. The Admiralty says betw[een 600] and 800 have already been landed at Clonakilty in th[e Kin-] sale, coming into the latter port in a string of boats tow[ed by a] Greek steamer. Motor fishing boats hovered near the sc[ene of the] wreck, picking up what boats they could and turning the[m into] the powerful ocean going tug Stormcock.

Huge crowds till Cockspur Street near the Haymark[et, fac-] ing the Cunard offices for news. The women, who had be[en wait-] ing so bitterly, paused for a moment when an agent of [the] bellowed through a megaphone the following dispatch:

"Our Liverpool office says First Officer Jones from [the] Queenstown he thinks between five hundred and six hundr[ed] been saved. This includes passengers and crew, and h[e] estimate."

A reward in the first boat which landed at Kinsale [re-] feared that 900 lives had been lost.

PASSENGERS WERE AT LUNCHEON.

The tug Stormcock returned to Queenstown, bring[ing] one hundred and fifty survivors, principally passengers, o[f] whom were many women, several of the crew and one ste[ward.]

Describing the experience of the Lusitania, the stew[ard said:]

"The passengers were at luncheon, when a submarine a[ppeared] and fired two torpedoes, which struck the Lusitania on [the] board side, one forward and the other in the engine room [which] caused terrific explosions.

"Captain Turner immediately ordered the boats to [be] ship began to list badly immediately.

"Ten boats were put into the water, and three boa[ts, one] dred and five hundred passengers aboard them. The [fourth] which I was approached the land within three other boats, were picked up shortly after 4 o'clock by the Stormcock.

"I fear that few of the officers were saved." [he said] bravely.

WENT DOWN BY BOW.

"There were only fifteen minutes from the time the [ship] struck until the foundered, going down bow foremost. It [was a] dreadful sight."

More dispatches brought word that the hotel and [private] houses are being canvassed in an effort to obtain more or [less au-] thoritative lists of the survivors.

One of the first persons landed from the ship by a bo[at that] reached Kinsale Head was General H. R. Lassetter, late c[om-] mander of an Australian Light Horse Brigade. George A. [Smith,] were returning from a trip to Los Angeles. George A. [Smith,] the New York wine agent, and Mrs. J. T. Smith, of B[raceville,] Ohio, were also reported among the saved.

The Admiralty gave out the official news about midni[ght that the] attack was made in broad daylight and with ideally c[alm] warning.

A Queenstown dispatch to "The Daily Chronicle" s[ays that] seven torpedoes were discharged from the German craf[t aimed at] one of them struck the Lusitania amidships.

There is no question in anyone's mind here that it [was a] marine which caused the disaster. There is information [...]

THE LUSITANIA, SUNK BY GERMAN TORPEDO, WITH HEAVY LOSS OF LIFE.

ATLANTIC OCEAN

QUEENSTOWN

SOUTH COAST OF IRELAND.

Showing where the Lusitania was attacked and the points where survivors of the passengers and crew were landed.

Dying and Injured Brought in with Survivors to Queenstown—Some La[nded] at Kinsale and Clonakilty.

14. One of two stern docking telegraphs located on the starboard side seabed at a depth of 93 metres. Note a section of stern safety rail above. *(Leigh Bishop)*

15. These bollards still remain *in situ* on the starboard side of *Lusitania's* intact foredeck located immediately alongside her now collapsed bridge. *(Leigh Bishop)*

17. This propeller was salvaged from the wreck and now serves as a permanent memorial to the *Lusitania*. It is located at the Albert dock in Liverpool.

(Lusitania Online)

16. Gregg Bemis Jr., owner of the *Lusitania*, emerging from a Delta minisub after visiting the ship in 1993. *(F. Gregg Bemis Jr.)*

18. Pier 54 in New York harbour as it is today. The pier's new decking is clearly visible while to the left of it are the rotting remains of the other former Cunard berth, pier 56.

(J. Andrews via Lusitania Online)

19. US Collector of Customs for the Port of New York, Dudley Field Malone. A shady character to say the least, Malone knew exactly what was being loaded as cargo aboard westbound liners, but was quite happy to turn a blind eye to the practice due to his personal and political allegiances.

(Library of Congress)

20. Front of an original Karl Goetz medal. Goetz produced the medal as a form of political satire against both the British and the German Governments. The heading 'Keine Bann Ware' means 'No Contraband', yet the deck of the sinking liner is depicted loaded with war materials. The date is given as '5 Mai' intimating that the sinking was pre-meditated.

(Lusitania Online)

21. Reverse of an original Goetz medal. Under the heading 'Geschaft Über Alles', meaning 'Business as usual', Death is pictured as a Cunard Agent still selling tickets to prospective passengers, despite a friendly German trying to warn those purchasing the ticket.

(Lusitania Online)

22. Porthole recovered from the wreck.
(Aiden Bowe, Leicestershire/Lusitania Online)

24. Last survivor of the *Lusitania* disaster Audrey Lawson-Johnson, pictured here donating a new lifeboat at Newquay. The photo was taken a few years before she passed away. Audrey was a lifelong supporter of the RNLI.

(Dara Gannon, RNLI,
by kind permission, Lusitania Online)

23. Cushion from a sofa in the ship's First Class Music Room. The cushion was salvaged from the sea the day after the disaster by a young Royal Navy seaman, Henry Grew. Henry was among those sent out to recover bodies. He kept the cushion, eventually passing it on to his son David, who kindly donated it to us. We in turn donated it to the Merseyside Maritime Museum, Liverpool, where it is now on public display.

(Lusitania Online)

25. Silver plated three-handled friendship cup. Such items were purchased aboard the ship as a memento of the voyage. This one was from First Class.

(Furness Private Collection,
Lusitania Online)

27. Recovered from the Bridge Wheelhouse, this telemotor once held the ship's wheel.

(Eoin McGarry, by kind permission, Lusitania Online)

6. An example of the ship's stationery or passenger use.

(Mary-Jo Dennis/Lusitania Online)

8. The wreck of *U-20*. She stranded in fog at Vrist on the coast of Denmark whilst trying to assist another U Boat. She resisted all attempts to refloat her so Schwieger had one of her torpedoes detonated in a forward tube, to prevent her falling into enemy hands. The Danes eventually cut up and removed most of the wreck. Her deck gun, conning tower and one propeller today reside in the Strandings Museum nearby. Her keel and motors still lie in the mud where she stranded.

(Library of Congress, George Bain Collection, Lusitania Online)

29. Recovered from the wreck in 2008, this .303 bullet is part of a consignment of four million such bullets the ship was carrying as part of her cargo. The serial number U15 VII identifies it as having been made in the USA by the Union Metallic Co. for the British Government.

(Eoin McGarry, by kind permission, Lusitania Online)

30. A handful of the four million .303 bulle found in the ship's cargo hold during the 2008 season's dives.

(Eoin McGarry, by kind permissio Lusitania Onlin

31. Postcard commemorating the ship's maiden arrival in New York.

(Carole Trottere/Lusitania Onlin

LUSITANIA ENTERING N. Y. HARBOR ON HER MAIDEN TRIP
SEPTEMBER 13th, 1907

2. An unexploded WW2 Royal Navy depth charge. The wreck's debris field is literally ttered with these unexploded 'Hedgehog' type depth charges. Proof that the wreck was peatedly used for target practice.

(Eoin McGarry, by kind permission, Lusitania Online)

3. Photographed in 2013, a window from one of the First Class Staterooms lies mongst the wreckage.

(Eoin McGarry, by kind permission, Lusitania Online)

34. Photographed in 2013, one of the ship's telegraphs still *in situ* on the Bridge area of the wreck.
(Eoin McGarry, by kind permission, Lusitania Online

35. One of the ship's triple chime whistles lying on the ocean floor.
(Eoin McGarry, by kind permission, Lusitania Online

Case of the Wreck of the _Lusitania_

on the ___7th___ day of ___May___ 19_15_

DETAILS OF EXPENSE.

1. Life-Boat's Crew of _____ Men at _____ shillings each man
2. _____ Persons for assisting to launch and haul up the Life-Boat at _____ each Person
3. Allowance to Signalman
4. Allowance to Messenger (if any)
5. The Hire of _____ Horses a distance of _____ miles, at _____ shillings each horse

TOTAL ... ... £

We HEREBY CERTIFY that these Services were actually performed and that the items specified are correct.

Given under our hands this _____ day of _____ 190_

_____ Honorary Secretary.

_____ Coxswain of Life-Boat.

To the Secretary of the
Royal National Life-Boat Institution.

REMARKS, &c. BY THE HONORARY SECRETARY, OR THE LOCAL COMMITTEE, ON THIS SERVICE.

[handwritten remarks, largely illegible]

36. Copy of the original 'call out sheet' for the Courtmacsherry lifeboat. The lifeboat _Ketzia Gwilt_ was a sailing vessel. In the calm conditions that prevailed on the day of the disaster, the lifeboat had to be rowed the twelve miles out to the scene, a fact that did not deter the volunteer crew.

(Dara Gannon, RNLI, by kind permission, Lusitania Online)

37. Full extent of the possible area of the torpedo strike, as revealed by the computer simulation performed in Germany. The highlighted area shows the maximum scope, given factors such as torpedo deviation. Given that all reliable witness statements put the torpedo's impact behind the foremast, the area is effectively halved.

(Lusitania Online)

38. Memo to President F D Roosevelt from his personal secretary, to accompany the original 27 page cargo manifest. In January of 1940, Roosevelt had demanded to 'know everything' and had sent for the manifest. The Mr Durning mentioned in the memo was Collector of Customs in New York at the time. Everything on the manifest of interest to the President (ie. contraband) was marked with an 'X'.

(FDR Archive/Lusitania Online)

THE WHITE HOUSE
WASHINGTON

1-26-40

MEMORANDUM FOR THE PRESIDENT:

This is from Mr. Durning, and is the original manifest of the S. S. Lusitania. He wanted me to open it but I was afraid to do it until you had seen it. I have thanked Mr. Durning.

E. M. W.

CUNARD STEAMSHIP COMPANY, Limited

PIER 54 NORTH RIVER, NEW YORK.

OUTWARD CARGO SHEET   S.S. Lusitania   Voy. 101   Bound for Liverpool

Sheet No. 18   Tons   Crew   Commander   Sailing May 1   191 5

Receipt No.	SHIPPER	MARKS and NUMBERS		QUANTITY and DESCRIPTION	MEASURE-MENT	REMARKS
1	Remington U.M.C.Co.	R A.U.M.C.Co. London	✓	200 cases Cartridges	183 4	@ 13200 lbs X
3	— " —	"	✓	2000 "	2000	@ 132000 "
40	— " —	"	✓	800 "	800	@ 52800 "
76	— " —	"	✓	200 "	183 4	@ 13200 "
74	— " —	"	✓	600 "	600	@ 40200 "
153	— " —	"	✓	200 "	183 4	@ 13200 "
151	— " —	"	✓	200 "	200	@ 13400 "
79	C.P. Rose & Co.	⟨NR⟩ KW 42649/98 42699/99 42714/843	✓ ✓ ✓	50 Bxs Aluminum 94 cases " 50 " Bronze Powder	1197 9	@

39. Sheet 18 of the cargo manifest obtained from President Roosevelt's archives. This sheet details the four million .303 bullets shipped by The Remington Co. Note the 'X' next to the listing.

(FDR Archive/Lusitania Online

40. Sheet 2 of the cargo manifest obtained from President Roosevelt's archive. This sheet details the shrapnel shells (shown as just shrapnel) and fuses for other artillery shells, all shipped by Bethlehem Steel. Note the 'X's' by the listings.

(FDR Archive/Lusitania Online

CUNARD STEAMSHIP COMPANY, Limited

PIER 54 NORTH RIVER, NEW YORK.

OUTWARD CARGO SHEET   S.S. Lusitania   Voy. 101   Bound for Liverpool

Sheet No. 2   Tons   Crew   Turner Commander   Sailing May 1   191 5

Receipt No.	SHIPPER	MARKS and NUMBERS		QUANTITY and DESCRIPTION	MEASURE-MENT	REMARKS
10	Robert Barrett	Mrs H. Healey Co. Kingston	✓	1 case Morris chair	19 3	@
4	Brooks Bros	Wm Kemp & Co. purced	✓	1 Bale Woolen Samples	1 11	@
33	Belmont Steel Supplies	W E	✓	100 cases Salt Brick	116 8	@
37	Booth & Co	⟨W Co 26⟩ ⟨3 Co 30⟩ 1226/1239 2291/...	✓	14 cases Accoutrements	231.	@
43	"	— " — 2421/2431	✓	25 " "	412 6	@
44	"	— " — 2421/2431	✓	11 " "	181 6	@
54	"	— " — 2432/2446	✓	15 " "	247 6	@
75	"	2447/2469	✓	23 " "	379 6	@
94	"	⟨W Co⟩ ⟨3 Co⟩ 2340/53	✓	14 " "	231 0	@
114	"	2470/54	✓	15 " "	247 6	@
155	"	" 2475/2509	✓	25 " "	412 6	@
166	"	" 2510/2544	✓	13 " "	214 6	@
165	"	⟨S W Co 20⟩ ⟨3 Co 20⟩ 1354/1363	✓	10 " "	165	@
188	"	2524/46	✓	12 " "	206	@
181	"	" 2523/2534	✓	12 " "	206	@
194	H.W. Baker Green Co	7 Z Clark Rugby	✓	2 cases Dry Goods	78 1	@
170	Bethlehem Steel Co	⟨BS⟩ Royal Arsenal Woolwich	✓	1250 cases Shrapnel	1041 8 103828	@ X
171	"	⟨RA⟩ Woolwich	✓	12 cases Fuses	19	@ X
174	"	" "	✓	6 " — " —	9 6	@ X
125	E. Bury & Co	R 495	✓	7 Bales Scrap Rubber	237 5	@

clung to hope in the water, some of them noticed a warship which seemed to be heading directly for them. Their spirits lifted momentarily, but their hope quickly turned to despair, as the warship suddenly turned around and then headed back to whence it came.

It was the second time that day that HMS *Juno* had been urgently recalled to Queenstown by the Admiralty in London. Upon receipt of Coke's report, Fisher had suddenly become available. He ordered *Juno* to be recalled at once, in case the submarine added the cruiser to its already considerable tally. It would take another two hours for the fastest of the fishing boats out of Kinsale to reach the scene of the disaster, though many currently in the water would never know.

Captain Turner had found a chair to cling to. He was one of the first to be found by the steamer *Bluebell*. He was brought aboard after almost three hours in the water then wrapped in a hot blanket and given a mug of something hot to drink. He sat alone, huddled into a corner, feeling an overpowering sense of loss.

Sometime later, the crew of the *Bluebell* fished Bestic out of the water. He was the first to actually recognize the Captain. Bestic sat down next to him and said, 'I'm glad to see you made it, sir.' Turner looked at him and said coldly, 'Why should you be? You're not that fond of me.' Bestic felt hurt by the remark, but put it down to the ordeal they'd been through. 'All the same sir, I'm glad to see you alive,' he said. Then Bestic thought it best to just leave the Captain alone, so he moved off somewhere else.

As Bestic left, someone else recognized the lonely figure of Captain Turner. She was a passenger whose young son had been drowned when one of the starboard lifeboats, hastily lowered, had hit the water bows first and been smashed to pieces. She accused him of a lack of organization and discipline among the crew of the *Lusitania*. She told him flatly that her son's death had been completely unnecessary. But her words seemed to wash over Captain Turner who, staring blankly into his drink, never looked up from the mug he held in his hands, his mind seemingly quite unable to come to terms with the enormity of what had happened.

When *Bluebell* docked in Queenstown, Turner shuffled down the gangplank still wrapped in the blanket, and looking for all to see like a ragged old Indian from the Wild West. There were subdued cheers from the townspeople on the quay, but he never heard them as he was shepherded off to temporary accommodation in a hotel.

Meanwhile, the dead as well as the living were being brought ashore. Buildings were hastily requisitioned for use as temporary morgues, for even at that early stage it was obvious to anyone watching that the dead far outnumbered the living.

The final casualty figures were 1,201 men, women and children dead out of a total of 1,962 persons onboard. The official figures of 1,959 persons aboard and 1,198 dead, obviously do not include the three Germans who were locked in the most comfortable cells now at the bottom of the Atlantic Ocean. To divide the figures again, of the 159 Americans on board, 128 had perished and of the 129 children aboard the *Lusitania*, ninety-four perished. Included in that figure were thirty-one infants out of a total of thirty-five on board. Only four were saved.

Public Enquiries: The Crown v The Truth

With the *Lusitania* now at the bottom of the Atlantic and *U-20* on her way home, those whose task it had been to protect the ship began the fight for their political lives. One thousand two hundred and one souls may have perished along with the *Lusitania*, but those in power were not going to relinquish their privileged positions easily. Indeed, from that point on, they would do their utmost to ensure that the full blame for this disastrous event was attached solely to the ship's master, Captain Turner.

Admiral Oliver, upon receiving the disastrous news, immediately contacted Captain Richard Webb, the Director of the Admiralty's Trade Division, and the two began concocting the Admiralty's version of events. They worked all that Friday night and into the weekend gathering all the signals and advices that had been sent to, and received from, the *Lusitania* and generally constructing their case against Captain Turner. They were to compile a lengthy and for Captain Turner a damning report, for the consideration of the Board of the Admiralty, who were awaiting Churchill's return from France on Monday.

Oliver's problem was twofold. Firstly, the *Lusitania* had been successfully attacked by a German submarine, which the Admiralty knew to be operating in that area; after all measures to protect the ship had been withdrawn. Secondly, the *Lusitania* had gone down in a mere eighteen minutes with appalling loss of life due to the explosive nature of the cargo which the Admiralty's Trade Division had loaded aboard her. If either or both of those facts were to become public knowledge, the buck would stop at the Admiralty. All sorts of awkward questions would be asked and heads would undoubtedly roll from the highest positions. The higher they fell from, the harder they would land. So, a scapegoat seemed to be urgently needed and who better to fill that position than the *Lusitania*'s Captain?

Reading the collective correspondence in its original, unedited state would have made it abundantly clear to anyone that Captain Turner had in fact acted well within his controlled remit; that is to say, he had followed his Admiralty instructions to the letter. This is why Oliver and Webb were now busily 'tailoring' the Admiralty signals register, the Admiralty advices and even the questions that the London inquiry would ultimately be asking.

Another thorn in the Admiralty's side was the unfortunate fact that the bodies of five of the *Lusitania*'s victims had been landed at Kinsale, in southern Ireland. The Kinsale coroner was John Horgan, a known Sinn Fein sympathizer, which did not sit well with those in London, particularly as Horgan would not release the bodies until he had discharged his official duty as coroner. This meant that he would have to hold an inquest.

Horgan was now in a perfect position to cause maximum embarrassment to the Admiralty in London as well as HM Government and was unlikely to waste the golden opportunity with which he had been presented. Or so the Admiralty thought. Horgan originally set the inquest date for Monday, 10 May. His next task was to subpoena as many of the survivors as he could, including Captain Turner.

Upon hearing that a date had been set for this inquest, Admiral Oliver contacted the Crown Solicitor-General, Sir Frederick Smith and quickly secured the agreement to hold an official public enquiry in London. Lord Mersey, HM Receiver of Wrecks, had agreed to conduct it. This immediately made the whole *Lusitania* subject, *sub judice*. The press up to this point had widely reported that survivors had heard a second explosion. Now, the press had to content itself with tales of British and American heroism aboard the doomed liner, or anti-German stories with which to feed the public. The British Government now seized the propaganda opportunity and the Ministry of Information went into overdrive.

Meanwhile, Sir Frederick Smith quickly contacted the Crown Solicitor for Cork and ordered him to stop Horgan's inquest immediately. Once again those in authority were too late. Horgan had somehow heard of these machinations and hurriedly rescheduled his inquest for Saturday afternoon at the Old Market House,

Kinsale. With a jury comprised of twelve local shopkeepers and fishermen, the inquest he desired went ahead.

Captain Turner gave evidence, referring in the course of his testimony to a second, internal explosion immediately following that of the torpedo and that this second explosion rent the ship. Other survivors also testified to the second explosion. He steadfastly refused to divulge the content of his Admiralty instructions, however.

Captain Turner's time in the witness box did not last too long as the stress he was under forced him to break down. Not only had Turner lost his ship and a good many of his passengers and crew, he had also lost his very dear friend Archie Bryce, the ship's Chief Engineer. Captain Turner at this juncture was unaware of the goings on at the Admiralty. The events of Friday, 7 May would ultimately leave their mark upon him for the rest of his life.

While this was going on, some of the dead were still being brought into Kinsale. That was until the Royal Navy, under orders from the Admiralty, stopped all boats from entering Kinsale and ordered them to Queenstown. The reason for this was so that any post-mortem evidence that was likely to show that the deceased had been killed by the second explosion could not then be used at the inquest.

In the event, Coroner Horgan had merely wanted to be seen 'doing his bit'. He got his headlines with a verdict that formally indicted the Kaiser on a charge of 'Wilful and Wholesale murder'. Just after the conclusion of his inquest, in true Admiralty style, Harry Wynne, from the Crown Solicitor's office in Cork, arrived at the Kinsale Market House with instructions to stop the inquest. Horgan wryly commented that the Admiralty were 'as belated on this occasion as they had been in protecting the *Lusitania*'.

After truly Herculean efforts over the weekend, Admiral Oliver and Captain Richard Webb had finally managed to complete the official Admiralty version of the sinking of the *Lusitania* by Monday morning. Churchill was due back from France that day and the Admiralty's case had now been fully prepared for his return and for the subsequent Board of Trade enquiry which was to be held in four weeks time, under Lord Mersey. The first casualty of their report was the truth; the second casualty was to have been Captain Turner.

The one piece of evidence that could save Turner was the coded message sent by Vice Admiral Coke to the *Lusitania* at 11.02 hours that Friday morning, diverting her into Queenstown. This signal was withheld from Cunard and their legal representatives at the Mersey enquiry. It should be noted that the page on which that signal was recorded is the only page missing from the main Admiralty signals log for the whole of the First World War.

Before Lord Mersey's enquiry was convened, Captain Turner had to attend an interview with the Board of Trade's solicitors. Also present at the interview was a representative of the Admiralty. The details of Captain Webb's report were set out for Turner and he was told that at no time had he been ordered to divert into Queenstown. The Admiralty list of signals drawn up by Admiral Oliver was shown to him and he could see for himself that the vital signal, the one sent to him in naval code, wasn't there.

As all his papers, including the *Lusitania*'s log and her signals register, had gone down with the ship, there was nothing in Turner's possession with which to counter Webb's allegations. The chart he'd saved, on its own, would not be sufficient and he could hardly stand up in court and accuse such an august institution as the British Admiralty of lying, without having overwhelming evidence to support him.

Now Turner should have known exactly where he stood. They were going to blame him for the loss of his ship; the ship they had failed to protect. But he seems to have been unable to grasp this situation fully, as was later evidenced by his manner at the enquiry.

Representing Cunard and Captain Turner at the enquiry was Butler Aspinall, KC, who had been selected by Cunard's lawyers Messrs. Hill, Dickinson and Co. He was to be assisted by two other barristers: Mr C. Lang, KC and Mr A.H. Maxwell.

The barristers for the Board of Trade were the Crown Solicitor-General, Sir Frederick Smith, the Attorney General, Sir Edward Carson with Mr P. Branson and Mr I. Dunlop to assist them. The solicitor to the Board of Trade was Sir Ellis Cunliffe.

On the bench presiding was HM Receiver of Wrecks, Lord Mersey, assisted by four naval assessors, two from the Royal Navy and two from the Merchant Navy.

One of the Royal Navy assessors needs to singled out at this juncture. He was Admiral Sir Frederick Inglefield, lately in overall command of the Auxiliary Coast Patrol, that force recently charged with the duty of protecting one RMS *Lusitania*. Inglefield also deserves mention on another point. He was in sole possession of the master set of case documents prepared by the Admiralty. Sir Frederick Smith had the only other copy. We must mention this now because it was to have a direct bearing on the outcome of the enquiry.

The enquiry was convened at Central Hall, Westminster on 15, 16 and 18 June and 1 July 1915; also at the Westminster Palace Hotel on 17 July, though that hearing was announced only after it had taken place. In total there were seven sittings over five days. Four were held in public, two in camera, that is to say behind closed doors and one at the hotel.

Prior to the commencement of the enquiry Captain Webb, on behalf of the Board of the Admiralty, had already asked Lord Mersey to blame Captain Turner. Sir Frederick Inglefield had also of course been briefed by the Admiralty and instructed to find Turner guilty.

Unknown to Lord Mersey at this point was the fact that ALL the evidence had been carefully sifted and any references to explosions taking place forward of No. 1 funnel had been removed. Any passenger and crew depositions that put the impact of the torpedo forward of the bridge were simply not used.

The opening days of the hearing dealt with the *Lusitania*'s construction and then the attack. This was followed by Captain Turner taking the stand. He was asked a total of 160 questions, mostly quite general in nature. After then being questioned by Clem Edwards, who was representing the National Sailors' and Fireman's Union, on the subject of lifeboats, Turner was questioned by Butler Aspinall.

Aspinall questioned him on the precautions he had taken upon entering the danger zone and then returned to the subject of the crew's proficiency at boat handling. It must be remembered of course that Aspinall was also representing the Cunard line as well as Captain Turner. It will be seen from the following dialogue that Aspinall's technique was to put Captain Turner into the position of merely confirming what Aspinall wanted him to say.

Aspinall: 'I want you to explain that a little. Is it your view that modern ships with their greasers and their stewards and their firemen, sometimes do not carry the old-fashioned sailor that you knew of in the days of your youth?'

Turner: 'That is right.'

Aspinall: ' And you preferred the man of your youth?'

Turner: 'Yes, and I prefer him yet.'

Thus Aspinall had demonstrated to the court that there was no suggestion of the crew's incompetence in boat handling, merely inefficiency.

It was the hearings that were held in camera which dealt with the important issues such as the cargo, wireless instructions, anti-submarine measures and Captain Turner's actions. It was to be in this arena that Captain Turner was to have been thrown to the lions. The source of our information at this point in the story has largely been drawn from our published biography of Captain Turner, *Lusitania and Beyond* which was taken from the private papers of Lord Mersey and which gives a much more detailed account of the Admiralty's attempt to blame Captain Turner for the loss of his ship.

From the start of the in camera hearings, the Admiralty strove to prove to the court that they had kept Captain Turner fully informed at all times as to enemy submarines, that they had given him definite instructions and that he had deliberately disobeyed them, thereby placing his ship in grave danger, with the tragic result which the court was now addressing.

If Captain Turner thought he might have had an ace up his sleeve in the shape of the Marconi operator who had received the twelve-word 'divert' message from Vice Admiral Coke, he was to be bitterly disappointed. Mr McCormick was not called to testify. Mr Leith, the Marconi operator who was on duty at the time of the attack but off duty at 11.02 hours when Coke's message came in, was called instead, as he could truthfully confirm the ship's receipt of the later Admiralty messages. Captain Turner was quite alone and for him, it was all a nightmare. Alfred Booth, Cunard's chairman observed, 'Poor Will appears thoroughly bemused by the whole affair. He consistently clings to Aspinall for support.'

Initially, Aspinall was having an exasperating time trying to get Captain Turner to give answers of more than one word. Turner just could not, it seems, understand fully what the Admiralty were doing to him or why they were doing it. He was constantly confused about the evidence and gave his answers reluctantly. This, of course, only served to further the nature of the Admiralty's case against him.

For example, when pressed on the question of the Admiralty's now famous 16 April memo about zig-zagging, he reluctantly admitted that he must have seen it, although Aspinall later managed to drag out of him after the memo had been read out in court for a second time: 'Now that it has been read to me again, it seems a different language.' Of course it was! Turner was thinking of the earlier advice note dated 10 February, which said to steer a serpentine course if a submarine was sighted, which of course he had seen. But this was part of Captain Webb's handiwork. The other memo, though bearing the draft date of 16 April wasn't circulated until 2 May. Turner and the *Lusitania* were one day out from New York on their way home at that point. Still, it was a useful round to his opponents initially.

The Admiralty, through Webb's efforts, had so far successfully persuaded the court that although he'd been instructed to avoid headlands, Turner had deliberately come close inshore. He had disobeyed the instruction to pass harbours at full speed and had in fact, by his own admission, reduced speed. He was not zig-zagging but steering a straight, undeviating course, nor was his ship in 'mid-channel.' As far as the Admiralty had ascertained, 'The vessel appears to have been on her usual trade route and the only instruction the master appeared to have obeyed was to aim to make his port at dawn'.

Lord Mersey had the list of signals, which he had been told was complete. No other signals had been sent. Though 'of a general and negative nature', the court was further persuaded that these signals constituted specific warnings.

The only defence so far offered for Captain Turner's 'incredible' actions, was that he wanted to fix his position before entering St George's Channel. Not very credible to the court given the wealth of information and specific instructions said to have been in his possession. When pressed to reveal the nature of his Admiralty instructions, Turner could only respectfully refer the enquiry to the Admiralty, as he was not of course allowed to divulge any operational orders. The court was therefore left to rely almost solely on Captain Webb's memorandum. It was not looking good for Captain Turner. Yet ironically, it was the court's reliance on Webb's dirty work, coupled with Lord Mersey's diligence that ultimately saved Captain Turner.

Butler Aspinall concluded his case for Captain Turner's defence to the best of his abilities. He knew he was having to make the best of a bad job. He emphasized all the precautions that Turner had taken before the *Lusitania* entered the danger zone. He admitted that the ship was not zig-zagging, but he did manage to convince Lord Mersey that Captain Turner had acted throughout with the safety of his passengers uppermost in his mind and that his policy had been one of passenger safety first, Admiralty advices second. As a finale, Aspinall read out a long list of the names of all the ships that had suffered the same fate as the *Lusitania*, in the same waters, within the six weeks prior to the *Lusitania*'s sinking.

Next it was the turn of Sir Frederick Smith to sum up his case for the Admiralty and the Board of Trade. He concentrated on the signals which had been sent to the *Lusitania* and it was at this point that the Admiralty's case was dramatically scuppered.

Smith, during the course of his monologue, referred to a message that apparently told Captain Turner to avoid a particular area by keeping well off the land. Lord Mersey interjected because he could not find this message in his papers. Mersey asked Smith if he was reading from the Admiralty memorandum headed '*Lusitania.*' Smith confirmed that he was. Lord Mersey then called Smith to the bench and asked him to point it out on the copy Mersey had in front of him. Smith could not, for the simple reason that the message was not present on Mersey's copy.

Mersey then asked Aspinall to approach the bench and bring his copy of the memorandum with him. It was not on Aspinall's copy either. Aspinall thought it must be new evidence of which he, and apparently Mersey, were unaware for some reason. Smith assured them that it was not new, as he had been working from it throughout the proceedings.

Lord Mersey then leaned across and took Admiral Inglefield's file from him. Contained in Inglefield's file was the sending log of the Naval Wireless Station at Valentia. There on the log was Vice Admiral Coke's twelve-word signal to 'MFA', the *Lusitania*, in naval code, timed at 11.02 hours on Friday, 7 May 1915.

Mersey reacted instantly. Summoning the Board of Trade solicitor, Sir Ellis Cunliffe to the bench, Mersey icily demanded an immediate explanation. Sir Ellis couldn't offer him a satisfactory reply. He asked Sir Ellis which was the correct file. Sir Ellis told him that Inglefield's was the master file so therefore the correct one.

If Lord Mersey was furious at the discovery, Sir Frederick Smith was doubly so. 'I do not want it!' he said, dismissing Inglefield's file. 'I think it would be very unfair of me when this has not been put to the Master (Captain Turner) and has not been produced in evidence.' He was now specifically referring to the 11.02 hours message in naval code sent to Captain Turner. Smith instantly realized he'd been conducting his 'prosecution' on a basis of falsified evidence. He refused to proceed further.

Lord Mersey was not slow to realize that the Admiralty had made a determined attempt to mislead his enquiry. Going back over the questions submitted by the Board of Trade (via the Admiralty), Mersey now realized that they had been specifically tailored for the given purpose of making Captain Turner appear negligent. This was especially so in the case of the question that asked whether or not any instructions had been sent to the Master of the *Lusitania* and whether those instructions had been carried out. The logical progression of the question is 'what were those instructions?' But that part of the question was of course, left out.

Lord Mersey was now quietly seething. After a further discussion with the counsels he decided to end the enquiry by simply adjourning it. He then asked his four assessors to give him their written opinions in separate sealed envelopes, as to Captain Turner's guilt or innocence. Only Admiral Sir Frederick Inglefield returned a verdict of guilty, the other three decided that Captain Turner was not to blame.

Inglefield, not happy that the scapegoat had escaped, complained about this 'whitewashing' of Captain Turner to the secretary to the Admiralty. But there had been changes at the Admiralty during the course of the enquiry.

On 15 May, First Sea Lord John Fisher had formally resigned yet again. Fearing he would be made jointly to blame for the disaster that the Dardanelles campaign was fast becoming, he made a strategic withdrawal to Scotland, though in fact he had only got as far as taking a room at the Charing Cross Hotel. The failure of the campaign brought down the Asquith government and First Lord of the Admiralty, Winston Churchill, lost his job.

With a new Board of the Admiralty headed by A.J. Balfour, Inglefield's complaint fell on deaf ears. The Admiralty had not only changed its body, it had changed its mind.

On 17 July 1915 the court was assembled to hear the final verdict. The court found that 'torpedoes fired by a submarine of German nationality' had caused the sinking of the *Lusitania*. The court opined, '. . . that this act was done not merely with the intention of sinking the ship, but also with the intention of destroying the lives of the people on board'.

In the annexe to his report, Lord Mersey stated that whilst Captain Turner may have disregarded some of the Admiralty's advices, he had most definitely followed his Admiralty instructions. The advices, said Lord Mersey, were 'not intended to deprive him of the right to exercise his skilled judgement'. Lord Mersey went on to say that 'he exercised his judgement for the best. It was the judgement of a skilled and experienced man, and although others may have acted differently . . . he ought not, in my opinion, to be blamed.'

Outside in the street, Alfred Booth and Captain Turner shook hands for the benefit of the press photographers who were present. The court had publicly exonerated Cunard and Captain Turner.

Given what Lord Mersey had discovered for himself during the course of his enquiry, it is hardly surprising that he should end this exhaustive hearing by merely concurring with the Kinsale coroner's verdict. Though he would not give the Admiralty their scapegoat, he did have to publicly blame the Germans for this dastardly act.

So, the 'beastly Hun' was found guilty and justice, at least to some, appeared to have been done. But it was a fundamentally unsound justice, as Lord Mersey knew only too well. Two days after reaching his verdict, Lord Mersey waived his fee for the case and formally resigned from his position as HM Receiver of Wrecks, stating that he no longer wished to serve. His last words on the subject were, 'The *Lusitania* case was a damned, dirty business'. But he did have one small consolation. However much they tried, then or in the future, the Admiralty would never be able to completely cover their tracks. Lord Mersey, in his wisdom, had confiscated the entire contents of Admiral Inglefield's master file.

The Wreck of the *Lusitania*

Today, RMS *Lusitania* lies in 290 feet of water at the bottom of the Atlantic Ocean. Her final resting place is 11.2 miles south and 3 degrees west of the Old Head of Kinsale, Ireland.

A diver named Jim Jarrett was the first to visit the wreck, in October 1935. However, he was only able to make one brief descent, during which he actually stood on the port side hull plates, before the weather turned bad and the dive had to be abandoned. Jarrett returned to the surface, but never returned to the wreck.

Then came the Second World War, during which the Admiralty took the 'precaution' of depth-charging the wreck site on a regular basis, just in case U-boats used it for shelter. After the war, anti-submarine exercises were held annually until 1949, using the wreck of the *Lusitania* as an extremely oversized target 'submarine'. What speaks volumes about their standard of marksmanship is that the hull of their 790-foot long 'target' is still largely intact to this day.

The Admiralty made the first salvage operations in 1948, and continued them on an intermittent basis until 1955. To this day, the Admiralty strongly deny that these operations ever took place, but enough local people, including the Irish coastguard and Kinsale fishermen, had witnessed the Royal Navy's salvage vessels at work on the wreck site to discount that claim.

Throughout the 1960s, an American diver by the name of John Light made several, largely underfunded descents to the wreck using basic scuba equipment. Descending to such depths in this manner was bravery to the point of foolhardiness, but his explorations attracted a wealth of media and other interest.

It was as a result of Light's involvement that the original disputes over the wreck's ownership came about. Today, having had his ownership of the wreck confirmed before three separate courts in England, Ireland and the United States, the undisputed legal owner of the wreck is millionaire American businessman Mr F. Gregg Bemis Jr. But although he is the wreck's owner, the Irish government have placed a heritage order on the site occupied by Mr Bemis' property, which means that this difficult situation now appears to have resulted in a mutual stand off while both parties try to work out a clear way forward.

Salvage operations, under contract with Mr Bemis, were carried out in 1982 by a firm called Oceaneering International Limited, of Houston, Texas. Among the items recovered were:

Three of the four 23-ton, four-bladed propellers
Two anchors
The ship's foghorn
One bridge telegraph
The ship's bell
Assorted bronze, brass and copper items
Some silver dishes
A quantity of silver-plated spoons
Some china plates and dishes
Some pieces of picture frames
A quantity of watchcases and boxed mechanisms
Percussion fuse parts for 4.7-inch and 6-inch high-
    explosive shells

Unfortunately, most of these items were auctioned off to private collectors shortly after recovery, but some are now in the hands of Peter Boyd-Smith, proprietor of that treasure trove of ocean liner memorabilia, *Cobwebs* of Southampton, England. We contacted Peter who willingly allowed us to visit his emporium and photograph these and some other *Lusitania* related items in his possession.

Sadly, apart from one of the salvaged propellers rescued from a scrapyard and now used as a *Lusitania* memorial at the Albert Dock, Liverpool, these few remnants are just about all that visibly remains of this once majestic liner. Occasionally however, another long lost item or artefact turns up. A silver-plated cigarette case, originally purchased as a souvenir from the ship's barber's shop, was found some years ago on a New York building site by local photographer Neil De Crescenzo.

Dr Robert Ballard, famous for his co-discovery with the French team from Ifremer, of the wreck of the *Titanic*, visited and filmed the *Lusitania* in 1993. His exploration resulted in a National Geographic sponsored video and a 'coffee table style' book, neither of which, despite Dr Ballard's 'investigative reporting', actually revealed anything new about the ship and, if anything, actually gave rise to further untruths about her.

For example, there is no long trail of coal on the seabed leading to the wreck, as Dr Ballard claims in his video and his book. This seems to have been invented to support the rather weak 'coal dust explosion theory' created by Captain Cyril Spur RN (retired) and Dr Ballard, in their joint effort to explain the possible cause of the second explosion. Mr Bemis explained to me that Dr Ballard's expedition never ventured much more than 150 feet or so astern of the wreck, whereas his own ongoing survey expeditions have covered the ground from the wreck back to the point of the torpedo's impact. Mr Bemis' explorations have revealed that although there are some small amounts of coal lying near to the wreck, which probably spilled out as the ship struck the bottom, no such trail of coal exists as that which Dr Ballard claimed to have found. Dr Ballard has since claimed, 'It doesn't really matter what caused the second explosion', a viewpoint which, although wholly his own, is one with which we cannot agree.

Today, the once majestic *Lusitania* lies on her starboard side, effectively hiding the fatal damage that was inflicted upon her. She rusts on the ocean floor, slowly becoming an integral part of the element that once supported her. The state and condition of the wreck can only be described as lamentable. Bent, bombed and festooned with snagged fishing nets, she lies with her bows pointing roughly north-east toward Ireland, as if she were still trying to make a landfall that will never, ever come.

What Sank the *Lusitania*?

So now we come to the $64,000 question, namely, why exactly did such a well found ship as the *Lusitania*, sink in a mere eighteen minutes, after being hit with a single torpedo? That question has been the cause of much speculation and controversy ever since Friday, 7 May 1915 and although we are by no means experts in marine forensics it is nonetheless a question that we thought we ought to address in a book such as this. During the course of our research we were of course, fortunate in making some very useful contacts along the way, some of whom are indeed experts in their fields. It is with the help of such people that we now endeavour to explain the events of the sinking.

The cause of the sinking is really due to the culmination of five elements. Firstly, the design of the *Lusitania*; secondly, the type of torpedo that Schwieger used; thirdly, the impact site of that torpedo and lastly, the nature of the *Lusitania*'s cargo. All four of these factors are linked together and combine with the fifth element, the inrushing seawater, to culminate in the sinking of the vessel. So let us consider each of the first four elements separately, in order, before we assemble them into a final analysis of the sinking.

In this endeavour we are most grateful for the expert advice and guidance given to us by a small band of experts; Dr John Bullen, maritime curator of the Imperial War Museum and a leading expert on matters maritime such as ship construction and torpedoes; Stan Walter, former curator of the Royal Artillery Museum and a foremost expert on Great War munitions; Colonel J.M. Phillips and his staff at the Royal Artillery Historical Trust's library, who supplied all the relevant technical information regarding the manufacture, packing, shipping, performance and behavioural characteristics of the 13-pounder shrapnel shell of 1915, and finally, Frederick Peeke, a former gunner with the Royal Artillery.

The first element we have to consider is the design of the *Lusitania*. In the crucial area, below the waterline, she was of the Royal Navy's pre-dreadnought type of construction, with hull plating of only one-inch thick unarmoured mild steel and with additional coalbunkers flanking the ship. It will be recalled that the main bunker was located forward of boiler room No. 1 and ran clear across the ship. Ahead of this vast bunker was the forward cargo hold. Today, a ship design such as the *Lusitania*'s would not be permitted as it has a number of inherent weaknesses, the main of which we outlined earlier, but in 1907 this design was very much at the cutting edge of shipbuilding technology.

As Dr Bullen explained to us, the pre-dreadnoughts ultimately proved to be extremely vulnerable to torpedo attack, as was evidenced by the 'livebait squadron debacle'. Having relatively thin skins and no underwater armour, a good torpedo such as the German G-type had no trouble penetrating the mild steel plate used to build these ships, as long as the torpedo was fired in the correct manner. Which leads us to the second element, the torpedo itself.

The German G-type torpedo was a refinement of the British Whitehead design. It carried a warhead of 440lbs of an explosive called Trotyl, a TNT derivative. The torpedo was propelled at 38 knots by a compressed air motor while gyroscopes kept it running true. The nose section of this underwater missile had a long threaded rod protruding from it. This rod was a contact-operated firing pin. Once the torpedo had been fired and was running, a small propeller-shaped locknut started to spin its way along the rod until it fell off the forward end. The torpedo was then armed, as the rod would now be able to slam back into the internal detonator as soon as it hit the target hull.

Though the G-type was undoubtedly the best torpedo in service with any navy during the Great War, it did have its faults. If the range between the U-boat and the target was much greater than 700 metres (756 yards), the performance of the torpedo was prone to being ineffective, inasmuch as it began to slow down. By gradually losing its momentum, a corresponding amount of the torpedo's 'punch' effect was lost, as was some of its destructiveness on impact with the target hull. In a number of cases, this meant that the target ship was not so badly damaged and sometimes even escaped. Another frustrating fault with the G-type was that if the torpedo were launched at anything other than a near 90-degree angle of intersection to its target, the forward motion of the very hull it was trying to penetrate could deflect the missile.

U-boat commanders noticed these maddening traits quite early on and accordingly, adopted a practice of making their submerged attacks from under 700 metres and at right angles to the target. Under these two conditions, the G-type torpedo usually proved to be devastatingly effective against a pre-dreadnought type of vessel.

A particularly good illustration of a text book U-boat attack on a pre-dreadnought type warship is the example of the attack made against a French cruiser only eleven days prior to the *Lusitania* disaster. The torpedo attack upon, and ultimate fate of, the 12,518-ton *Leon Gambetta* was so similar to that of the *Lusitania* that it is worth a slight digression at this point, as the episode illustrates the first two elements very well. It also illustrates the fact that surprise, tinged with a little luck, was the key element in the U-boat's success. Even a trained naval crew could be caught out, as indeed were the crews of the three British cruisers involved in the 'livebait squadron debacle', the *Aboukir*, *Hogue* and *Cressy*. The only differences from the attack upon the *Lusitania* is that two torpedoes were used against the French cruiser and that the attack upon the *Leon Gambetta* took place by the light of a full moon on a calm, clear night.

In the early evening of the 26 April 1915, in the Straits of Otranto, *Kapitänleutnant* Georg Ritter von Trapp, (yes, the very same man of the *Sound of Music* fame) commanding the Austrian submarine *U-5*, sighted the distant *Leon Gambetta* leading a patrol and sailing parallel to his direction. Because of the *U-5*'s generally poor performance characteristics, (*U-5*'s maximum submerged speed was just 5 knots and her maximum speed on the surface was only 10 knots) he could not hope to manoeuvre his submarine into a favourable position to attack the enemy force at such extreme range, especially as *Leon Gambetta*'s top speed was listed as being 22 knots.

However, the Straits of Otranto are reasonably narrow, which gave von Trapp the advantage of knowing approximately where his enemy would reappear on the return leg of their patrol. *U-5* therefore waited patiently, moving gently though the water, to minimize the glow of her wash in the bright moonlight.

Just before midnight, a lookout on *U-5*'s conning tower spotted a dark shape on the horizon. Von Trapp recognized the moonlit silhouette of the French flagship from the distinctive spacing of her funnels. The *Leon Gambetta* and her attendant ships were indeed returning and this time, as luck would have it, she was heading directly toward the waiting U-boat. The sea swallowed *U-5* as she submerged to lie in wait for the oncoming prize.

Most of the *Leon Gambetta*'s crew were asleep at their action stations in case of a surface attack and her nocturnal speed had unwisely been reduced to 6 knots, to conserve coal. Her lookouts scanned and rescanned the horizon, continually searching for any sign of marauding Austrian or German destroyers. They were not expecting to be attacked from below the waves.

Von Trapp allowed the *Leon Gambetta* to move squarely into his periscope sights, thus keeping the deflection angle to a minimum. At 00.20 hours, he gave the deadly orders: 'Fire one! Fire two!' and the torpedoes cleared their tubes, streaking towards the still unsuspecting cruiser. The *Leon Gambetta* now had only minutes to live.

As the first torpedo hit the *Leon Gambetta* and exploded in the dynamo compartment, the ship was instantly plunged into darkness. The second torpedo struck an instant later, penetrating a boiler room and stopping the engines. The stricken vessel lost momentum, listed noticeably to port and began settling rapidly by the head. Her commander, *Capitaine* Andre, gave orders to flood the starboard compartments in a frantic attempt to keep her on an even keel, as he had already realized that his ship was doomed and that all efforts to save her would be fruitless. His actions had little effect however, so he therefore ordered the crew to abandon ship.

The cruiser had taken on an incredible 30 degree list to port, rendering the starboard lifeboats useless. The crew did not panic, but their boat drill appears to have gone by the board as the port side lifeboats were hastily launched. Some were smashed against the hull while others got caught under the davits, killing, crushing and injuring those desperately seeking to escape from the doomed cruiser. The death toll among her crew was high, as the *Leon Gambetta* capsized and sank in just twenty-two minutes. Not one officer was saved.

After witnessing his success, von Trapp closed the periscope down and stole silently away from the scene, thus avoiding the vengeful attentions of the other ships in *Leon Gambetta*'s patrol.

Just seven months after the Royal Navy's 'livebait squadron debacle', its lessons obviously still had not been learned. A mere eleven days later, *Kapitänleutnant* Walther Schwieger would drive that lesson forcibly home to the world with a terrible clarity.

So now we come to examine the third element in the *Lusitania*'s sinking, namely the impact point of the torpedo on the *Lusitania*'s hull. Schwieger's torpedo actually found its mark in the forward cargo hold. The site of impact can be fairly accurately placed by four pieces of evidence, three of which are eyewitness statements.

Our first witness is *Kapitänleutnant* Walther Schwieger. It will be remembered that he fired his torpedo with the running depth set at 3 metres (about 10 feet) and after observing and noting the effects of his torpedo through the periscope, he in fact revised the initial observations he made. Having overestimated the speed of his target, he realized that his shot had struck the ship further forward of where he had first thought (he was aiming for a hit in the *Lusitania*'s foremost boiler room) and he therefore amended his log to reflect this. His revised log is today held in the *Bundesmilitärarchiv*, in Freiburg.

Our second witness is Able Seaman Thomas Quinn, the starboard lookout in the *Lusitania*'s crow's nest at the time of the attack and a trained observer. He stated in his mandatory deposition to the Board of Trade, (which wasn't used at the subsequent enquiries but is today held in the Public Record Office) that: 'The torpedo struck the ship on the starboard side, abaft the foremast.' The word 'abaft' is a nautical term, which means 'immediately aft of' or 'immediately behind'.

Our third witness is Captain William Thomas Turner. He knew exactly where the torpedo struck his ship, as the Pearson's Fire and Flood alarm system had told him. As well as testifying to the second explosion at Coroner Horgan's inquest, Captain Turner went to see the Cunard superintendent at Queenstown, Captain Dodd, on the Monday after the disaster. He visited Dodd primarily to complain about his naval escort being withdrawn, but when Dodd asked him what he thought had caused the second explosion, Turner told him he was convinced that the torpedo he had seen from the bridge had caused part of the cargo to explode, which means Turner knew that the torpedo had struck his ship in the forward hold.

So, we have Schwieger's statements from *U-20*'s log and we have Quinn's and Turner's statements. All three are the statements of cool-headed, trained observers. This leaves no doubt in our minds that the impact area was immediately behind the foremast and 10 feet below the waterline.

On the profile plans of the *Lusitania*, you would therefore be looking to place the impact somewhere between frames 251 and 256 and 10 feet below the waterline. This area is the top of the forward hold (aft end, starboard side) abaft the foremast and immediately below the baggage room. Which brings us to our fourth piece of evidence. There were no survivors from the baggage room working party.

Now we turn to the fourth element, the *Lusitania*'s cargo. This is perhaps the most controversial aspect of the whole episode. For some time since war had been declared, the *Lusitania* had been used as a high-speed munitions carrier by the Admiralty's trade department. On her final voyage, she was carrying considerably more contraband than usual, including eighteen cases of fuses for various calibre artillery shells, which were listed on her manifest, and a large consignment of gun-cotton, an explosive used in the manufacture of propellant charges for big-gun shells, which wasn't listed on the manifest. These two items caused a minor sensation when their presence aboard the *Lusitania* was first revealed in the American press shortly after the sinking.

The fuses carried in eighteen cases as cargo aboard the *Lusitania* were far from complete fuses and formed part of a mixed consignment of percussion fuse mechanisms for the British Army's 4.5-inch and 6-inch calibre high explosive shells, and the 13-pounder shrapnel shell. Despite being incomplete, they did contain a small quantity of explosive, which is why all eighteen cases were stored in the ship's magazine, aft.

The gun-cotton was quite a large consignment and was stored in part of the new space created by the Admiralty, forward on E deck. It is worth recording that this large consignment was not packed in the proper containers usually employed to transport this explosive, due to a sudden shortage of them.

In the immediate area of the torpedo's impact there was, according to the ship's manifest, only a generally harmless cargo listed as being, '1,248 cases of shrapnel', (supposedly just the lead musket balls with which to fill shrapnel shells) surrounded by three large consignments, one of butter, one of cheese and the other being lard. The last three items were kept unrefrigerated for the entire voyage.

However, thanks to Colin Simpson's detective work in his excellent 1972 book *Lusitania*, it transpires that two of the three items stowed next to the shrapnel, namely the large consignments of unrefrigerated butter and cheese, were in fact consigned to the Liverpool box number of the Royal Navy's weapons testing establishment at Shoeburyness, Essex. This immediately begs the question, what on earth would such an establishment want with approximately 90 tons of unrefrigerated dairy products? The exact nature of these two consignments has never been firmly established but curiously, as Colin Simpson discovered, both were insured at the special government rate and furthermore, the insurance money was never claimed.

The cases of shrapnel, situated at the heart of the torpedo's impact point, are easier to trace though, thanks once again to Colin Simpson's initial detective work. The 1,248 cases of shrapnel listed on the manifest of the *Lusitania* came from the Bethlehem Steel Corporation and Simpson found that their shipping note was a little more specific than the ship's cargo manifest.

The shipping note, dated 28 April 1915, shows 'consignment number 23' as being '1,248 cases of three-inch calibre shrapnel *shells*, filled; four shells to each case'. These shells were consigned to the Royal Arsenal at Woolwich and as our own subsequent research, aided by the Royal Artillery Historical Trust has revealed, they were for use by the Royal Artillery in the 13-pounder field gun. So why was such a large consignment of live artillery shells being carried aboard the *Lusitania*, a passenger liner?

It must be remembered that due to the deepening munitions crisis, speed was of the absolute essence. The British Army, it will be recalled, was firing more shells per week than the factories produced. Britain's factories were producing only one quarter of the daily output of shells that French munitions factories produced. Even more lamentable was the fact that Germany's armament factories were producing more than double the amount of the combined daily production totals of the British and French factories. Therefore, corners had to be cut and usual, time-consuming peacetime practices such as stockpiling and using shells in rotation according to date of manufacture, were of necessity quickly abandoned, in the desperate rush to get the shells to the front.

The American-made shells were indistinguishable from their British-made counterparts apart from the manufacturer's mark, and to save a considerable amount of precious time, as Colonel Phillips' staff confirmed to us in writing, they were imported from America as complete rounds, with a simple transit plug in place of the 'Type 80 Time and Percussion fuze'. It is therefore important at this point to properly explain the difference between a shell and a complete round, and to explain a little about the anatomy of this ammunition and how it was packed, transported and used.

The shell, or more properly, 'projectile', actually weighed 12.5 pounds and contained 234 lead musket balls, forty-one of which combined to weigh one pound, which were suspended in resin. The projectile itself contained only a small 'burster' charge, designed to discharge the shrapnel balls in flight, ahead of advancing enemy troops, like a shotgun blast. Against advancing troops, a fusillade of shrapnel was unrivalled as a killer of men en masse.

The complete round, as imported from America, was made up of the unfused projectile, fitted with its cartridge, which contained a propellant charge of 1.25 pounds of cordite MD extruded into rods or 'cords'. Cordite MD was a modification to standard cordite and was designed to help prevent erosion of the gun's barrel. The propellant charge was sufficient when the gun was fired, to give the 12.5 pound projectile a maximum range of 5,900 yards and the 13-pounder field gun a muzzle velocity of 1,675 feet per second. Each of these unfused complete rounds weighed 16.5 pounds. Hereafter, for the sake of convenience, we shall simply refer to the complete round as a 'round'.

The wooden crates containing the imported rounds were also made in America, to the War Office specification. They were made of deal (untreated pine) with elm ends, had two metal bands running around them and two heavy wire handles, one at each end. The crates were unlined, contained no packing other than two wooden support spacers, and each empty crate weighed 6 pounds. A crate containing four complete 13-pounder shrapnel rounds without fuses would therefore weigh a hefty 72 pounds, hence the thick wire handles.

The Type 80 time and percussion fuse was peculiar to shrapnel and anti-aircraft shells, both of which were designed to explode in flight. The fuse carried a percussion mechanism in case the timer failed and the projectile returned to earth.

Upon receipt of the imported shrapnel rounds at the Royal Arsenal, they would simply be mixed in with other outbound consignments of ammunition destined for the front. In the case of the imported fuse parts though, it was a little different. The workers at the arsenal had to assemble and then arm each fuse. This involved inserting the fuse detonator into the imported percussion mechanisms and, in the case of those fuses destined to be fitted to shrapnel and anti-aircraft shells, fitting this assembly into a nose cone, which would also include the powder-operated timer rings. The now complete fuse would then be fitted with a protective soft lead cover. The assembled fuses would be packed into their own, separate, wooden boxes.

The fuses were never packed with nor fitted to, the rounds until the two separate lots reached the gun battery's fusing station in the reserve lines. It was there, as former gunner Frederick Peeke explained to us, that the round's transit plug was removed and the fuse, still with its protective cover, was finally fitted to the round to make it ready. Each round was then stencilled with the word 'fused', reboxed again in their original wooden crates (four rounds per crate) and then sent on the short journey up the line, for immediate use.

The consignments of shrapnel rounds and fuse mechanisms carried aboard the *Lusitania*, were just part of a very large order supplied by Bethlehem Steel, totalling 214 consignments.

So now we can return to the *Lusitania*'s cargo hold. Stored one deck above the shrapnel rounds on the *Lusitania* was another large consignment from the Remington Small Arms Co. consisting of 4,297 boxes of .303 rifle ammunition, each box containing 1,000 rounds.

These were just the loads that were in the immediate vicinity of the torpedo strike. Also aboard the *Lusitania* in the forward hold were seventy-four barrels of fuel oil, 1,702 copper 'bullion bars', 178 cases of brass rods, 206 reels of wire, numerous barrels and boxes containing metallic elements such as brass tubes, copper tubes and bronze and aluminium powders. There were also loads such as fifty-nine cases of shotgun cartridges, a very large consignment of quarters of beef and many other cases, barrels or packages of sundries, most of which were destined for either the British Army or the Royal Navy. There were other consignments carried in the new areas on the decks above, such as the 349 bales of raw furs consigned to a company who, as Colin Simpson discovered, had absolutely no connection with the fur trade.

Such then is the nature of the first four elements. Now, guided once again by our experts, we shall attempt to reconstruct what happened to the ship from the moment Schwieger's torpedo penetrated the cargo hold to the ship's foundering, and examine the contribution each of the elements made to the likely chain of events that culminated in the sinking of the ship.

The torpedo struck the *Lusitania* exactly in the manner, though not in the location, that Schwieger intended. It struck the ship square on at 38 knots, thus delivering its full 'punch effect', penetrating the hull and exploding its 440lb warhead. This was the first, or initial explosion that people aboard the *Lusitania* heard. Given that we also now have a better idea of the site of the torpedo's impact (between frames 251 and 256) and the nature of the cargo stored in this area, we can now proceed with the most likely chain of events.

The second, almost instantaneous explosion, which was universally described by the survivors as being much louder was, as Stan Walter described to us, almost certainly due to the explosion of a substantial part of the consignment of shrapnel rounds, their propellant charges (not the small internal 'Burster' charge) set off by the torpedo exploding among the crates containing them, near the top of the stack. Given that the unlined packing crates containing the shrapnel rounds were only made from softwood (deal), Stan Walter expressed the opinion that those rounds contained in the crates in the immediate vicinity of the torpedo strike would, without a shadow of doubt, have exploded, though by no means the entire consignment would have been affected. The sound of this second explosion would have been quite different to the sound of the torpedo's explosion.

Taking that as the most likely cause of the second explosion, and here a second expert, (Dr Bullen) agreed with the possibility, the bulkhead between the hold and the main coalbunker, which was only 20 feet away from the heart of this double explosion, would have suffered catastrophic damage. Though strong, the bulkhead was never designed to withstand the force of the double explosion that had just occurred. Consequently, the starboard end of it would have given way, or more precisely, was probably blown away. The outward force of the second explosion would have followed the line of least resistance, which meant that the starboard hull plating, already substantially weakened by the ingress and initial explosion of the torpedo, now suffered catastrophic damage on both sides of where the end of the bulkhead had once stood. The rest of the cargo in the hold would most likely have acted in the manner of a blast wall, thus preventing the port side of the ship from being damaged by the double explosion.

The fifth element was now added to the overall picture as seawater, at a rate measured in hundreds of tons per minute, came rushing in and the *Lusitania* began rolling over to starboard and going down rapidly by the head.

Therefore, with both the cargo hold and the main coalbunker breached and filling rapidly, the *Lusitania*'s list increased at a dramatic rate. As the list increased, the remaining coal in the main bunker, as well as the cargo in the hold, would all have shifted 'downhill' to starboard, together with such immensely weighty items as the copper bars, the remaining crates of shrapnel rounds, the cases of rifle ammunition, the brass rods, the barrels of fuel oil and the dubious 90-ton consignments of butter and cheese. The very considerable weight of these cargoes, plus the coal in the main bunker, was now in totally the wrong place. The *Lusitania*, with her unusually high freeboard, would have been particularly suscep-tible to having her delicate balance altered by such a dramatic and uneven shift in weight distribution. The added weight of the inrushing seawater now combined with these factors to ruin her stability and effectively seal her fate.

Although Captain Turner had ordered all watertight doors to be closed, it made little difference. All the internal bunker hatches were open as were quite a few of the portholes on the starboard side, thus effectively bypassing the watertight doors. The further she rolled, the faster she sank. It was totally impossible for her ever-increasing list to starboard to have been checked or countered at any stage. Had her bows not struck the bottom first, the *Lusitania* would have capsized completely.

Given that this mighty 45,000-ton liner rolled over and sank in only eighteen minutes it is nothing short of miraculous that the initial death toll wasn't higher. If rescue vessels had been able to reach the scene more quickly, more lives would undoubtedly have been saved. If the forward hold had not been filled with explosive munitions, the lives of all on board, as well as the ship herself, would undoubtedly have been saved, for Schwieger's single torpedo, hitting the ship where it did, could not have caused sufficient damage to sink the *Lusitania*. It was the second explosion that caused the fatal damage.

Our investigations into the cause of the *Lusitania*'s rapid demise are based upon the careful sifting of all the currently available documentary evidence. Having the invaluable help of experts from such august bodies as the Imperial War Museum and the Royal Artillery Historical Trust, as well as F. Gregg Bemis Jr., dedicated owner and surveyor of the *Lusitania* wreck, has perhaps enabled us to analyse the event of her loss from a more advantageous position than anyone previously. But the only way anyone will ever know for sure what really happened to her will be, as Mr Bemis said in the foreword to this book, when a thorough underwater examination of the affected area of the wreck is made.

With the *Lusitania* resting on her starboard side, effectively hiding the fatal damage, any such detailed examination is obviously rendered that much more difficult, dangerous and therefore of course, more costly.

The technology required to conduct such an examination, previously out of reach, is today available, although at considerable cost. The earlier explorations of the wreck, lacking today's technology and equipment, could not therefore be comprehensive and were thus confined to easily accessible areas only. The crucial area of the wreck has yet to be explored, so our best estimation of the damage she sustained as a result of the two explosions remains, for the present, just that; a highly educated estimation.

Until the necessary proper undersea examination of the wreck is undertaken and completed, the *Lusitania* will keep her final secret and it would, as Walter Lord once said of the *Titanic*, '... be a rash man indeed who would set himself up as being the final arbiter on all that happened'.

Epilogue

Such then, is the story of RMS *Lusitania*. A story of pride, triumph, of great achievements and technological advancements, but ultimately of great tragedy. Today, with the exception of a few select books, all that is left in her wake is a brief, and usually inaccurate mention, in a handful of history books and encyclopaedias.

Even the very real tragedy of the 1,201 lives lost in the disaster is largely forgotten. The physicality of her sinking has seemingly eclipsed almost every aspect of her story, except perhaps for the almost endless controversies that seem destined to be forever recycled. Was she armed? Did she carry munitions? Did Winston Churchill engineer the disaster to bring the Americans into the war? Was Captain Turner to blame? We believe that those questions have now been fully answered.

Once the historical barrier of the disaster is passed however, it becomes immediately apparent just what a truly pioneering ship the *Lusitania* was. The first ever quadruple-screw turbine-driven passenger liner. It was she that set the standard all subsequent liners would follow. Great liners like the *Queen Mary*, *Queen Elizabeth*, *France* and *United States*, all owed their heritage to the *Lusitania*.

We know what happened to the *Lusitania*, but what of some of the people and places that are forever connected with her story?

The company that built her, John Brown and Co. have not built a ship for well over thirty years. Absorbed by Kvaerner Industries, they are now in the energy business as their experiences with the Parsons marine turbine engine lead them to even greater things, namely building power station engines and more latterly, gas turbine engines.

The company that owned her, the Cunard Line, is still in business. In 1922, under the terms of the Treaty of Versailles, the Germans were forced to hand over the Hapag Line's 52,000-ton flagship *Imperator* to Cunard, in reparation for the loss of the *Lusitania*. Cunard renamed her *Berengaria*. In 1934 Cunard were forced, at the behest of the British government, to merge with their great rival, the White Star Line. This was a condition made upon them in order to obtain the necessary government funding required to complete 'No. 534', the *Queen Mary*, then on the stocks at John Brown's Clydebank yard. Henceforth, they became known as the Cunard-White Star Line and moved their head office to Southampton. Thereafter, they gradually phased out the use of the White Star part of the name. Today, Cunard is American-owned, and famed as the owners and operators of the *QE2*.

Of the men who had commanded the *Lusitania*, Captain James Watt retired in 1908. Following Captain Watt's achievement on the *Lusitania*'s second voyage, the Blue Riband remained a Cunard held honour until the advent of the German liner *Bremen*, in 1929. When James Watt retired in 1908, the Lloyds list of captains, it will be recalled, had the following noted on his record:

Captain Watt, Commodore of the Cunard fleet, who is retiring after 35 years service, completed his last trip in the *Lusitania* which arrived in Liverpool yesterday. The passengers under the presidency of speaker of the Canadian House of Commons, presented him with an address, in which they said that he and his brother-commanders, who had done so much to promote the comfort and safety of Atlantic travel, were deserving of the deepest gratitude from all ocean voyagers.

Captain William Turner, her second captain and the man who commanded her on her fateful last voyage, remained with Cunard after the disaster. Captain Turner recovered from the incident and the British Admiralty's despicable attempts to blame him alone for the disaster that befell his ship, and went on to serve his country again during the 1914–1918 conflict, commanding troopships. He was torpedoed again on New Year's Day 1917, whilst in command of the *Ivernia*, which sank. At the end of the war, and at the behest of Cunard chairman Alfred Booth, Turner was awarded the OBE. Captain Turner retired in 1919 after a long and distinguished career and died in 1933 after losing his battle against cancer.

Captain James T.W. Charles, *Lusitania*'s third captain was

highly decorated by the time his career ended. Captain Charles was appointed an Officer of the Military division of the Most Excellent Order of the British Empire, in recognition of his valuable services rendered in connection with the war on 1 January 1919. In 1920, he was further decorated by being appointed Knight Commander of the Civil division of the Most Excellent Order of the British Empire, also for services in connection with the war. He also held the Royal Naval Reserve Officers Decoration. Captain Charles was in command of Cunard's latest and most luxurious ship, *Aquitania*, when he died suddenly in 1928.

Lusitania's fourth captain was Daniel Dow. His service record appears free from blemishes, although that return sailing from New York in 1915, when he misused the stars and stripes '. . . due to the presence of influential Americans on board' and dashed to Liverpool because of a U-boat threat, was noted on his file. After the somewhat providential leave that he was granted, during which the *Lusitania* was sunk, he was appointed to Cunard's newest and grandest ship, the *Aquitania*. After *Aquitania* he had one voyage in command of the *Mauretania*. Command of the *Thracia* and finally the *Royal George* followed this. Captain Dow retired from Cunard in 1919 after a long and distinguished career. He was a holder of the Royal Naval Reserve Officers Decoration and died in 1931.

The fate of the man who put the *Lusitania* on the bottom is also worth recording at this point. In July 1917, *Kapitänleutnant* Walther Schwieger was awarded the *Pour Le Mérite* medal, or 'Blue Max' as it was more popularly known. It was Germany's highest award for gallantry in the face of an enemy and was given in recognition of his having sunk a total of 190,000 tons of Allied shipping.

The commendation for Schwieger's award made no mention at all of the sinking of his largest victim, the *Lusitania*. He was, by virtue of being a holder of this coveted award, officially a U-boat ace, ranking sixth in the league table of U-boat commanders. He died with his entire crew, six weeks after receiving his medal, when in command of the *U-88*. Whilst being pursued by the Q-ship HMS *Stonecrop*, the submerged *U-88* struck a British-laid mine off the island of Terschelling in the North Sea, on 5 September 1917. He was thirty-two years of age when his worst nightmare came true.

In Germany, the sinking of the *Lusitania* was cause for widespread celebration initially, though one German, a medal maker from Munich by the name of Karl Goetz, wasn't overly impressed by this latest deed of his country's navy. He struck a special limited edition medal, of his own design, as a form of political satire aimed at Cunard and the German government. Unfortunately, his satirical comment backfired somewhat, as examples of his medal found their way into British hands. The British government seized the propaganda initiative with both hands, striking thousands of copies and circulating them with a very anti-German flyer, advertising Goetz's medal as a callous commemorative piece, thereby labelling his production of it as a deplorable act equal in repugnance to the event his medal depicted. There were even some people who actually believed that Goetz had specially produced this medal for the commander and crew of the *U-20*; a myth that persists even today.

The sinking of the *Lusitania* was roundly condemned almost everywhere outside Germany. In Queenstown, Ireland, the German owner of a large hotel locked himself in his cellar as the *Lusitania*'s dead were brought ashore, for fear of reprisals. In London, anti-German riots were rife. Police were called out in large numbers as German-owned shops and businesses, or even ones with a German sounding name, were attacked and looted by the angry mobs.

In the United States, the American press whipped up a frenzy of public anger at the 128 American deaths on the *Lusitania*. The US government sent strongly worded notes of protest to the German government, but American opinion and anger stopped short of a declaration of war. There was, said President Wilson, '... such a thing as being too proud to fight'. It would take another two years, the deaths of many more American citizens crossing the Atlantic, and finally the infamous Zimmermann telegram, before America, as President Wilson finally concluded, 'found herself'. But in the end, it was simply humanity that had lost itself, as the 1,201 men, women and children who perished in the sinking of the *Lusitania*, would attest.

The city of New York has changed a good deal since the *Lusitania* left there for the last time. Pier 54, scene of both her maiden arrival and her final departure, still stands today, though in a state of semi-dereliction. The large Cunard transit shed that stood atop the pier was demolished in 1990 after a survey revealed that it was on the point of collapse. Pier 54 has recently been given a new deck and currently awaits its planned redevelopment as a museum to historic shipping, surrounded by a large park.

Today, Liverpool is also a very different place from the bustling port of the *Lusitania*'s heyday. Large ocean liners making regular Atlantic crossings are a thing of the past, made redundant by the advent of the jet age. Those select few transatlantic liners still in service now use the port of Southampton as their terminal. Liverpool, like the *Lusitania*, is largely forgotten too, it seems. Today, the city of Liverpool has the appearance of having been drained, long ago milked for all of her commercial worth. Though admirable regeneration schemes are in progress, to the casual observer the effects appear to be largely piecemeal in nature. It is almost as if everybody over the last few hundred years has taken whatever they wanted from Liverpool, without bothering to put much back.

Yet despite this, the *Lusitania* lives on in her homeport. At the once busy Albert Dock, within sight of the former Cunard building and the Prince's landing stage, one of her four 23-ton propellers salvaged from the wreck and further rescued from a scrapyard, stands as a dedicated and permanent memorial to all those who lost their lives in the disaster, as well as to the ship herself. Every year, on the closest Sunday to 7 May, a remembrance service is held at this monument to ensure that at least in Liverpool, if nowhere else, the victims of the sinking and the *Lusitania* herself are never forgotten.

Appendix I

PASSENGER AND CREW LIST

for the final voyage of

RMS *LUSITANIA*

which sailed from

NEW YORK to LIVERPOOL on SATURDAY, 1 MAY 1915

under the command of Captain William Thomas Turner

and was torpedoed and sunk by the

German Submarine, *U-20*

off the Old Head of Kinsale, Ireland, on FRIDAY, 7 MAY 1915

Contents

Preface to the Passenger and crew list

The information contained in the following pages is based on Cunard's final return of all the passengers and crew aboard the *LUSITANIA*, from New York, 1 May 1915.

After much cross-checking and referencing, spurious and erroneous names as featured on the original Cunard passenger list have now largely been successfully edited out and where known, the full names of passengers have been entered to give a much more accurate record. The crew list is shown exactly as it appeared on the hastily compiled original Cunard list. I am deeply indebted to Geoff Whitfield for the painstaking research he has done in connection with the names on this list.

Kevin Walsh-Johnson, Northwich, Cheshire. April 2001.

The names of all those who survived are shown in bold type.

Saloon Passengers on Board

Passengers' name	Point of Origin	Nationality
Adams, Henry	England	British
Adams, Mrs Annie Elizabeth	England	British
Adams, Arthur Henry	London, England	US
Adams, William McMillan	London, England	US
Allan, Lady Marguerite Ethel	Montreal, Canada	British
and maid (**Davis, Emily**)		British
Allan, Miss Anna Marjory	Montreal, Canada	British
Allan, Miss Gwendolyn Evelyn	Montreal, Canada	British
and maid (**Walker, Annie**)		British
Alles, Nicholas N.	New York, USA	US
Ayala, Julian de	Liverpool, England	Cuban
Baker, James	England	British
Baker, Miss Margaret A.	New York, USA	British
Baldwin, Harry Bradley	New York, USA	US
Baldwin, Mrs Mary Margaret	New York, USA	US
Barnes, Allan Byron	Toronto, Canada	British
Bartlett, George Walter Bowers	London, England	British
Bartlett, Mrs Irma	London, England	British
Bates, Lindon Wallace, Jr.	New York, USA	US
Battersby, James Johnson	Stockport, England	British
Bernard, Oliver	Boston, USA	British
Bernard, Clinton P.	New York, USA	US
Bilicke, Albert C.	Los Angeles, USA	US
Bilicke, Mrs Gladys	Los Angeles, USA	US
Bistis, Leonidas	Greece	Greek
Black, James Joseph	Liverpool, England	British
Bloomfield, Thomas	New York, USA	US
Bohan, James	Toronto, Canada	British
Boulton, Harold, Jr.	Chicago, USA	British
Bowring, Charles Warren	New York, USA	British
Braithwaite, Miss Dorothy Douglas	Montreal, Canada	British
Brandell, Miss Josephine	New York, USA	British
Broderick, Carlton Thayer	Boston, USA	US
Brooks, James Ham	Bridgeport, USA	US
Brown, Mrs Mary Catherine Wolf	New York, USA	US
Brown, William Henry Helm	Buffalo, USA	British
Bruno, Henry Augustine	Montclair, USA	British

Bruno, Mrs Annie	Montclair, USA	British
Burgess, Henry G.	England	British
Burnside, Mrs Josephine S.	Toronto, Canada	British
and maid (Waites, Mattie)	Toronto, Canada	British
Burnside, Miss Iris	Toronto, Canada	British
Buswell, Peter	England	British
Byington, Albert Jackson	London, England	US
Byrne, Michael G.	New York, USA	US
Cairns, Robert Wishart	Booked on board	British
Campbell-Johnston,		
Conway Seymour	Los Angeles, USA	British
Campbell-Johnston, Mrs Ida Amelia	Los Angeles, USA	British
Campbell, Alexander	London, England	British
Chabot, David L.	Montreal, Canada	British
Chapman, Mrs Ellen Elizabeth	Toronto, Canada	British
Charles, John H.	Toronto, Canada	British
Charles, Miss Doris Maud	Toronto, Canada	British
Clarke, Rev. Charles Cowley	London, England	British
Clarke, Alfred Russell	Toronto, Canada	British
Cloete, William Brodrick	San Antonio, USA	US
Colebrook, Harry G.	Toronto, Canada	British
Conner, Miss Dorothy	New York, USA	US
Copping, George Robert	Toronto, Canada	British
Copping, Mrs Emma	Toronto, Canada	British
Crichton, Mrs Mabel	New York, USA	US
Crompton, Paul	Philadelphia, USA	British
Crompton, Mrs Gladys Mary	Philadelphia, USA	British
Crompton, Stephen	Philadelphia, USA	British
Crompton, Miss Alberta	Philadelphia, USA	British
Crompton, Miss Catherine Mary	Philadelphia, USA	British
Crompton, Master Paul Romelly		
(9 years)	Philadelphia, USA	British
Crompton, Master John David		
(6 years)	Philadelphia, USA	British
Crompton, Master Peter (infant)	Philadelphia, USA	British
and nurse (Allen, Dorothy D.)	——	US
Crooks, Robert William	Toronto, Canada	British
Cross, Ambrose Betham	F. Malay States	British
Daly, Harold Mayne	Ottawa, Canada	British
Dearbergh, Robert Edward	New York, USA	British
Depage, Madame Marie	Belgium	Belgian
Dingwall, Charles Arthur	London, England	British
Dougall, Miss Catherine	Guelph, Canada	British
Drake, Bernard Audley Mervyn	Detroit, USA	British
Dredge, Joseph Alan	British Honduras	British

114

Dredge, Mrs Evelyn	British Honduras	British
Dunsmuir, James	Toronto, Canada	British
Emond, Walter A.	Quebec, Canada	British
Fenwick, John	Switzerland	British
Fisher, Dr Howard	New York, USA	US
Forman, Justus Miles	New York, USA	US
Fowles, Charles Frederick	New York, USA	British
Fowles, Mrs Frances May	New York, USA	British
Freeman, Richard R., Jr.	Boston, USA	US
Friedenstien, Joseph	London, England	British
Friend, Edwin W.	Farmington, USA	US
Frohman, Charles	New York, USA	US
and valet (Stainton, William)		US
Gauntlett, Frederick John	New York, USA	US
Gibson, Matthew Orr	Glasgow, Scotland	British
Gilpin, George Arthur	England	British
Gorer, Edgar Ezekiel	London, England	British
Grab, Oscar F.	New York, USA	US
Grant, Montague Tassell	Chicago, USA	British
Grant, Mrs Chastina Jane	Chicago, USA	British
Hammond, Frederick Sydney	Toronto, Canada	British
Hammond, Mrs Kathleen Saunders	Toronto, Canada	British
Hammond, Ogden Haggerty	New York, USA	British
Hammond, Mrs Mary Picton	New York, USA	British
Hardwick, Charles Cheever	New York, USA	US
Harper, John Henry	New York, USA	British
Harris, Dwight Carlton	New York, USA	US
Hawkins, Frederick Williams	Winnipeg, Canada	British
Hickson, Miss Katharyn	New York, USA	US
Hill, Charles Tilden	London, England	US
Hodges, William Sterling	Philadelphia, USA	US
Hodges, Mrs Sara	Philadelphia, USA	US
Hodges, Master William Sterling (8 years)	Philadelphia, USA	US
Hodges, Master Dean Winston (5 years)	Philadelphia, USA	US
Holt, William Robert Grattan	Montreal, Canada	British
Home, Thomas	Toronto, Canada	British
Hopkins, Albert L.	New York, USA	US
Houghton, Dr James Tilley	Saratoga Springs, USA	US
Hubbard, Elbert	E. Aurora, USA	US
Hubbard, Mrs Alice	E. Aurora, USA	US
Hutchinson, Miss Phyllis	England	British
Jacobaeus, Anton Sigurd	Sweden	Swedish
Jeffrey, Charles Thomas	Chicago, USA	US

Jenkins, Francis Bertram	New York, USA	British
Jolivet, Miss Rita	Paris, France	French
Jones, Miss Margaret Drutler	Honolulu, Hawaii	British
Keeble, Wilfred R.	Toronto, Canada	British
Keeble, Mrs	Toronto, Canada	British
Kellett, Francis Cranston	Tuckahoe, USA	US
Kempson, Maitland	Toronto, Canada	British
Kenan, Dr Owen	New York, USA	US
Kennedy, Mrs Catherine Hickson	New York, USA	US
Keser, Harry J.	Philadelphia, USA	US
Keser, Mrs Mary Bringhurst	Philadelphia, USA	US
Kessler, George A.	New York, USA	US
King, Thomas Boyce	New York, USA	US
Klein, Charles	London, England	British
Knight, Charles Harwood	Baltimore, USA	US
Knight, Miss Elaine Harwood	Baltimore, USA	US
Knox, Samuel McIlhenny	Philadelphia, USA	US
Lane, Sir Hugh Percy	England	British
Lassetter, Mrs Elizabeth Anne	London, England	British
Lassetter, Frederick Macquarie	London, England	British
Lauriat, Charles Emilius, Jr.	Boston, USA	US
Learoyd, Charles Alfred	Sydney, Australia	British
Learoyd, Mrs Mabel Kate	Sydney, Australia	British
and maid (Hurley, Margaret)		British
Leary, James	New York, USA	US
Lehmann, Isaac	New York, USA	US
Leigh, Evan Arthur	Liverpool, England	British
Letts, Gerald Arthur	New York, USA	British
Levinson, Joseph, Jr.	Canada	British
Lewin, Frederick Guy	England	British
Lobb, Mrs Mary Beatrice	New York, USA	British
Lockhart, Reginald R.	Toronto, Canada	British
Loney, Allan Donnellan	New York, USA	US
Loney, Mrs Catherine Wolf Brown	New York, USA	US
and maid (Bouteiller, Elsie)		French
Loney, Miss Virginia Bruce	New York, USA	US
Luck, Mrs Charlotte	Worcester, USA	US
Luck, Master Eldridge (9 years)	Worcester, USA	US
Luck, Master Kenneth (7 years)	Worcester, USA	US
Macdona, Mrs Amelia	New York, USA	US
Mackworth, Lady Margaret H.	Cardiff, Wales	British
MacLennan, Frederick Ebeneezer	Glasgow, Scotland	British
Mason, Stewart Southam	Boston, USA	British
Mason, Mrs Lesley Hawthorne	Boston, USA	British

Matthews, Arthur T.	Montreal, Canada	British
Maturin, Rev. Basil William	Oxford, England	British
Maurice, George	London, England	British
McConnel, John W.	Manchester, England	British
McLean, Walter	France	British
McMurray, Louis Leonard	Toronto, Canada	British
McMurtry, Fred A.	New York, USA	British
Medbury, Maurice Benjamin	New York, USA	US
Miller, Capt. James Blaine	Washington, DC, USA	US
Mills, Charles Veith	New York, USA	US
Mitchell, James Duncan	England	British
Moodie, Ralph Troupe	Gainesville, USA	British
Morell, Mrs M.S.	Toronto, Canada	British
Morrison, Kenneth J.	Canada	British
Mosley, George G.	England	British
Munro, Mrs C.	Liverpool, England	British
Myers, Herman A.	New York, USA	US
Myers, Joseph Laurence	New York, USA	US
Naumann, Frank Gustavus	England	British
Nyblom, Gustaf Adolf	Canada	Swedish
Orr-Lewis, Frederick	Montreal, Canada	British
and valet (**Slingsby, George**)		British
Osborne, Mrs Irene	Hamilton, Canada	British
Osbourne, Mrs Alexandra	Glasgow, Scotland	British
Padilla, Frederico G.	Liverpool, England	Mexican
Padley, Mrs Florence M.	Liverpool, England	British
Page, John Harvey	New York, USA	US
Pappadopoulo, Michael N.	Greece	Greek
Pappadopoulo, Mrs	Greece	Greek
Partridge, Frank	New York, USA	British
Paynter, Charles Edwin	Liverpool, England	British
Paynter, Miss Irene Emily	Liverpool, England	British
Peardon, Frank Arthur	Toronto, Canada	British
Pearl, Major Frederick Warren	New York, USA	US
Pearl, Mrs Amy Lea	New York, USA	US
Pearl, Miss Audrey (infant)	New York, USA	US
and maid (Lorenson, Greta)		Danish
Pearl, Amy W.W. (2 years 6 months)	New York, USA	US
Pearl, Susan W. (1 year 6 months)	New York, USA	US
and nurse (**Lines, Alice**)		US
Pearl, Master Stuart Duncan Day		
(5 years)	New York, USA	US
Pearson, Dr Frederick Stark	New York, USA	British

Pearson, Mrs Mabel	New York, USA	British
Perkins, Edwin	England	British
Perry, Fred John	Buffalo, USA	British
Perry, Albert Norris	Buffalo, USA	British
Phillips, Wallace Banta	New York, USA	US
Pierpoint, William John	Liverpool, England	British
Pirie, Robinson	Hamilton, Canada	British
Plamondon, Charles Ambrose	Chicago, USA	US
Plamondon, Mrs Mary Letitia	Chicago, USA	US
Pollard, Henry	Washington, DC, USA	British
Pope, Miss Theodate	Farmington, USA	US
and maid (Robinson, Emily)	London, England	US
Posen, Eugene H.	New York, USA	British
Powell, George A.	Toronto, Canada	British
Rankin, Robert	New York, USA	US
Ratcliffe, Norman Albert	England	British
Rhys-Evans, Arnold L.	Cardiff, Wales	British
Robinson, Charles E.	Philadelphia, USA	British
Robinson, Mrs Prudence Mary	Philadelphia, USA	British
Rogers, Frank Albert	Toronto, Canada	British
Rogers, Mrs Agnes	Toronto, Canada	British
Rogers, Percy William	Toronto, Canada	British
Rumble, Thomas Walter	Toronto, Canada	British
Ryerson, Mrs Mary Amelia	Toronto, Canada	British
Ryerson, Miss Laura Mary	Toronto, Canada	British
Schwabacher, Leo M.	Baltimore, USA	US
Schwarcz, Max M.	New York, USA	US
Schwarte, Fred W. August	New York, USA	British
Scott, Alick John	Manila, Philippines	British
Seccombe, Percy W.	Peterboro, USA	British
Seccombe, Miss Elizabeth	Peterboro, USA	British
Shields, Victor E.	Cincinnati, USA	US
Shields, Mrs	Cincinnati, USA	US
Shymer, Mrs R.D.	New York, USA	US
Silva, Thomas James	Temple, USA	US
Slidell, Thomas	New York, USA	US
Smith, Mrs Jessie Taft	Braceville, USA	US
Sonneborne, Henry Becker	Baltimore, USA	US
Stackhouse, J. Foster	London, England	British
Stephens, Mrs Frances Ramsey	Montreal, Canada	British
and maid (Oberlin, Elsie)		Swiss
Stephens, Master John Harrison		
Chattan (infant)	Montreal, Canada	British
and nurse (Millen, Carolina)		British

118

Stewart, Duncan	Montreal, Canada	British
Stone, Herbert Stewart	New York, USA	US
Strauss, Julius	Hamilton, Canada	British
Stuart, Alex	Glasgow, Scotland	British
Sturdy, Charles Frederick	Montreal, Canada	British
Taylor, Richard Lionel	Montreal, Canada	British
Tesson, Frank B.	Philadelphia, USA	US
Tesson, Mrs Alice	Philadelphia, USA	US
Thomas, David Alfred	Cardiff, Wales	British
Thompson, Elbridge Blish	Seymour, USA	US
Thompson, Mrs Maud	Seymour, USA	US
Tiberghien, Georges	France	French
Timmis, Robert James	Gainesville, USA	British
Tootal, Frederick Edward Owen	London, England	British
Townley, Ernest Ethelbert	Toronto, Canada	British
Trumball, Issac B.	Bridgeport, USA	US
Turner, Scott	Lansing, USA	US
Turton, George Henderson	Melbourne, Australia	British
Vanderbilt, Alfred Gwynne	New York, USA	US
and valet (Denyer, Ronald)		US
Van Straaten, Martin	London, England	British
Vassar, William A.F.	London, England	British
Vernon, George L.P.	London, England	British
Wakefield, Mrs Mary Gertrude	Honolulu, Hawaii	British
Walker, David	New York, USA	British
Watson, Mrs Katharine	Montreal, Canada	British
Watson, Mrs Florence Stancliffe	England	British
Willey, Mrs Catherine E.	Lake Forest, USA	US
Williams, Thomas Henry	Liverpool, England	British
Williamson, Charles Francis	New York, USA	US
Winter, William Herman	Liverpool, England	British
Witherbee, Mrs Beatrice	New York, USA	US
Witherbee, Master Alfred Scott		
(4 years)	New York, USA	US
Withington, Lothrop	Boston, USA	US
Wright, Walter	Scotland	British
Wood, Arthur John	England	British
Wright, Robert Currie	Cleveland, USA	US
Young, James M.	Hamilton, Canada	British
Young, Mrs Georgina	Hamilton, Canada	British
Yung, Philip J.	Antwerp, Belgium	Belgian

119

Analysis of saloon passengers' nationality

British	173
United States Citizens	104
Greek	3
Swedes	2
Swiss	1
Belgian	2
Mexican	1
Cuban	1
French	3
Danish	1
Total	291

Second Cabin Passengers on Board

Passengers' name	Point of Origin	Nationality
Abas, Mrs Beatrice	New York, USA	Dutch
Abas, Miss Isabel (6years)	New York, USA	Dutch
Abas, Miss Beatrice (2 years)	New York, USA	Dutch
Abercromby, Ralph Frank	Cincinnati, USA	British
Abramowitz, Samuel	Paris, France	Russian
Ackroyd, Mrs Hannah	Brooklyn, USA	British
Ackroyd, Master Frederick (3 years)	Brooklyn, USA	British
Adams, H. Allan	Winnipeg, Canada	British
Adams. Mrs A.E.	Edmonton, Canada	British
Adams, Miss Joan M. (2 years)	Edmonton, Canada	British
Aiston, Joseph	Brooklyn, USA	British
Aitken, James	Merritt, Canada	British
Aitken, Jarvie	Merritt, Canada	British
Aitken, Master Jarvie (7 years)	Merritt, Canada	British
Aitken, Miss Chrissie	Merritt, Canada	British
Allen, John	Philadelphia, USA	British
Amory, Mrs Phoebe	Toronto, Canada	British
Anderson, Mrs Margaret Armstrong	Pittsburg, USA	British
Anderson, Mrs Emily	Bridgeport, USA	British
Anderson, Miss Barbara Winifred		
(2 years)	Bridgeport, USA	British
Armitage, Mrs Florence G.	New York, USA	British
Arnott, Robert	Kearney, USA	British
Arter, Joseph Sidney	Seattle, USA	British
Arthur, George Herbert	Minneapolis, USA	British
Bailey, Walter George	Nelson, Canada	British
Bailey, Mrs Jessie Annie	Nelson, Canada	British
Bailey, Miss Ivy	Nelson, Canada	British
Baker, Miss Eva	New York, USA	British
Bancroft, William B.	New York, USA	US
Barber, Miss Constance	Winnipeg, Canada	British
Barbour, Miss Bessie	Victoria, Canada	British
Barchard, Edmund E.	Columbus, USA	British
Barker, Mrs Martha Ann	Trenton, USA	US
Barker, Miss Winifred (9 years)	Trenton, USA	US
Barr, James	Toronto, Canada	British
Barr, Mrs Catherine Symington	Toronto, Canada	British

Barrett, Miss Mae	New York, USA	British
Barrie, Edward	New York, USA	British
Bartlett, Edmund Thomas	New York, USA	British
Baxter, William	Welland, Canada	British
Baxter, Mrs Annie E.	Welland, Canada	British
Baxter, Master William (6 years)	Welland, Canada	British
Beattie, Rev. James A.	New York, USA	British
Beattie, Mrs Margaret	New York, USA	British
Beattie, Mrs Grace S.	Winnipeg, Canada	British
Beattie, Allam Martin	Winnipeg, Canada	British
Beaumont, James	England	British
Bilbrough, George W.	Smith Fall, Canada	British
Bingham, Miss Alice Winnifred	Toronto, Canada	British
Bingley, Mrs Catherine	New York, USA	British
Birchall, Henry	Roslyn, USA	British
Bird, Mrs Rose	England	British
Booth-Jones, Edward	New York, USA	British
Booth-Jones, Mrs Millichamp	New York, USA	British
Booth-Jones, Miss Ailsa (8 years)	New York, USA	British
Booth-Jones, Master Percival (4 years)	New York, USA	British
Booth, John	Alexandria, USA	British
Booth, Mrs H. Emily	Ottawa, Canada	British
Booth, Nigel Frederick (infant)	Ottawa, Canada	British
Bourke, Mrs Mabel Juliet	Winnipeg, Canada	British
Boyd, Miss Margaret L.	Hamilton, Canada	British
Braddick, Sidral William	Minneapolis, USA	British
Brammer, Mrs Elizabeth Jane	Trenton, USA	British
Brammer, Miss Edith Francesca (8 years).	Trenton, USA	British
Bretherton, Mrs Noah Edith	Los Angeles, USA	US
Bretherton, Elizabeth (infant)	Los Angeles, USA	US
Bretherton, Master Paul (3 years)	Los Angeles, USA	US
Brilly, Louis	New York, USA	Italian
Brown, Daniel Taylor	Los Angeles, USA	British
Brownlie, Thomas	Freeport, USA	British
Brownlie, Mrs Margaret	Freeport, USA	British
Bryce, Hugh B.	Syracuse, USA	British
Bryce, Mrs Arabella	Syracuse, USA	British
Buchanan, Miss Mary	Pottstown, USA	British
Bull, Mrs Elizabeth	Hamilton, Canada	British
Bullen, Henry Garnet	Winnipeg, Canada	British
Burdon, Mrs Ellen	Winnipeg, Canada	British
Burdon, Master Robert P. (14 months)	Winnipeg, Canada	British
Burley, Rueben	Hamilton, Canada	British

122

Burley, Mrs Florence	Hamilton, Canada	British
Burley, Reginald (infant)	Hamilton, Canada	British
Burley, Miss Doris F. (9 years)	Hamilton, Canada	British
Busvine, William Robert	New York, USA	British
Butler, Mrs Margaret	Whitefish, USA	British
Butler, T. O`Brien	Ireland	British
Butters, Miss Margaret Hill	Toronto, Canada	British
Callan, Patrick	Chicago, USA	US
Campbell, Kennedy	Boston, USA	British
Campbell, William	Chicago, USA	British
Campbell, Mrs Amy E.	Chicago, USA	British
Campbell, Miss Tina F.	Calgary, Canada	British
Campbell, Miss Ada M.	New York, USA	British
Candlish, Arthur	Pawtucket, USA	US
Candlish, Mrs Ellen	Pawtucket. USA	US
Carson, Miss Henrietta	Sherbrooke, Canada	British
Catherwood, John	Philadelphia, USA	US
Catherwood, Mrs Maria	Philadelphia, USA	US
Cattley, Colin	Edmonton, Canada	British
Chalmers, Mrs Blanche	Winnipeg, Canada	British
Chalmers, Guy	Boston, USA	British
Chambers, Mrs Ethel	Boston, USA	British
Chantry, Harold	Nelson, Canada	British
Chantry, Mrs Mina	Nelson, Canada	British
Chantry, Elizabeth Ellen (infant)	Nelson, Canada	British
Charles, Miss Eleanor	New York, USA	British
Chatt, Miss Anna	New York, USA	British
Chirgwin, Mrs Maud Gertrude	Havana, Cuba	British
Chirgwin, Richard (infant)	Havana, Cuba	British
Clarke, Mrs Nore	Toronto, Canada	British
Clay, Miss Elizabeth Alice	San Francisco, USA	British
Clayton, William	Vancouver, Canada	British
Clayton, Mrs	Vancouver, Canada	British
Cockburn, Guy R.	Pasadena, USA	British
Colbert, William	New York, USA	US
Colbert, Mrs Helena	New York, USA	US
Coleman, Miss Susan	Brooklyn, USA	British
Collis, Edwin Martin	Riverside, USA	US
Condon, Miss Della Josephine	New York, USA	US
Costello, Miss Mary	New York, USA	British
Cowper, Ernest S.	Toronto, Canada	British
Cox, Mrs Margaret Elizabeth	Winnipeg, Canada	British
Cox, Master Desmond Francis (2 years)	Winnipeg, Canada	British
Critchison, Stanley	Hamilton, Canada	British
Critchison, Mrs Lillian	Hamilton, Canada	British

Critchison, Master Bernard (13 months)	Hamilton, Canada	British
Crosby, Miss Ellen	Vancouver, Canada	British
Crosby, Miss Annie	Vancouver, Canada	British
Crossley, Cyrus	Toronto, Canada	British
Crossley, Mrs Sylvia	Toronto, Canada	British
Dale, William	Toronto, Canada	British
Dalrymple, David	Hoboken, USA	British
Davies, George F.	Wales	British
Davis, Miss Annie	Welland, Canada	US
De Boissierre, Etienne T.	San Francisco, USA	Belgian.
Dewhurst, William	Fall River, USA	British
Dixon, Arthur	England	British
Dixon, Mrs Bertha	England	British
Dixon, Master Stanley (6 years)	England	British
Docherty, Mrs Mabel	New York, USA	US
Docherty, William Thomas (infant)	New York, USA	US
Dodd, Miss Dorothy	Edmonton, Canada	British
Dolphin, Miss Avis (11 years)	St Thomas, Canada	British
Donahue, Miss Sarah	Boston, USA	British
Donald, Archibald Douglas	Cambridge, USA	British
Duguid, George	Toronto, Canada	British
Duncan, Mrs Robert	Montreal, Canada	British
Dyer, Robert	Pittsburg, USA	US
Egana, Vincente	New York, USA	Spanish.
Ehrhardt, Herbert	Toronto, Canada	British
Elliott, Arthur W.	Calgary, Canada	British
Elliot, Mrs Annie Louise	Calgary, Canada	British
Ellis, John	Edmonton, Canada	British
Ellis, Miss Hilda	St Thomas, Canada	British
Ellis, William Herbert	England	British
Ewart, Robert James	Brooklyn, USA	US
Exley, Miss Ida	N. Braintree, USA	British
Fentiman, Miss Nellie	Manchester, USA	British
Ferguson, John	New York, USA	US
Ferrier, Alexander Hubert Buxton	Penticton, Canada	British
Ferrier, Mrs Elizabeth Margaret	Penticton, Canada	British
Ferrier, Sheila (infant)	Penticton, Canada	British
Finch, Mrs Eva E.	Lynn, USA	British
Fish, Mrs Sarah Mary	Toronto, Canada	British
Fish, Joan (infant)	Toronto, Canada	British
Fish, Miss Eileen (10 years)	Toronto, Canada	British
Fish, Miss Marian (8 years)	Toronto, Canada	British
Foley, Arthur R.	Trenton, USA	US

124

Foss, Carl Elmer	New York, USA	US
Fox, Francis	Trenton, USA	British
Fox, Mrs Emily	Trenton, USA	British
Freeman, John	Saskatoon, Canada	British
Freeman, Mrs Rachael	Saskatoon, Canada	British
French, Miss Grace	Passaic, USA	British
Friedman, Samuel	Brooklyn, USA	US
Frost, Harry R.	Regina, Canada	British
Fulton, John N.	Montreal, Canada	British
Fyfe, Mrs Jennie	Holyoke, USA	British
Gadsden, Arthur	Chicago, USA	British
Galligan, Miss Margaret	New York, USA	British
Gardner, James	New Zealand	British
Gardner, Mrs Edith	New Zealand	British
Gardner, Eric	New Zealand	British
Gardner, Master Willie (11 years)	New Zealand	British
Garry, Christ	Cleveland, USA	US
Gauthier, Carlos	Montreal, Canada	Argentinian
Gilhooly, Mrs Catherine	New York, USA	British
Gill, Miss Catherine	Gillespie, USA	British
Gilsenan, Hugh	Long Island City, USA	US
Glancy, Joseph	Toronto, Canada	British
Goodman, A.	Rochester, USA	British
Grandidge, Mrs Lydia May	Yonkers, USA	British
Grandidge, Miss Eva Mary (3 years)	Yonkers, USA	British
Gray, James Paul	Oakland, USA	British
Gray, Robert D.	Brooklyn, USA	British
Gray, Mrs Florence Terrance	Los Angeles, USA	US
Gray, Master Stewart James (4 years)	Los Angeles, USA	US
Greenwood, Master Ronald (11 years)	Lawrence, USA	US
Griffiths, Christopher William	Winnipeg, Canada	British
Grimshaw, Arthur	Brooklyn, USA	British
Groves, Sidney	Toronto, Canada	British
Groves, Mrs Clara	Toronto, Canada	British
Groves, Master Frederick William (18 months)	Toronto, Canada	British
Gwyer, Rev. Herbert Lindford	Saskatoon, Canada	British
Gwyer, Mrs Margaret Inglis Adams	Saskatoon, Canada	British
Haigh, James Harold	Winnipeg, USA	British
Haldane, James Cargill	Boston, USA	British
Hamilton, Mrs Isabella	New Haven, USA	British
Hampshire, Miss Elizabeth Eleanor	Boston, USA	British
Hanes, Duncan Arthur Walpole	Saskatoon, Canada	British
Hanson, Samuel	Central Falls, USA	British

Hanson, Mrs Mary	Central Falls, USA	British
Hardy, Miss Elsie	Montclair, USA	British
Hare, Miss Bessie	New York, USA	British
Harris, Reuben	Toronto, Canada	British
Harris, Mrs Emma	Toronto, Canada	British
Harrison, Herbert K.	Chicago, USA	British
Harrison, James	New York, USA	British
Hastings, Mrs Margaret	New Rochelle, USA	British
Henderson, Mrs Violet	New Rochelle, USA	British
Henderson, Master Huntley		
(10 years)	Montreal, Canada	British
Hendricksen, Knud I.	Edmonton Canada	British
Henn, Ernest George	Saskatoon, Canada	British
Henn, Mrs Edith Mabel	Saskatoon, Canada	British
Henshaw, Mrs Mabel Iris	Saskatoon, Canada	British
Henshaw, Mary (infant)	Saskatoon, Canada	British
Herbert, Mrs Florence	London, Canada	British
Hertz, Douglas G.	St Louis, USA	British
Higginbottom, Miss Mary	Fall River, USA	British
Hill, William Spencer	Wales	British
Hill, Mrs Caroline	Schenectady, USA	British
Hogg, Mrs Ellen	New York, USA	British
Holborne, Ian Bernard Stoughton	Yonkers, USA	British
Holland, Mrs Nina	New York, USA	US
Homewood, William	Toledo, USA	British
Hopkins, Miss Alice	Boston, USA	British
Hopkins, Miss Kate	Boston, USA	British
Hopkins, David Thomas	Wales	British
Horsburgh, Miss Martha	Bernardsville, USA	British
Horton, Mrs Elizabeth	Cleveland, USA	British
Hoskins, Arthur	Montreal, Canada	British
Hounsell, Edgar Cyril	England	British
Hubbard, Frederick Cole Amos	New York, USA	British
Hull, Mrs Winnifred	Winnipeg, Canada	British
Hume, Mrs Mary A.	Harrison, USA	US
Humphreys, Henry G.	Los Angeles, USA	British
Hunt, Miss Isabella	Haverford, USA	British
Hunter, George H.	Atlanta, USA	British
Hunter, Mrs Maggie	Atlanta, USA	British
Huston, Miss Nellie	Chicago, USA	British
Inch, William E.	New York, USA	British
Jackson, Percy Thornton	Buffalo, USA	British
Jackson, Isaac	Paterson, USA	British
Jones, Patrick L.	England	British
Jones, Fred R.	Winnipeg, Canada	British

Jones, William Gwynne	Wales	British
Jones, Issac T.	Wales	British
Jones, Mrs Ellen	Toronto, Canada	British
Jones, William Edward (infant)	Toronto, Canada	British
Jones, Miss Gwendolyn	San Francisco, USA	British
Judson, Frederick S.	New York, USA	US
Kaltenbach, Miss Alice M.	Toronto, Canada	British
Kay, Mrs Marguerita	New York, USA	British
Kay, Master Robert (7 years)	New York, USA	British
Kaye, Miss Kathleen	Toronto, Canada	British
Keely, Miss Annie	Toronto, Canada	British
Kelly, James Robert	New York, USA	British
Kelly, Miss Margaret S.	Pittsburg, USA	US
Kenney, Mrs Margaret	Charlestown, USA	British
Kenney, Miss Mary Bridget (2 years)	Charlestown, USA	British
Kinch, William Mostoe	Cleveland, USA	British
Kinch, Mrs Eunice	Cleveland, USA	British
King, Mrs Martha Frances	Lockport, USA	British
Kuebellick, Samuel Max	Montreal, Canada	British
Ladd, Owen	Winnipeg, Canada	British
Lakin, Miss Martha M.	Saskatoon, Canada	British
Lambie, Mrs Mary	Roslyn, USA	British
Lambie, Miss Elizabeth (8 years)	Roslyn, USA	British
Lambie, Miss Mary (2 years)	Roslyn, USA	British
Lancaster, Miss Annie	Montreal, Canada	British
Lancaster, Miss Dorothy	Montreal, Canada	British
Lancaster, Francis William	Toronto, Canada	British
Lander, Edward Harries	New York, USA	British
Lane, George B.	England	British
Lawranson, Edward	Michel, Canada	British
Lawranson, Mrs Elizabeth	Michel, Canada	British
Lawrence, Miss Ella Woods	Winnipeg, Canada	British
Lee, Miss Bridget	New York, USA	British
Lertold, Miss Catherine M. E.	Chicago, USA	British
Leverich, Mrs Rosina T.	New York, USA	US
Leverich, Miss Rosina P.	New York, USA	US
Lewis, John	New York, USA	British
Lewis, Mrs Jane	New York, USA	British
Lewis, Miss Edith (5 years)	New York, USA	British
Lines, Stanley L. B.	Toronto, Canada	British
Lines, Mrs Ethel Moore	Toronto, Canada	British
Lintott, Roy Iver	Calgary, Canada	British
Little, Mrs Margaret	Brooklyn, USA	British
Little, Alice (infant)	Brooklyn, USA	British
Lohden, Mrs R. Mary	Toronto, Canada	British

Lohden, Miss Elsie (11 years)	Toronto, Canada	British
Longdin, Arthur	Toronto, Canada	British
Longdin, Mrs Matilda	Toronto, Canada	British
Lovett, Miss Mary	Fall River, USA	British
Loynd, David	Ottawa, Canada	British
Loynd, Mrs Alice	Ottawa, Canada	British
Lucas, Francis John	Pittsburg, USA	British
Lund, Charles	New York, USA	US
Lund, Mrs Sarah	New York, USA	US
MacFarquhar, Mrs Jane Ann	Stratford, USA	US
MacFarquhar, Miss Grace Marie	Stratford, USA	US
MacGregor, Arthur Samuel	New York, USA	British
MacGregor, Mrs Betsy	New York, USA	British
Mackay, Hamish	New York, USA	British
Macky, Joseph	New Zealand	British
Macky, Mrs Mary	New Zealand	British
Maclay, Miss Bessie	Ridgefield Park, USA	British
Mainman, Alfred Reid	Edmonton, Canada	British
Mainman, Mrs	Edmonton, Canada	British
Mainman, John V.	Edmonton, Canada	British
Mainman, Alfred S.	Edmonton, Canada	British
Mainman, Miss Molly	Edmonton, Canada	British
Mainman, Miss Elizabeth (7 years)	Edmonton, Canada	British
Mainman, Master Edwin (7 years)	Edmonton, Canada	British
Manby, Miss Ada	Montreal, Canada	British
Manion, Martin	Albany, USA	British
Marichal, Joseph P.	Kingston, Canada	British
Marichal. Mrs Jessie	Kingston, Canada	French
Marichal, Miss Yvonne (5 years)	Kingston, Canada	French
Marichal, Miss Phyllis (4 years)	Kingston, Canada	French
Marichal, Master Maurice (2 years)	Kingston, Canada	French
Martin, Charles	Pittsburg, USA	British
Martin, Miss Ruby	New York, USA	British
Martin-Davey, William	Vancouver, Canada	British
Martin-Davey, Mrs Elizabeth Cumbe	Vancouver, Canada	British
Martin-Davey, Arthur	Vancouver, Canada	British
Mathewson, Mrs Maud E. S.	Springfield, USA	British
Matthewson, Joseph (infant)	Springfield, USA	British
Matthews, Robert	Winnipeg, Canada	British
Matthews, Mrs Annie	Winnipeg, Canada	British
Maycock, Miss Mary	Harrison, USA	British
McClintock, Miss Margaret	New York, USA	British
McClure, Miss Margaret	New York, USA	British
McColm, Mrs Christina	Ottawa, Canada	British

McCorkingdale, Mrs Elizabeth	Chrome, USA	British
McCorkingdale, Mary (infant)	Chrome, USA	British
McCorkingdale, Master Duncan (7 years)	Chrome, USA	British
McCreedy, Dr Ralph J. R.	Battle Creek, USA	British
McDonnell, Miss Kate	New York, USA	British
McEvoy, Henry	New York, USA	British
McFadyen, Hugh	Galt, Canada	British
McGinley, Patrick Vincent	New York, USA	British
McGovern, Miss Mazie	Bloomfield, USA	US
McHardy, Mrs Annie	New York, USA	US
McIlroy, Archibald	Edmonton, Canada	British
McKensie, Mrs Mary A.	New Bedford, USA	US
McKetchan, Mrs R. Elizabeth	Gillespie, USA	British
McKetchan, Campbell (infant)	Gillespie, USA	British
McKetchan, Master James (5 years)	Gillespie, USA	British
McKinnon, Mrs Robert	Toronto, Canada	British
McLellan, Miss Sarah	Lake Forest, USA	British
McPartlin, Myles	New York, USA	US
Menzies, Miss Isabella	Yakima, USA	British
Meriheina, Uno	New York, USA	Russian
Michael, Dewi	England	British
Middlemast, Mrs Elizabeth L.	Regina, Canada	British
Middleton, Miss Alice (upgraded from third-class)	New York, USA	British
Milford, Frederick J.	Hancock, USA	US
Miller, Mrs Aubrey M.	New York, USA	British
Mitchelhill, William	St Joseph, USA	British
Mitchell, Arthur Jackson	Toronto, Canada	US
Mitchell, Walter Dawson	Newark, USA	British
Mitchell, Mrs Millicent Jeanette	Newark, USA	British
Mitchell, Walter (infant)	Newark, USA	British
Moffatt, William	Winchester, USA	British
Molloy, Miss Margaret	New York, USA	British
Moody, Mrs Martha	San Francisco, USA	British
Moody, Miss Martha	San Francisco, USA	British
Moore, John	Manchester Green, USA	British
Moore, Ernest	Moose Jaw, Canada	British
Moore, Dr Daniel Virgil	New York, USA	US
Moore, Edwin	Central Falls, USA	British
Morris, Rev. Hugh C. S.	Toronto, Canada	British
Mounsey, William	New York, USA	US
Muir, Matthew	Philadelphia, USA	British
Murdock, Miss Jessie	Westbury, USA	British
Murray, Mrs C. Rose	New York, USA	US
Myers, Ellason	Hamilton, Canada	British

Naisch, Theodore	Kansas City, USA	US
Naisch, Mrs Belle Saunders	Kansas City, USA	US
Neatby, Miss Frieda	Saskatoon, Canada	British
Needham, Henry E.	New York, USA	British
Negus, Edward	New York, USA	British
Neilson, Henry	Brooklyn, USA	British
Neilson, Mrs Frances	Brooklyn, USA	British
Neilson, Charles H.	Brooklyn, USA	British
Neimark, Abraham	New York, USA	Russian.
Neville, Albert Charles	Toronto, Canada	British
Neville, Mrs Mabel Frances	Toronto, Canada	British
Neville, Master Charles (11 years)	Toronto, Canada	British
Neville, Miss Evelyn	Toronto, Canada	British
Neville, Miss Muriel (4 years)	Toronto, Canada	British
Nicholson, Charles Duncan	Edmonton, Canada	British
Nicol, Miss Mary F.	Chicago, USA	British
Nicoll, George	Philadelphia, USA	British
Norman, Robert	New York, USA	British
North, Miss Olive	Saskatoon, Canada	British
O`Donnell, Patrick	Hoboken, USA	US
Owens, Mrs Cecilia	Ellwood City, USA	British
Owens, Master Ronald (10 years)	Ellwood City, USA	British
Owens, Master Reginald (8 years)	Ellwood City, USA	British
Page, Andrew	Medicine Hat, Canada	British
Palmer, Albert	Toronto, Canada	British
Palmer, Mrs Annie	Toronto, Canada	British
Palmer, Albert (infant)	Toronto, Canada	British
Palmer, Master Edgar (6 years)	Toronto, Canada	British
Palmer, Miss Olive (4 years)	Toronto, Canada	British
Palmer, Frank Arthur	N. Augusta, USA	British
Palmer, Miss Kathleen	N. Augusta, USA	British
Parlett, Mrs Amy	New York, USA	British
Partlett, Miss Enid	New York, USA	British
Parsons, Archibald Ernest	New York, USA	British
Pavey, Miss Lorna	Fort Qui Appelle, Canada	British
Payne, Martin S.	Springfield, USA	British
Peacock, Edward	Jerome, USA	British
Peacock, Mrs Elizabeth F.	Jerome, USA	British
Pells, Cyril Elmore	Vancouver, Canada	British
Pells, Mrs Mary Anita	Vancouver, Canada	British
Pells, John (infant)	Vancouver, Canada	British
Phair, Rev. Ernest Edward Maxwell	Winnipeg, Canada	British
Pirie, Mrs Annie	Lynn, USA	British
Pirie, Miss Margaret (10 years)	Lynn, USA	British
Pirie, Master Arthur (4 years)	Lynn, USA	British

Pirrie, Miss Henrietta	Ottawa, Canada	British
Plank, Mrs Harriet	Toronto, Canada	British
Poole, Mrs Gertrude Kate Elizabeth	New York, USA	British
Potter, Walter	Calgary, Canada	British
Prescott, Mrs Bertha	Toronto, Canada	British
Press, Miss Mary Jane	New York, USA	British
Prichard, Richard B.	Montreal, Canada	British
Proudfoot, Samuel Lamond	Belle Vernon, USA	British
Purse, Reginald	Chattanooga, USA	British
Purse, Mrs Gertrude Alice	Chattanooga, USA	British
Pye, Mrs Charlotte	Edmonton, Canada	British
Pye, Marjorie (infant)	Edmonton, Canada	British
Readdie, James R.	Brooklyn, USA	British
Reid, Peter	Little Rock, USA	British
Richards, Thomas H.	Butte, USA	British
Richards, Mrs Phyllis	Butte, USA	British
Richards, Miss Dora (infant)	Butte, USA	British
Richards, Master Percy (6 years)	Butte, USA	British
Richards, Master Cecil (4 years)	Butte, USA	British
Richardson, Mrs Annie	Philadelphia, USA	British
Ritchie, William Joass	Winnipeg, USA	British
Robertson, Andrew	New Orleans, USA	British
Robinson, Thomas H.	Vancouver, Canada	British
Robinson, Mrs Edith	Vancouver, Canada	British
Robson, Kenneth Hamilton Stewart	Mt. Vernon, USA	British
Robson, Miss Annie	Mt. Vernon, USA	British
Rogers, Richard James	Toronto, Canada	British
Rogers, Miss Elizabeth	Toronto, Canada	British
Rolfe, George	Hamilton, Canada	British
Rooney, Miss Mary	Brooklyn, USA	British
Rose, Fred J.	Baltimore, USA	British
Rowell, Thomas Reuben	New York, USA	British
Ryan, Miss Mary	New York, USA	British
Salt, Henry J.	Boston, USA	US
Samoilescu, David	New York, USA	US
Sandells, Thomas	Winnipeg, Canada	British
Scott, George	Toronto, Canada	British
Scrimgeour, William	New York, USA	British
Secchi, Mrs Bert	New York, USA	British
Semours, Charles T.	Buffalo, USA	British
Semple, Mrs Agnes	Toronto, Canada	British
Semple, John (infant)	Toronto, Canada	British
Shaw, Miss Emily	Winnipeg, Canada	British
Shineman, James	New York, USA	US
Shineman, Mrs Margaret	New York, USA	US

Simpson, Rev. Henry Wood	Roseland, Canada	British
Slater, Frank William	New York, USA	British
Slattery, Patrick John	New York, USA	US
Smart, George Mercer	Vancouver, Canada	British
Smith, Albert R.	New York, USA	British
Smith, Mrs Gladys	New York, USA	British
Smith, Dorothy (infant)	New York, USA	British
Smith, George Arthur	Rochester, USA	British
Smith, Alfred F.	Ellwood, USA	British
Smith, Mrs Elizabeth A.	Ellwood, USA	British
and infant	Ellwood, USA	British
Smith, Miss Helen (6 years)	Ellwood, USA	British
Smith, Harry A.	Toronto, Canada	British
Smith, David J.	England	British
Smith, John Preston	England	British
Smith, Miss Sarah	St. Thomas, Canada	British
Sorenson, Soren	Edmonton, Canada	British
Spillman, John B.	Wyandotte, USA	British
Spillman, Mrs Eliza	Wyandotte, USA	British
Stanley, Henry William	Trenton, USA	British
Stevens, Charles Henry	Atlantic City, USA	US
Stevenson, Mrs Janet	Cleveland, USA	British
Stevenson, Elizabeth (infant)	Cleveland, USA	British
Stewart, Mrs Christina	Toronto, Canada	British
Stewart, John (infant)	Toronto, Canada	British
Stokes, George Edward	Victoria, Canada	British
Stokes, Mrs Mabel	Victoria, Canada	British
Stokes, Master William (30 months)	Victoria, Canada	British
Stones, Norman	Vancouver, Canada	British
Stones, Mrs Hilda Mary	Vancouver, Canada	British
Storch, Walter R.	San Francisco, USA	British
Stroud, Edwin P. W.	Mexico	British
Stroud, Mrs Constance	Mexico	British
Stroud, Miss Helen (3 years)	Mexico	British
Sullivan, George	Groton, USA	British
Sullivan, Mrs Emily	Groton, USA	British
Sullivan, Florence	Boston, USA	British
Sullivan, Mrs Julia	Boston, USA	British
Sumner, Thomas	Quincy, USA	British
Surman, Mrs Mabel Annie	England	British
Sutherst, Thomas	England	British
Sweeney, John Martin	Watertown, USA	US
Sweet, Frank H.	Toronto, Canada	British
Taft, Sidney	Needham, USA	British
Tarry, Edward	Toronto, Canada	British
Taylor, Mrs Annie Sarah	Boston, USA	US

Taylor, Stanley Robert	Boston, USA	US
Thomas, Ernest	Winnipeg, Canada	British
Thomas, Mrs Mary Hannah	Winnipeg, Canada	British
Thompson, Miss Muriel	Miami, USA	British
Thompson, Robert Joseph	Holdridge, USA	British
Thompson, Albert	Toronto, Canada	British
Thurston, John	Bridgeport, USA	British
Tierney, Mrs James Mary	Vandegrift, USA	British
Tierney, Miss Nina (5 years)	Vandegrift, USA	British
Tijou, Walter Edgar	Toronto, Canada	British
Tijou, Master Howard Walter (10 years)	Toronto, Canada	British
Todd, David	Philadelphia, USA	British
Treverrow, Mrs Caroline	Butte, USA	British
Tullock, James	Kendall, USA	British
Tullock, Mrs Agnes	Kendall, USA	British
Tullock, Hannah (infant)	Kendall, USA	British
Turpin, Thomas Keith	Victoria, Canada	British
Turpin, Mrs Maud	Victoria, Canada	British
Twigg, Frederick Alexander	Winnipeg, Canada	British
Tyers, Frederick Charles	Nottingham, England	British
Vance, John	New York, USA	US
Varcoe, Mrs Lavinia	Kansas City, USA	British
Varley, Miss Alice	E. Northfield, USA	British
Venn, Harold Stanley	San Francisco, USA	British
Viscovi, Silvio de	New York, USA	Italian.
Walker, John	Toronto, Canada	British
Walker, Mrs Gertrude	Toronto, Canada	British
Walker, Miss Mary	San Francisco, USA	British
Wallace, Cyril John George	Holyoke, USA	British
Wallace, Miss Margaret	New York, USA	British
Wallace, Miss Delia	New York, USA	British
Walsh, Miss Ellen	New York, USA	British
Ward, Michael	Pittsburg, USA	US
Ward, James L.	Wilkie, Canada	British
Waring, Charles	Winnipeg, Canada	British
Warner, Tertius S.	London, Canada	British
Waters, Miss Katherine W.	Elcentra, USA	British
Waters, Miss Margaret	Elcentra, USA	British
Webb, Miss Minnie	New York, USA	British
Webster, Frederick G.	Toronto, Canada	British
Webster, Mrs Margaret and two infants (Frederick and Henry)	Toronto, Canada	British
Webster, Master William (3 years)	Toronto, Canada	British
Wier, Cecil H.	Victoria, Canada	British

133

Whaley, Robert William	Victoria, Canada	British
Whitcombe, Hugh D.	Havana, Cuba	British
Whitehead, Miss Florence	Boston, USA	British
Whyatt, Mrs Martha Ann	New Bedford, USA	British
Wickham, Mrs Nina	New Zealand	British
Wickings-Smith, Cyril	Victoria, Canada	British
Wickings-Smith, Mrs Phyllis	Victoria, Canada	British
Wickings-Smith, Phyllis (infant)	Victoria, Canada	British
Wickings-Smith, Basil G.	Victoria, Canada	British
Wiggins, Mrs Sarah H.	Toronto, Canada	British
Wilde, Miss Evelyn Norbury	Paterson, USA	British
Wilde, Miss Agnes	Paterson, USA	British
Williams, Robert	Calgary, Canada	British
Williams, Mrs Jane	Toronto, Canada	British
Williams, Thomas J.	Wales	British
Williams, Miss Beatrice	Rock Island, USA	British
Wilson, John	Cambridge, USA	British
Wilson, Mrs Minnie	Moosejaw, Canada	British
Wilson, Miss Sarah	Brooklyn, USA	British
Winter, Miss Thirza	New York, USA	British
Wise, Sister Isabella	Jamaica	British
Wolfenden, John Charles	Pawtucket, USA	US
Wolfenden, Mrs Dora	Pawtucket, USA	US
Woodcock, Miss Sarah Emma	Fall River, USA	British
Woolden, Mrs Nellie	Edmonton, Canada	British
Worden, Mrs Jane	Lowell, USA	US
Wordsworth, Osmund Bartle	Toronto, Canada	British
Wordsworth, Miss Ruth Mary	Toronto, Canada	British
Wright, Miss Mary E.	New York, USA	British
Wylie, Mrs Emma	Jersey City, USA	British
Yardley, Lewis Frank	Toronto, Canada	British
Yeatman, Charles Aylmer Luttrell	New York, USA	British
Yeatman, Mrs Cora	New York, USA	British

Analysis of second cabin passengers' nationality

British	520
United States Citizens	65
Belgian	1
Dutch	3
Russian	3
French	5
Italian	2
Spanish	1
Argentinian	1
Total	601

Third Class Passengers on Board

Passenger's name	Point of origin	Nationality
Agnew, Thomas	Monessen, USA	British
Agnew, Mrs Thomas	Monessen, USA	British
Alexan, Babajan	New York, USA	Russian
Ameraiof, Benjamin	Chicago, USA	Persian
Andersdotter, Mrs Carolina B.	Walden, USA	Swedish
Andreastos, Marinos	New York, USA	Greek
Andrijine, Anisyon	New York, USA	Russian
Antilla, Mrs Amoo		
Antilla, Carl		
Antilla, Jan		Russian
Antilla family,		
deported passengers		Russian
Aprin, Joseph	Gary, USA	Russian
Ashman, Henry Clifford	Butte, USA	British
Baba, Abraham	Chicago, USA	Persian
Baba, Frank	Chicago, USA	Persian
Baba, George	Chicago, USA	Persian
Babeicz, Jakim	New York, USA	Russian
Babiczuk, Siemion	Windsor, Canada	Russian
Babka, Matthew	Canada	Russian
Bailey, Fred	Orange, USA	British
Ballantyne, Miss Margaret	New York, USA	British
Bannerji, Induprakas	Princeton, USA	Indian
Barclay, George	Canada	British
Barrow, Donald	Maple Creek, Canada	British
Barrow, Mrs May	Maple Creek, Canada	British
Bartley, George N.	Welland, Canada	British
Bartley, Mrs Ellen	Welland, Canada	British
Bartley, Master Arthur	Welland, Canada	British
Bartley, Gordon (infant)	Welland, Canada	British
Beauchamp, William	Otsego, USA	British
Benjamin, Miss Queenie	Roland Park, USA	British
Bennett, William	Canada	British
Bevan, Jack	Bellaire, USA	British
Bialans, Stefan	Waterbury, USA	Russian
Bishop, Joseph	Hamilton, Canada	British
Bishop, Mrs Alice	Hamilton, Canada	British
Bishop, William	Knowles, USA	British

Blackburn, George R.	Canada	British
Blackshaw, Mrs Alice	St Thomas, Canada	British
Blackshaw, Master John J.	St Thomas, Canada	British
Blackman, Judka	New York, USA	Russian
Bodell, Thomas	Toronto, Canada	British
Bodell, Mrs Florence	Toronto, Canada	British
Bodell, Master Thomas	Toronto, Canada	British
Boreskevecs, Folop	Palmerton, USA	Russian
Bottomley, Fred	New York, USA	British
Boyle, Nicholas	Chicago, USA	British
Boyle, James	Canada	British
Bozenof, Denis	Chicago, USA	Russian
Bozenof, Philate	Chicago, USA	Russian
Brown, Miss Constance	Philadelphia, USA	British
Brown, Miss Evelyn	Philadelphia, USA	British
Brown, William	Toronto, Canada	British
Budrin, Antoni	Greaville, USA	Russian
Burke, Ernest J.	Central Falls, USA	British
Butler, William M.	New York, USA	British
Byrne, Miss Nellie	Boston, USA	British
Canigan, Miss Margaret	Boston, USA	British
Caracitsos, George	New York, USA	Greek
Carlson, C. J.	Chicago, USA	Swedish
Cattew, Miss Emily	New York, USA	British
Charkowski, Porflri	E. St Louis, USA	Russian
Chwysink, Pawel	Chicago, USA	Russian
Clift, Horace	Chicago, USA	British
Connolly, Michael	New York, USA	British
Cook, William George	Toronto, Canada	British
Cooper, Mrs Nellie Elizabeth	New Bedford, USA	British
Cooper, Joseph E. (infant)	New Bedford, USA	US
Coughlan, John J.	Butte, USA	British
Coughlan, Mrs Catherine	Butte, USA	British
Coughlan, Master John	Butte, USA	US
Coughlan, Miss Margaret	Butte, USA	US
Coughlan, Bernard (infant)	Butte, USA	US
Coxon, Geoffrey Thornley	New York, USA	British
Crosbie, Miss Agnes	Wilmette, USA	British
Cross, Charles	Camden, USA	British
Crutchley, William Henry	E. Liverpool, USA	British
Cunniff, Miss Hannah	Brooklyn, USA	British
Curley, Miss Alice	New York, USA	British
Czertowicz, Marcin	Philadelphia, USA	Russian
Dawsley, David	New York, USA	British
Dawson, Walter	Lowell, USA	British

Deickey, Ewstafey	New York, USA	Russian
Delaney, Miss Mary	New York, USA	British
Dhenin, Thomas	New York, USA	British
Dhenin, Mrs Evelyn	New York, USA	British
Dhenin, Master Thomas	New York, USA	British
Dhenin, Miss Isabella	New York, USA	British
Diamandis, Theodor	New York, USA	Greek
Dick, Miss Annie	New York, USA	British
Dixon, Alfred	El Paso, USA	British
Doyle, Miss Anna	New York, USA	British
Doyle, Michael	Gt. Barrington, USA	British
Duckworth, Mrs Elizabeth A.	Norwich, USA	British
Duncan, Mrs Kate Cassie	New York, USA	British
Dunn, Thomas W.	Canada	British
Duplex, Miss Kate M.	New York, USA	British
Driscoll, Timothy	Boston, USA	US
Edwards, Isaac	Greensburg, USA	British
Eshoo, Benjamin	Yonkers, USA	British
Farrow, Robert	Canada	British
Faulds, Andrew	Yonkers, USA	British
Faulds, Mrs Maragaret	Yonkers, USA	British
Feeley, Mrs Teresa	New York, USA	British
Feely, Joseph	New York, USA	British
Ferguson, Mrs Mary Agnes	Newark, USA	US
Ferguson, Edward (infant)	Newark, USA	US
Ferrick, John	New York, USA	British
Ferrick, Mrs Maragaret	New York, USA	British
Flaherty, Thomas	Brooklyn, USA	British
Flynn, John	New York, USA	British
Frankum, Joseph	Detroit, USA	British
Frankum, Mrs Anna	Detroit, USA	British
Frankum, Master Francis	Detroit, USA	British
Frankum, Master Fred	Detroit, USA	US
Frankum, Miss Winifred	Detroit, USA	US
Galvin, Michael	New York, USA	British
Gately, John	New York, USA	British
Gibbons, Michael	Chicago, USA	US
Gililen, Ellie	Yonkers, USA	Persian
Gleason, Miss Catherine	Chicago, USA	British
Goodhall, William	Kearny, USA	British
Goodhall, Mrs Beatrice	Kearny, USA	British
Goodhall, Leonard	Kearny, USA	British

Goodhall, Jack (infant)	Kearny, USA	US
Goode, George	Kearny, USA	British
Goodwin, Miss Rose	Baltimore, USA	British
Gordon, George	Calgary, Canada	British
Graham, Gordon	San Francisco, USA	British
Granahan, Michael	Chicago, USA	British
Greenshields, A.J.	Unknown	British
Grigorian, Majlim	New York, USA	Russian
Grinstead, Cyril	New York, USA	British
Griwaczewski, Mikhail	New York, USA	Russian
Groves, George	New York, USA	US
Gryszkiewicz, Antoni	Three Rivers, USA	Russian
Hancock, Thomas	Bisbee, USA	British
Hanley, Peter	Brooklyn, USA	British
Hanus, Charles	Chicago, USA	British
Hanus, Mrs Mary	Chicago, USA	British
Harkens, Alexander	Philadelphia, USA	British
Harrison, George W.	Fernie, Canada	British
Harvey, William	New York, USA	US
Hebden, Robert	New Bedford, USA	British
Hebden, Mrs Clara	New Bedford, USA	British
Henry, Mrs John	New York, USA	British
Hesketh, Alfred W.	Welland, Canada	British
Hogan, Miss Jane	New York, USA	British
Hook, George	Canada	British
Hook, Miss Elsie	Canada	British
Hook, Master Frank	Canada	British
Houston, Frank	Auburn, USA	British
Howard, William	St Louis, USA	British
Howley, Mrs Rose	New Rochelle, USA	British
Hurley, Charles E.	Boston, USA	US
Inman, John E.	Park City, USA	British
Ireton, Edward	New York, USA	British
Isherwood, Fred	New York, USA	British
Ivannik, Peter	Jamaica, USA	Russian
Iwanuk, Emilian	New York, USA	Russian
Jacobs, Mrs Liba Bella Cohen Klass Schmidt	Chicago, USA	British
James, Miss Violet Isobel	Edmonton, Canada	British
Jenkins, Alfred	Canada	British
Johannsen, Sven	Chicago, USA	Swedish
Johnson, Albert E.	Canada	British
Johnson, Herbert K.	New York, USA	British

138

Johnson, John	New York, USA	British
Jones, Evan	Chicago, USA	US
Junczyk, Egor	Hoosik Falls, USA	Russian
Kaperalia, Nikola	Chicago, USA	Persian
Kasiaran, Mirja	New York, USA	Russian
Kelly, Miss Marie	Boston, USA	British
Kelly, Miss Annie	Deported Passenger	British
Kenny, Miss Agnes	New York, USA	British
Kevorke, Ahajan	New York, USA	Russian
Kilkenny, Miss Delia	Cambridge, USA	British
Kilkenny, Miss Annie	New York, USA	British
Killawe, Miss Winifred	Pittsburg, USA	British
King, George	W. Frankfort, USA	British
King, Harry	Chicago, USA	British
King, Sarah (Mrs Michael Doherty)	Deported Passenger	British
Koczurko, Wilkenti	Chicago, USA	Russian
Komaryshyn, Hryhory	S. Ste. Marie, USA	Russian
Kornejczyk, Andrej	Clarksburg, USA	Russian
Koweretz, Naum D.	Chicago, USA	Russian
Kozlowski, Kost	Clarksburg, USA	Russian
Kulicz, Stegan	Chicago, USA	Russian
Lambert, Mrs Delia	New York, USA	British
Lambert. Master, Robert	New York, USA	US
Leyland, William	San Francisco, USA	British
Lichaczow, Ignatii	Windsor, USA	Russian
Light, Herbert	Camden, USA	British
Lindley, Harry	Toledo, USA	British
Lizawczuk, Alexaj	Philadelphia, USA	Russian
Lockhart, James	New York, USA	British
Lockwood, Mrs Florence	Harrison, USA	British
Lockwood, Master Clifford	Harrison, USA	British
Lockwood, Miss Lily	Harrison, USA	US
Logan, Mrs Ruth	New York, USA	British
Logan, Robert (infant)	New York, USA	US
Logunietz, Wasili	New York, USA	Russian
Long, Harry	Detroit, USA	British
Losevicz, Fadej	Woodhaven, USA	Russian
Lucko, Timofej	Hastings, USA	Russian
Luker, Francis John	Canada	British
Lukianowicz, Wawren	Chicago, USA	Russian
Lyons, Miss Annie	Newark, USA	British
MacKenzie, Robert Anderson	New York, USA	British
Malicz, Pawel L.	Chicago, USA	Russian

Marchewka, Josef	Three Rivers, USA	Russian
Marks, Mrs Elizabeth	Chicago, USA	British
Marks, Miss Georgina	Chicago, USA	British
Marsh, Mrs Thomas	Canada	British
Marsh, Mrs Annie	Canada	British
Marsh, Thomas (infant)	Canada	British
Marshall, Mrs Fannie	Canada	British
Martin, Mrs Laura	New Philadelphia, USA	British
Mason, Joseph H.	Detroit, USA	British
Matthews, Thomas	Calumet, USA	British
Mazurak, Iwan	Waterbury, USA	Russian
McAfee, Thomas	Canada	British
McAneny, John	New York, USA	British
McCallum, Albert Alexander	New York, USA	British
McClamond, Samuel	New York, USA	British
McCormick, Thomas	Nashua, USA	British
McCready, Robert G.	Canada	British
McDermott, Andrew	Boston, USA	British
McKeon, Miss Jane	New York, USA	British
McLoughlin, Patrick J.	Hartford, USA	British
McNulty, Steve	New York, USA	British
Meaney, George Peter	Thomas, USA	British
Michalkowicz, Iwan	Chicago, USA	Russian
Molly, Robert J.	Deported Passenger	British
Moses, Mrs Janet	Wilkinsburg, USA	British
Muirhead, William	New York, USA	British
Muraszko, Boris	Oxford Furnace, USA	Russian
Murray, Mrs Margaret	Chicago, USA	British
Murray, Master Walter	Chicago, USA	British
Murray, Mrs Mary	Cuba	British
Neilson, Miss Violet	Deported Passenger	Norwegian
Nieborski, Gregory	Oxford Furnace, USA	Russian
Nielson, Miss Gerda	Brooklyn, USA	British
Nikander, Gunnar	Deported Passenger	Finnish
Norman, Jasper	Rochester, USA	British
O'Connor, John	New York, USA	British
Oginski, Danil	Hartford, USA	Russian
Ohannia, Aziz	Chicago, USA	Persian
O'Kelly, John J.	New York, USA	British
Oleszko, John	Chicago, USA	Russian
Olivar, Diego	New York, USA	Mexican
Ordyniez, Andrej	Syracuse, USA	Russian
Owens, Patrick	St Louis, USA	British

140

Palmer, Charles	Camden, USA	British
Parkes, William Henry	Canada	British
Perka, Maxim Antanow	Canada	British
Petrenok, Andrej	Mechanicsville, USA	Russian
Petrosian, Kahraman	New York, USA	Russian
Phillips, William	Hillcrest, Canada	British
Pickard, Fred	New York, USA	British
Podrubleny, Aleksij	Niagra Falls, USA	Russian
Polubinski, Mikentii	North Easton, USA	Russian
Pryor, John	New York, USA	British
Pulik, Mychail	S. Ste. Marie, USA	Russian
Rawen, Miss Annie	Chicago, USA	British
Reid, Mrs Ellen	New York, USA	British
Reid, John H.	Trenton, USA	British
Riley, Eddie	Boston, USA	British
Riley, Mrs Annie	Boston, USA	British
Riley, Master Sutcliffe	Boston, USA	British
Riley, Miss Ethel	Boston, USA	British
Robinson, Alan William	Clay Centre, USA	British
Robshaw, Miss Edith	Kearney, USA	British
Sargis, Pera	Gary, USA	Persian
Scott, Mrs Alice Ann	No. Adams, USA	British
Scott, Master Arthur	No. Adams, USA	British
Seferien, Levon	Troy, USA	Persian
Seisian, Karatioum	Troy, USA	Persian
Self, James	Canada	British
Self, Mrs Florence	Canada	British
Sergis, George	Yonkers, USA	Persian
Shackell, William George	New York, USA	British
Sharp, Miss Annie	Boston, USA	British
Sharpe, Samuel S.	Crooksville, USA	British
Sharpe, Mrs Mary J.	Crooksville, USA	British
Sharpe, George	Crooksville, USA	British
Sheedy, Patrick	Deported Passenger	British
Shepperson, Arthur G.	New York, USA	British
Shirras, Robert Brown	Canada	British
Shkredoff, Archie	Pittsburg, USA	Russian
Shkredoff, Jacob	Pittsburg, USA	Russian
Sidwell, George	Hamilton, Canada	British
Sikiwicki, Andro	Franklin Furnace, USA	Russian
Sikora, Joseph	Buffalo, USA	Russian
Simpson, Edward	Lawrence, USA	British
Skelton, Fred	Hamilton, Canada	British

141

Smethurst, Harold	New Philadelphia, USA	British
Smethurst, Mrs Alice	New Philadelphia, USA	British
Smith, Mrs Minnie	Hamilton, Canada	British
Smith, George Arthur	Canada	British
Smith, Miss Agnes	Chicago, USA	British
Snowden, Thomas	Lynn, USA	British
Snowden, Fred A.	Toronto, USA	British
Sobolewski, Mitrofan	Lyndora, USA	Russian
Solonina, Stefan	E. St Louis, USA	Russian
Spendly, Mrs Kate	New York, USA	British
Stacey, Joseph Nelson	Canada	British
Stachula, Michal	Buffalo, USA	Russian
Standfast, Noel	Nanaimo, Canada	British
Stankicwicz, Anthony	Trenton, USA	Russian
Steele, George	New York, USA	British
Stenson, Miss Delia	Boston, USA	British
Stephens, Thomas Ohan	Chicago, USA	US
Stevens, George	Olean, USA	British
Stevenson, Hugh	Yonkers, USA	British
Stockton, Alfred	Marion, USA	British
Stolarenic, Vasili	Chicago, USA	Russian
Strulz, Theodor	Canada	Russian
Strynechuk, Sava	Palmerton, USA	Russian
Swallow, Allan	Hamilton, Canada	British
Tadus, Asset	Yonkers, USA	Persian
Taracsewics, Iwan	Palmerton, USA	Russian
Taylor, Harold William	Niagara Falls, USA	British
Taylor, Mrs Lucy	Niagara Falls, USA	British
Taylor, Arthur	Canada	British
Thompson, Joseph	Canton, USA	British
Thompson, Mrs Sarah Ann	Canton, USA	British
Thompson, Norman	Canton, USA	British
Tobin, Mrs Nora	Boston, USA	British
Tomaszewicz, Iwan	Bayonne, USA	Russian
Tomms, Miss Elizabeth	Toronto, Canada	British
Topping, Mrs Margaret	Brooklyn, USA	British
Topping, Miss Hilda	Brooklyn, USA	British
Travers, Mrs Jane	Newark, USA	British
Tucker, Albert	Hamilton, Canada	British
Tuohey, Miss Margaret	New York, USA	British
Twinning, Edwin	New York, USA	British
Tyler, Samuel	Whitehall, USA	British
Veale, Albert E.	Orange, USA	British
Veale, Mrs Agnes M.	Orange, USA	British

Waaranen, Miss Elli M.	Worcester, USA	Finnish
Ward, George	Newark, USA	British
Ward, Mrs Ellen	Newark, USA	British
Ward, Joseph	Blakely, USA	British
Wardle, Mrs Cissie	Adamsdale, USA	British
Watson, Mrs Kate	Seaforth, Canada	British
Webb, William	Medford, USA	British
Webb, Mrs Sarah	Medford, USA	British
Webb, Mrs Elizabeth	Medford, USA	British
Welsh, John	New York, USA	British
Wilks, Miss Alice K.	Chicago, USA	British
Williams, Mrs Annie	Newark, USA	British
Williams, Master John	Newark, USA	British
Williams, Miss Edith	Newark, USA	British
Williams, Master George	Newark, USA	British
Williams, Miss Ethel	Newark, USA	British
Williams, Miss Florence	Newark, USA	British
Williams, David (infant)	Newark, USA	US
Williams, David	Edmonton, Canada	British
Williams, James	New York, USA	British
Williams, Thomas	Johnstown, USA	British
Wilson, Mrs Emily L.	Toronto, Canada	British
Wilson, Master Frank	Toronto, Canada	British
Wilson, Miss Dorothy	Toronto, Canada	British
Woodworth, Robert	Niagara Falls, USA	British
Worrell, Fred A.	New York, USA	British
Yocab, Baba Jan	Chicago, USA	Persian
Yohama, Envia	Chicago, USA	Persian
Yohanan, Alevaretz	Chicago, USA	Persian
York, William	Brantford, Canada	British
Young, Mrs Charles	Chicago, USA	British
Zaliachanoff, Khaeho	New York, USA	
Diminguez, Manuel	Ex SS *Gileston*	D.B.S.*
Genanselm, A.	Ex SS *Gileston*	D.B.S.
Slight, H.	Ex SS *Shenandoah*	D.B.S.

*There was no explanation given on the original list but this possibly means Distressed British Seamen.

Analysis of third-class passengers nationality

British	256
United States Citizens	20
Russian	68
Finnish	2
Swedish	3
Norwegian	1
Persian	15
Greek	3
Indian	1
Mexican	1
D.B.S.	3
Total	373

There were also three Germans aboard who were caught spying just after *Lusitania* left New York. They were placed under armed guard and were to be handed to the British authorities at the journey's end. Locked in the ship's cells, they went down with the *Lusitania*.

Crew on Board – Deck Department

Name	Rank
Turner, W.T.	Commander
Anderson, J.C.	Staff Captain
Piper, John P.	Chief Officer
Stevens J.	Ex Chief Officer
Jones, A.R.	1st Officer
Hefford, P.	2nd Officer
Lewis, J.T.	3rd Officer
Bestic, A.A.	Junr. 3rd Officer
Robertson, Neil	Carpenter
Brown, John	Joiner
Davies, John	Bosun
Sikking, Florence	Bosun's Mate
Egan, William	Bosun's Mate
Quinn, Thomas	Bosun's Boy
Williams, William	Master-At-Arms
Smith, Peter	Master-At-Arms
McCubbin, J.A.	Purser
Draper, P.	2nd Purser
Burden, A.H.	Asst. Purser
Harkness, W. H.	Asst Purser
Sloane, L. H.	Junr. Asst. Purser
Harrod, A.	Junr. Asst Purser
Beesely, G. W.	Junr. Asst. Purser
McDermott, Dr Joseph	Surgeon
Garry, Dr Joseph	Asst. Surgeon
Leith, R.	Telegraphist
McCormick, D. W.	Asst. Telegraphist
Crank, J.	Baggage Master
Cannon, Robert H.	Inspector
Hale, Miss Sadie	Typist
Hughes, J.E.	Hospital Attendant

A.B. (Able bodied seamen)

Evans, Thomas	Sikking, James	Knight, C. T.
Johnston, H. R.	Roberts, Charles A.	O'Neil, F. H.
Yetts, W.	Anderson, John	Clinton, G.
Hennessy, Frank	Quinn, Thomas	Seagraves, P.
Thompson, L .H.	Malone, F.	Todd, James

Heighway, E. J.
Lockett, H.
Elliot, Fred
Quirk, W. E.
Cunningham, E.
Robb, Joseph
Hume, James
Roper, John
Elliot, A.G.

Herman, A.
Parry, Joseph
Jones, W.
Bowden, Joseph
Battle, James
Owens, Owen
Fleming, H.
Morton, Clifford

Clyde, Neil
Gunn, C.
Robins, T.
Ledene, Thomas
Hannan, John
Fayle, Edward
Heyes, J.
Morton, Leslie

Seamen

McGlade, George
McNally, Peter

O'Mahoney, Thomas
Reid, J.

Hume, James
Moore, Daniel

O.S. (Ordinary seamen)

Thompson, John

McLeod, Victor

Crew on Board – Engineering Department

Bryce, Archibald	Chief Engineer
Cockburn, Andrew	Senr. 2nd Engineer
Smith, W. T.	Int. 2nd Engineer
Duncan, Alex	Jun. 2nd Engineer
Duncan, R. H.	1st Senr. 3rd Engineer
Little, George	2nd Senr. 3rd Engineer
Hetherington, W.	3rd Senr. 3rd Engineer
Fairhurst, Wilfred George	1st Int. 3rd Engineer
Cole, W.H.	2nd Int. 3rd Engineer
Leech, T.	1st Junr. 3rd Engineer
Wylie, R. G.	3rd Junr. 3rd Engineer
Duncan, P. R.	Senr. 4th Engineer
Jones, R. E.	Junr. 4th Engineer
Anderson, W. A.	Senr 5th. Engineer
Kelly, S. C.	Int. 5th Engineer
Hayes, J. H.	Junr. 5th Engineer
Beggs, J.	Senr. 6th Engineer
Dunn, A. C.	Int. 6th Engineer
Morrice, D.	Junr. 6th Engineer
Lea, J.	Senr. 7th Engineer
Wheelhouse, A. T.	Junr. 7th Engineer
Paton, J. F.	Steering Engineer
Fenton, C. S.	Deck Engineer
Quarrie, W.	Ventilating Engineer
Hutchinson, George	1st Electrician
Latham, G. E.	2nd Electrician
Jones, W.	3rd Electrician
Gould, R.	Boilermaker
McLean, R.	Plumber
Fitzgerald, John E.	Electric Attendant
Sharkey, John	Electric Attendant
O'Hare, Owen	Engineers' Stores
Owens, Richard	Engineers' Stores
Dalrymple James	Refg. Greaser
McEvoy, John	Refg. Greaser
Pimblett, James	Refg. Greaser
Griffiths, William	Refg. Greaser
Fairclough, Robert	Donkeyman

Greasers

Gaul, R
Wood, John H.
Walsh, R.
Horrigan, M.
Wiencke, Paul
Ormrod, Thomas
Quine, George

Southwold, Henry
Jones, Hugh
McCarthy, Patrick
Moran, James
Larkin, James
Ormrod, James
Ennis , J.

Hughes, Owen
Melia, Patrick
McLoughlin, Joseph
Donoghue, P.
Brennan, Patrick
Horden, J.
Fearon, P.

Leading Firemen

Carroll, T.
Doyle, Peter
Martin, A.

Evans, David
Needham, Patrick
Grundy, George

Leathers, S.
Breen, James
Burns, John

Firemen

Crumby, Stephen
Madden, John
Stanley, H.
Farrell, John
Mitchell, D. J.
McCabe, A.
Toole, John
Newby, J.
Delvin, Henry
Whelan, John
Lewis, F.
Hughes, W.
Kelly, John
Lee, Daniel
Donnelly, P.
Elliot, James
Bowen, Henry
McCarthy, Bartle
Casey, James
Ward, John
O'Connell, John
Edwards, Thomas
Murphy, James
Molden, J.
Toner, F.
Hodder, James
Brown, John
Forrest, John
McCann, Thomas
Woods, Joseph
Donovan, William

Cassidy, Bernard
Rice, Michael
Butler, J.
Power, Daniel
Heaton, Patrick
Curran, P.
Keating, Phil
Ralph, M.
Sinnott, William
Corby, M.
Jones, John
McGowan, Joseph
Sheridan, Patrick
Sheppard, Ralph
Donnelly, John
Sheridan, Jeffrey
Murphy, Matthew
McGough, Mick
Dunn, Thomas
Payne, Michael
Grant, Michael
Duckworth, Thomas
McAteer, Francis
Barry, W.
Laffey, T.
Stanley, J.
Kenny, James
Manning, Peter
McMahon, P.
Collins, Patrick
McCormick, James

Campbell, P.
Rice, S.
O'Neil, Michael
Cross, Andrew
Dougherty, William
Dwyer, John
French, J.
Carribine, Bernard
Coady, James
English, Michael
Casey, Patrick
Ford, John
Cooney, Michael
Osborne, J.
Madden, Thomas
Ward, Michael
Cain, Thomas
Rowan, Fred
Costello, Thomas
O'Neill, James
McCabe, Richard
Robinson, William
Tierney, M.
McCutcheon, Thomas
McDonald, John
Brown, James
Waring, R.
McDermott, E.
Burns, Joseph
Plummer, Leslie
Sterberg, R. A.

McAdam, Michael
Chester, Michael
Ratcliffe, Peter
Mylaska, C.
Rafferty, Joseph
Barrett, Daniel
Culshaw, William
Scannell, Charles
Doyle, John
Rossiter, L.
Jenkins, James
Cooney, Michael
Keogh, P.
Bridge, William
Murphy, Dan
Gunther, Charles
Ross, E. W.
Norman, A. W.

Daley, Daniel
Casey, Joseph
Hutchinson, George
Mallin, W.
Hopkins, Patrick
Moran, Patrick
Savage, F.
Beattie, J.
O'Brien, Patrick
McFarland, Terrance
Rigby, G.
McAleavey, Thomas
Farrell, John
Scott, C.
McKenna, Patrick
Whitmore, G.
Reynolds, Patrick
McStay, John.

Kelly, Thomas
Norton, Bernard
Linton, Isaac
McMahon, Patrick
Rice, Edward
Sweeney, Jeremiah
Hussey, John
Orange, John
Chadwick, Jacob
Lockhart, Peter
Kearney, Thomas
Roach, James
Gallagher, George
Fernandez, Edouardo
Lawrence, William
O'Neil, Paul
Osterburg, August

Trimmers

Taylor, Chris
Griffiths, S.
Davies, John
Lee, Wiliam
Loughran, P.
Doyle, Joseph
McKenna, John
McAleer, James
Gardner, Alfred
Finnegan, E.
Hamel, George T.
Kennedy, John
King, Michael
Dyer, John
Thompson, John
Myles, Peter
Goodman, B.
Williams, Sydney
McKenna, F.
Rowe, John
Lemon, John
McNulty, Peter
McGuinness, B.
Thompson, John W.
Duggan, John
Brown, Patrick
Hillhouse, Hugh

Davies, J.
Colwell, W.
McBride, Peter
Wiencke, Paul F.
Webb, James
Brennan, John
Keegan, John
Harris, James
Lewis, Joseph
Evans, Robert
Hume, Archie
Cushion, Michael
Palmer, Thomas
Thompson, M.
Batt, George
Dwyer, James
Taylor, T.
Marrion, John
Slavin, O.
Welsh, Christopher
Rafferty, P.
Manning, John
Tear, Joseph E.
Collins, J.
Lawson, T.
Coyle, P.
Kearney, Patrick

Vose, George
McCabe, John A.
Turner, Joseph
Wynn, Peter
Campbell, Charles
Conlon, Bernard
McDermott, Eugene
Stafford, T.
Ruddan, Thomas
Brennan, Thomas
Lawton, John
Jones, Michael
Lyons, A.
Kehoe, D.

Traynor, P.
Burns, P.
McDonald, J.
Markey, P.
Kennedy, John James
McGugan, Donald
Hoey, James
Connelly, Owen
Davies, F.
Manan, Andrew
Welsh, Martin
Gavan, Peter

McKinley, Andrew McGugan, Walter Needhan, John
McKenna, Bernard McCann, Owen Burke, James
Ashe, John Hanlon, Patrick O'Neill, Bernard
Downey, E. Rogan, John Bradley, Tom
Horncastle, W. Morris, J. Powell, Edward
Gregory, J. McGinty, Thomas Malfait, Shef
Field, W. Trainor, A.

Stewards Department

Jones, Fred V.	Chief Steward
Ford, Arthur	Ex Chief Steward
Chisolm, Robert D. F.	Second Steward
Boyd, Fullerton R.	Barkeeper
Ross, Henry	Barkeeper
Houghton, Thomas.	Smokeroom Barkeeper
Newbold, Hubert H.	Cellarman
Nixon, Harold	Storekeeper
Hughes, Thomas Owen	Assistant Storekeeper
Penkeyman, Samuel J.	Pantry Steward
Wilmer, William	Pantry Steward
Sutton, Nugent M.	Pantry Steward

Assistant Pantry Stewards

Danson, Richard Wood, Henry E. German, Samuel K.
Davies, Charles Thornley, George Hughes, Edward
Prowse, Thomas

Owen, Thomas	Linenkeeper
Mitchell, William	Assistant Linenkeeper
Shiel, Michael S.	Saloon Steward
Allport, Harry	Second Saloon Steward
Davies, Fred	Printer
Mitchell, George	Printer

Barbers

Gadd, Lott Denton, Jonathan Nice, Reginald B.S.

Wiggins, William	Deck Steward
Orwin, Nicholas	Deck Steward
Parry, Frank	Assistant Deck Steward
Grisdale, Harry	Library Steward
Kent, John G.	Lounge Steward
Blythyn, Robert W.	Smokeroom Steward
Newport, William	Smokeroom Steward
Caldicott, Samuel	Assistant Smokeroom Steward
James, Oswald	First Class Steward

First Class Bedroom Stewards

Barnes, William
Charlton, George J.
Critchley, David
Williams, William H.
Bond, Edward
Settle, Vincent
Morse, Robert

Wood, Walter
Dawes, Thomas G.
Clegg, Arthur
Perry, John
Grant, James
Huther, Edwin
Ruffels, William

Wood, Alfred
Penny, Percy
Collins, James
McLeod, William
Randall, Charles
Fletcher, William S.

First Class Waiters

Touzel, Sidney G. le
Gorst, Fred
Conway, R.
Simpson, Malcolm
Hotchkiss, Charles
Archer, Joseph
Rylands, William D.
Henderson, John
McSane, Patrick
Deiner, Fred
Neems, William F.
Wilson, James R.
Livermore, Vernon
Kupfernagel, Alfred
Mills, J.
Currie, George
Smith, William
Holden, James W.
Baldwin, Edgar

Ashcroft, Gordon
Comerford, Thomas
Van Hoeck, J. E.
Hilton, George
Darcy, John
Glover, George
Kewley, Ernest
Adamson, T.
Lee, Richard
Browne, E. Bennett
Rushton, George
Fletcher, George
Brown, James H.
Godley, Tom G.
Stanley, David H.
Pringle, Thomas
Foster, John
Roach, John

McDonald, Charles
Baldwin, Thomas G.
Riston, William
Russell, Fred
Haybyrne, James
Hendry, William
McFarlane, Malcolm
Stringer, Harry

Moffatt, John
Almond, John
Finucane, Noel
Murphy, John H.
Lawson, Percy
Hagen, Francis J.
Marshall, James
Thorn, Alfred R.
Williams, R. W.

Night Watchmen

Cranston, George
McKenzie, Henry
Mudge, John

Jones, Alfred
Williams, Robert
Knight, Charles (since dead)

Chamberlain, R.
Aindow, Charles

Handlin, D. E.
Wood, Wallace

Second Class Steward
Second Class Smokeroom Barkeeper

Second Cabin Bedroom Stewards

Kidd, Frank
Cartwright, Harry
Christian, K.
Lake, W.

Jessop, Robert
Anderson, James
Casey, Martin
Stark, Robert

Hallam, Ernest
Eastwood, W.
Thomas, W. S.

151

Second Class Waiters

Quinn, Alfred
Gilroy, Charles
Stansfield, Leslie
Allen, Norman F.
Clarke, James
Matthews, Henry
Jones, William
Lewis Fred

Griffith, George
Rowbottom, Harold E.
Shevland, John
Edgar, William
Moss, J. B.
Williams, H.
Gardner, George

Gaul, Bart

McConkey, Chris
Rose, William
Sutton, Frank
Wallace, James
Thomas John

Boots

Maylor, George   Heap, Harry   **Anderson, William**

Scullerymen

Scantlebury, Samuel
Verdin, F.
Dewrance, Sydney
Wynne, Joseph

Edwards, Henry
Higgins, John
Kendrick, James

Knill, George
McLaughlin, Joseph
Iverson, Ambrose

Pederson, Adolph   Interpreter
Griffiths, John   Chief Third Class Steward

Third Class Waiters

Brooke, George
Driscoll, Cornelius
Shann, Sydney
Whalley, Leslie
Holman, Frank

Edwards, Joseph
Lamont, Charles
Williams, John
Reid, Alfred
Ledger, James

Dickinson, John
Ipsen, Owen A.
Allan, Ashley
Lapphane, Charles

Glover, Edwin   Officers' Mess Steward
Thomas, George W.   Assistant Officers' Mess Steward
Wilkinson, James   Engineers' Mess Steward

Assistant Engineers' Mess Stewards

Bostock, Joseph
Roberts, John

Johnstone, James
Hall Edwin

Davies, Kenneth

Cowan, Alex   Lift Attendant
Rourke, Stanley   Lift Attendant

Stewards' Boys

Horrigan, Cornelius
Steinberg, Arthur
Hughes, William
Burrows, William

Bates, George
Clark, Robert
Wright, Harold

Joynson, Edgar
Holton, Ben
Sharp, Phillip

Seurre, E.	Chef
Ulgar, Jean	Sauce Cook
Bertrand, Maurice	Ex Second Cook
McClelland, David	Ex Ex Second Cook
Beckett, Henry	Passenger Cook
Griener, Oscar	Roast Cook
Redmond, James	Vegetable Cook
McAteer, Matthew	Vegetable Cook
Hine, J.	Ex Vegetable Cook
Ottino, John	Larder Cook
Pratt, Richard	Grill Cook

Assistant Cooks

Duncan, Joseph	McArthur, W.	**Wynne, George**	Hughes, William

Smith, O.	Ship's Cook
Saultry, W.	Ship's Cook
NussBaum, Samuel	Soup Cook
Septon, William	Night Fireman's Cook
Swift, Edward	Third Cook
Connertin, Thomas	Extra Third Cook
Pinkerton, Robert	Chief Baker
Wiseman, James	Second Baker
Francom, James	Extra Second Baker
Ledson, John	Ex Ex Second Baker
Christian, W. E.	Third Baker
Gytenbuch, A.	Extra Third Baker
Cooper, Fred	Fourth Baker
Kennedy, John	Extra Fourth Baker
Harrias, George	Assistant Baker
Lemburg, Freid	Confectioner
Bird,Walter	Chief Butcher
Jones, Charles	Second Butcher
Crawford, Thomas	Third Butcher

Assistant Butchers

Harris, John	Ronnan, George	Geraghty, M.

Assistant Stewards

Stewart, Thomas E.	McIver, Jack	**Ferris, John**	Glancy, James W.

Stewardesses

Bird, Miss Marian	**Moorcroft, Mrs Fanny**	McCormac, Miss Margarita
Duncan, Miss Christina	Roberts, Miss Annie	**Machell, Miss Elizabeth**
Hull, Mrs Margaret	Morrow, Miss Isabel	**Hughes, Miss Ellen**

Richardson, Miss Annie	Jones, Miss Mary E.	Cassels, Miss Nora
Howdle, Mrs Jane E.	**Dewhurst, Mrs Elizabeth**	Dodwell, Miss Eleanor
Foulkes, Mrs Margaret	Irvine, Miss Catherine	

Stewardesses transferred in New York from SS *Cameronia*

Craigie, Mrs M.   McGregor, Miss A.   Weir, Mrs M.   **Phillips, Miss Mary**

Leitch, Mrs M.   Matron transferred from *Cameronia*
Enderson, Mrs Anna   Matron
Jargensen, Mrs Carrie   Assistant Matron

Waiters

Gouder, Charles	**Foden, Robert Earnest**	Burrows, F.
MacPherson, John	Banner, A.	Potter, Ben
Dingley, H. J.	Blend, John H.	Bain, Duncan
Nieman, Robert	Gowan, G.	**Osterman, Jacob**
MacKenzie, Kenneth	Kinshott, H. W.	**Freeman, Matthew**
Price, C.	**Shalvey, G.**	Mc.Iver, John ?
Hannah, T.	**Weigh, Edward**	MacKenzie, Henry
Varney, John	Spendley, D. M.	**Grainger, Robert**
Leach, John Neill	Toder, Ernest	**Leach, John F.**

Skay, Edward   Kitchen Porter

Scullions

Dimond, John   Cummings, John   Kelly, A.

Orchestra

Cameron, C.	Bandmaster
Drakeford, George	Bandsman
Carr-Jones, E.	Bandsman
Hawkins, H.	Bandsman
Hemmingway, J. W.	Bandsman

Analysis of Crew Onboard

Deck Department	78
Engineering Department	314
Stewards' Department	297
Orchestra	5
Total Crew	694

Appendix II

1903 Agreement
CUNARD OBLIGATIONS
(Excerpted from Cunard's memo)

Clause 3.

1) To build with all dispatch two steamships of large size capable of maintaining a minimum average speed of from 24 to 25 knots an hour in moderate weather.

2.a) To submit to the Admiralty before the building is started, the plans and specifications of the proposed **steamers**

b) To modify such plans and specifications if requested by the Admiralty within one month.

c) To construct each such steamship to the satisfaction of an inspector to be agreed upon between Admiralty and the company and to be employed at the joint expense of the Admiralty and the company.

Clause 4.

To hold, at all times during the term of the agreement all the company's vessels at the disposal of the government for hire or purchase.

Clause 5.

1) Not to alter the memorandum or articles of association (as revised in accordance of the agreement) without the consent of His

Majesty's Government. To observe the provision of the under noted.

Articles of Association:–

No.2) Providing the company is to be and remain under British control and that – No foreigner is to hold office as a Director. No foreigner to be employed as a principal officer of the company. No share to be held by or in trust for a foreigner or foreign corporation.

No.3) To carry on the company business to the best advantage.

No.4) Not to unduly raise freights or charges.

No.5) Not to give undue preference as against British subjects in the fixing of freights or charges.

No.6) To submit to the Admiralty the plans of any new vessels built to attain the speed of 17 knots or upwards and to modify such plans if so required by the Admiralty within one month.

No.7) To afford every facility to Admiralty for placing fittings on board in the event of any of the vessels being taken up for use as armed cruisers. To provide storage for fittings, not more than 15,000 cubic feet and 1000 feet of floor space and to keep and maintain the fittings in clean order.

No.8) Not to let out on charter except to the Indian Government any vessel of 17 knots or upwards.

No.9) a, To secure that on all the company's steamers the masters, officers and engineers in charge of a watch on board shall always be British subjects and that three fourths of the crew are British subjects.

b, That on the *Campania*, *Luciania* and *Umbria* as long as neither of the 2 fastest steamers have started on its first voyage, all certified officer other than engineers and not less than half of the crew shall belong to the RNR or the Royal Naval Fleet Reserve under a penalty of £12 per head. To furnish each year to the Admiralty a return showing the number of RNR or Royal Naval Fleet Reserve Officers, Engineers and men borne in each vessel.

To use the Company's best endeavours to secure the employment of the largest possible proportion of members of the Royal Naval Reserve or Royal Naval Fleet Reserve.

No.10) To keep the company's vessels in a thoroughly seaworthy condition and good repair.

To keep the two fastest steamers in such condition as to be capable of maintaining an average minimum ocean speed of 24.5 knots an hour in moderate conditions.

To permit His Majesty's Government at all reasonable times to inspect all the company's steamers in order to see that they kept in such condition.

No.11) To adduce to His Majesty's Government within three months after the expiration of every year calculated from the date the vessel starts on her first voyage such reasonable proof from the running of the vessel as His Majesty's Government may require that each vessel has been capable of maintaining a minimum average ocean speed of 14.5 knots per hour in moderate weather.

No.12) To permit the Admiralty to make at their cost and reasonable provision for the fittings of pillars &c.

No.13) To register and keep registered all the company's vessels under the British Flag and not to do anything to endanger the British Registry or the right to fly the British flag.

No.14) To sell no vessel of the speed of 17 knots or upwards without the previous consent in writing of His Majesty's Government, but such consent not to be unreasonably withheld under certain conditions, also not to sell any vessels (whether or not of the speed of 17 knot or more) which has during the previous

157

12 months been ordinarily employed as a mail ship subject to certain conditions.

No.15) To sell no vessel of the speed of 17 knots or upwards without giving seven days notice in writing to His Majesty's Government and allowing His Majesty's Government the option of purchase.

Clause 7

To adduce to the satisfaction of the Admiralty reasonable proofs from trials that the two fast steamers will be capable of maintaining a minimum average ocean speed of 24.5 knots in moderate weather, failing which the company will be liable to a reduction of the subsidy.

Clause 10.

a, To secure the loan advanced by His Majesty's Government by a charge upon the whole of the company's ships.

b, To secure the charge by a Trust Deed and by mortgages on the steamers particularised in the first schedule of the agreement and the two fast steamers.

c, The loan to be advanced to the company by instalments referred to in clause 3 certifying that the provisions of that clause have been complied with up to the date of the certificate.

d, The loan to carry interest as to one half from the date on which the first of the two fast steamers sails on her first voyage and as to the other half from the date on which the second fast steamer sails on her first voyage.

e, The interest payable by the company on so much of the loan as may be due to be at the rate of 2.75 per cent per annum.

f, The loan to be repaid by annual instalments equal to one twen-tieth of the total amount of the advance.

The issue to two nominees of His Majesty's Government as soon as the Articles of Association have been altered as provided for one twenty pound share with certain privileges.

Clause 13

To convey the mail from Liverpool via Queenstown to New York once in every week.

Clause 14.

To sail from Liverpool a mail ship every Saturday as soon as possible after the advertised hour and to put to sea and proceed direct to Queenstown and remain there until the mails are embarked and thence proceed without unnecessary delay direct to New York.

Clause 15.

1, To employ as mail ships in all cases vessels of adequate capacity, power and speed.

2, To employ as mail ships the fastest of the steamships for the time being belonging to or chartered by the company.

3, To employ in the event of the fastest of the company's steamers being disabled, hired by the Government or temporarily withdrawn for annual overhaul, the steamships ranking next in rate of speed, and to arrange for the annual overhaul of the fastest steamers to detract in the least possible degree from the rapidity of the mail service &c.

Clause 16.

To provide on each of the mail ships a separate room or rooms for the mail and to keep the parcel mails in a place of safety.

Clause 17.

To provide mail sorting accommodation on board the ships on certain terms if required by the Postmaster General.

Clause 18.

The Master of each ship to furnish to the Postmaster General the usual abstracts of his logs and certificates showing the due delivery of mails.

Clause 19.

Not to convey any letter other than mails.

Clause 20.

To convey all parcel mails from New York to Queenstown and Liverpool and all mails from the United Kingdom to the United States of America which the Postmaster General or his oficers may require to be conveyed.

Clause 21.

To contribute one third towards the cost of special service for conveyance of mails between London and Dublin.

Clause 22.

To observe quarantine and Public Health arrangements.

Clause 23.

Not to attempt to exercise any lien upon the mails for or in respect of a general average contribution.

Clause 24.

Not to convey in any steamships conveying mails any article which in the opinion of the Postmaster General is likely to endanger the mails.

Clause 25.

To be responsible for the loss or damage of an parcel or any registered postal packet provided the aggregate amount shall not exceed £500 in any one voyage.

Clause 30.

Not to assign, under lien or dispose of part 2 of the agreement without the consent of the Postmaster General.

Clause 35.

To subject any difference or dispute in connection with the agreement to arbitration.

Clause 38.

To execute and do all acts and things necessary for the carrying out this agreement as soon as the special resolutions have been passed by the company's shareholders.

TRUST DEED

Clause 3.

To issue to His Majesty's Government on its nomineers stock for an amount equal at par to the amount of equal instalment of the loan to be made under the agreement.

Clause 7.

To mortgage or cause to be mortgaged to the trustees the steamships referred to in the schedule of the trust deed and the new fast steamers.

Clause 8.

To charge in favour of the trustees the specifically mortgaged premises with payment of the stocks and the interest thereon.

Clause 9.

To charge with payment to the trustees of the stock and interest thereon the assets and undertakings of the company for the time being other than the specifically mortgaged premises.

Clause 20.

To establish a sinking fund for the redemption of the stock and at the expiration of each year from the date on which the second of the two fast steamers sails on the first voyage and on the same day in each succeeding year, pay to the trustees a sum equal to a twentieth of the amount of the stock issued.

Clause 21.

To invest all monies which under the trust ought to be invested in the names or under the legal control of the trustees in certain stocks or funds or banks.

Clause 22.

1) To conduct the business of the company during the continuance of the security in a proper and efficient manner and to the greatest possible advantage.

2) To keep the usual and proper accounts as provided in the company's Articles of Association.

3) To perform all obligations under the agreement with His Majesty's Government.

4) To keep the company's vessels in good seaworthy order and condition so as to comply with the requirements of the Board of Trade &c.

5) To permit the trustees and such persons as they shall from time to time appoint in writing to view the state and condition of all vessels and to inspect the company's books and accounts.

6) To keep all vessels in process of construction adequately insured and also all vessels for the time being forming point of the fleet insured in the aggregate to the extent of one half of the amount for the time being due to the stock.

7) To furnish to the trustees in every year a full and complete list of certificates by the secretary of the company and all the marines policies for the time being in force.

Clause 24.

To pay to each of the trustees in each and every year during the continuance of their security for their services the sum of £210.

SECOND SCHEDULE

Clause 2.

Provide that whenever the sinking fund established under the trustees amounts to £100,000 it shall be applied in redeeming at par an equivalent amount of stock.

Clause 3.

Any stock not previously redeemed to be redeemed at par the expiration of 20 years.

Clause 5.

Stock to carry interest at the rate of £2.15.0 per cent per annum payable on the 1st July and 1st January in each year.

Clause 6.

Every holder of stock to be entitled to a certificate unde the seal of the company.

Clause 22.

A register of the stock to be kept by the company.

After the agreement was signed and approved Cunard was effectively under the control of the British Government by way of Admiralty.

Appendix III

Lusitania Online: The *Lusitania* Historical Society on the web.

Lusitania Online was established in 1999 by the authors of this book, as the Lusitania Historical Society. The aim of *Lusitania* Online is to provide accurate information about the ship and her last Captain, William Thomas Turner, to those who seek to know the truth.

If you have enjoyed reading this book, you may like to visit our website

www.lusitania.net

Appendix IV

RMS *Lusitania*: Dimensions and Statistics

Chief designer – Leonard Peskett
Keel laid – May 1905
Builder – John Brown & Co. Ltd., Clydebank, Glasgow
Launch date – 7 June 1906
Launched by – Mary, Lady Inverclyde
Official Sea Trials commenced – 29 July 1907
Maiden Voyage – 7 September 1907
Length Overall – 785 feet
Beam – 88 feet
Gross tonnage – 31,550 tons
Displacement – 44,000 tons
Propulsion – Quadruple screw
Engines – Four direct drive Parson's steam turbines
Maximum Speed attained in service – 26.7 knots
Funnels – 4
Masts – 2
Rig – Schooner
Accommodation – 563 First-class, 464 Second-Class, 1,138 Third-
or steerage class
Lifeboat accommodation at time of final voyage – 48 boats
(22 boats from hanging davits and 26 collapsible boats) with
spaces for 2,605 persons
There were also 2,325 life jackets and 35 life buoys
Port of Registry – Liverpool

Appendix V.

The Legend of Charles Voegele:
An intriguing story of humanity in war?

In 2011, we were contacted via our website by a Mr Richard Heier in America, who asked if we had any information about a relative of his, who was supposed to have been a member of *U20*'s crew; a seaman by the name of Charles Voegele. For reasons that will become clear in a moment, we told him we didn't, as this was an aspect of the story that we'd purposefully left out of our book originally, but we put Richard in touch with our friends at the *BundesMilitarArchiv* in Germany whilst we searched elsewhere on his behalf. We also posted two specific requests for information about Voegele on *www.lusitania.net.*

Anyone who has read other books about the *Lusitania* disaster will have heard of Voegele. If the story about him is true, he apparently refused to relay Schwieger's order to prepare a torpedo forward to Raimund Wiesbach, *U20*'s Torpedo Officer, and after being shoved aside and the order duly relayed, Voegele was placed under arrest and subsequently court-martialled and jailed for his attack of humanity/cowardice, whichever way one chooses to view it.

The story of Charles Voegele was first widely printed in Des Hickey and Gus Smith's 1981 book, *SEVEN DAYS TO DISASTER*. (We later discovered however that the story was originally published in December of 1972 as an article by Prof. M A Ricklin of Strasbourg University, in the French newspaper *Le Monde*. Presumably, Hickey and Smith had originally got it from there). Despite making enquiries at the time, we could find nothing to either prove or disprove the story when we were writing *THE LUSITANIA STORY,* so we simply left it out of our book, but there have been other authors, one of whom wrote a *Lusitania* book at a similar time to ours, who were only too pleased to repeat this unsubstantiated "human interest" story in their work. Voegele has appeared in more than one television programme over the years, too. What follows now is the culmination of the research and the many email exchanges between us and Richard Heier on the subject. From Richard:

My mother's oldest brother Jakob Voelker (1900-1987) was married twice. His first wife Lucy Birchler (1900-1952), was descended from Swiss immigrants who had settled in Fulda, Indiana, shortly after 1848. In 1956, the widower Jakob had visited Switzerland and while there had married Gertrud (Trudy) Vögele 1918-living in 2011. Having previously done the seven Birchler family charts, I had then interviewed Trudy in 1983 about her family and transcribed all of her family data. One incident from that interview I still vividly recall, almost three decades later, was the Christian name of one of her many nephews. She said his name was <u>Charles</u> Vögele (1923-2002) and I challenged her, suggesting that in fact it was Karl and not the French form of that name. "No" she insisted, "It is Charles." At the time, I wrote it down as such, and that was the end of the story until late 2010. During that 1983 interview she had also mentioned that Charles, a shoemaker by trade, had some years or decades earlier started a very successful shoe factory in Switzerland.

Forward to autumn 2010: *I am scanning through the donated books in the library of our condo association and discover one which I had read, maybe a couple of years after it first appeared around the early 1980's. It is* **'Seven Days to Disaster, The Sinking of the Lusitania'** *by Des Hickey & Gus Smith ISBN 0-399-12699-6. In it, the book quotes the precise dialogue which supposedly transpired when in 1915, Kapitan-Leutnant Schwieger of the German submarine U20, gave the order to 'ready' the torpedo, which was then fired at the British passenger ship. Kapitan-Leutnant Schwieger had given that order to Charles Voegele to be then relayed by him to the torpedo officer (Raimund Wiesbach). Voegele in turn, had refused to comply on moral grounds and had afterward been court martialled and then jailed in Kiel until the end of the war in November of 1918. I noted the identical names of both my aunt's nephew and that of the sailor* *but mentally put these facts aside since I knew that Trudy's nephew had been born in 1923, i.e. eight years after the sinking and thus suspected no connection. Again time passed, but this time only a few months.*

Wishing to keep my German speaking skill from withering away, I currently participate in two independent conversation groups in downtown Milwaukee. During one of these meetings I had been given a copy of a then current German-American publication "Neu Yorker Staats-Zeitung & German Times" which featured an article about Charles Vögele Fashion Day in 2011. The main theme of the ad was the fact that Charles Vögele GmbH had recently signed the German film star and producer Til Schweiger as one of its several glamorous spokespeople. Apparently the once humble footwear entrepreneur had metamorphosed very successfully into a fashion clothing empire.

*The fact that the almost identical surnames Schwieger and Schweiger are suddenly associated with the names of the two different Charles Vögele's finally arouses my curiosity. As a result I read 'Lusitania, an Epic Tragedy' by Diana Preston ISBN 0-8027-1375-0, hoping to find a possible hint of a family connection between these two Charles Vögele's. The specific bibliographies on the Voegele names in both of these books are super sparse and found me contacting all the authors and publishers without getting their ear even once. Hickey & Smith are probably dead for all I know and Diana Preston could not be approached, even via her publisher. Hickey & Smith gave a brief credit for their Voegele data to a **Professor M.A. Ricklin**, but did not mention his full name, residence or academic affiliation. He was just Professor Ricklin. Thus this reference material could not be re-examined for additional details such as the birth date, birthplace & burial site of the supposed Alsatian sailor, Voegele.*

It was at about this point in his story that Richard contacted us at **Lusitania Online**, asking for our help. As mentioned earlier, we posted his request on our website, *www.lusitania.net* and put him onto the *BundesMilitarArchiv* first, whilst we made some enquiries on his behalf as well. He continues:

What is even more intriguing is the fact that both literature and television broadcasts have put precise, defiant and even treasonable quotes into this supposed sailor's mouth, yet not one *single locatable document hints at, or even supports the fact that he, as an actual person, ever existed. **The Sinking of the Lusitania: Terror at Sea** was aired in England in 2007 & in Germany in 2008, complete with Charles Voegele.*

Ultimately, even the German military archives in Freiburg came up with nothing on Voegele. As a result of this situation, a question arose: Is this Charles Voegele an urban legend that has metamorphosed into literary fact, without anyone wishing to challenge it? Did Des Hickey & Gus Smith fabricate the personage Voegele? If so, why? Somehow I found this scenario too difficult to accept.

If the sailor died indeed in 1920, then there is a fair possibility that his namesake, who was born 1923 in Switzerland, may have been named after him. This likelihood however diminishes considerably, should it prove that the sailor died in 1926. My effort to re-establish my previous 1983 contact with Switzerland, had thus far failed. I never did get a response to any of my emails.

At about this time, we informed Richard that we had found Professor M. A. Ricklin. He had in fact been a Language Professor at Strasbourg University and his article had appeared in the well known French newspaper *Le Monde* in December of 1972. The article was titled; *Last Victim of the Lusitania*. We also gave Richard the contact details for *Le Monde*. He continues:

*By early December 2011 most of the dust settled. I had previously found the birth certificate of the sailor Charles Vögele 1886-1926 and also by then, thanks to the information given by Lusitania Online, I had obtained the University of Strasbourg's records of Prof. M.A. Ricklin. Shortly thereafter, the **Marine Nachrichten Blatt** in Germany, who had seen my query on the* Lusitania.net *website, asked me to share my data, which I readily did. They in turn then tediously combed through all known military archives in Germany and they found the previously ever elusive sailor Karl Vögele, later known as Charles Voegele. Their findings on him were astounding. Yes, he had twice served as a sailor in the Imperial German Navy, but records revealed that he had **never, at any time**, served on a submarine, **nor had he ever been court martialled** as claimed in 'Seven Days to Disaster, The Sinking of the Lusitania' and he'd also **never** been jailed.*

Meanwhile, an entirely separate incoming enquiry about *U20*'s attack on the *Lusitania* was also about to contribute to this event. Herr Ralf Bartzke, an accomplished student of U-boat tactics from Germany, had contacted us via our website asking about the actual torpedoing of the ship. He was in the final stages of collecting data for a specialist computer simulation of the attack. Ralf was gathering and cross checking all the necessary information in order to reconstruct it as accurately as possible. During our exchanges with Ralf, we mentioned the Voegele story.

When Ralf ran the attack through the specially designed computer simulator, he used two scenarios. One, his original intention, the attack using all the available known data; and another introducing an estimated delay of 5 seconds in the firing of the torpedo, caused, if the story were true, by Voegele's refusal to obey the order and Wiesbach's delayed receipt of that order. The simulator showed that if the Voegele story was true, the delayed torpedo would have hit the ship well aft, which patently didn't happen, because of clear evidence to the contrary, plus the undeniable fact that the ship sank bows first. We passed Ralf's findings and the simulator data on to Richard, who concludes:

*The whole story has thus revealed itself to be a complete concoction by this Prof. M.A. Ricklin, which he had initially published in 1972 in the French newspaper **Le Monde**. This conclusion is further reinforced by all the facts now known about the U20's personnel, command procedure, the computer simulated attack and the tight physical structure within the small submarine.*

Richard continues:

The (captain) Schwieger - (actor) Schweiger name similarities, which had triggered this search in the first place, were nothing but a coincidence. I requested the university archivist in Strasbourg to continue searching for the supposed reference material used by Ricklin for his article, but seriously doubt if this was attempted, or if it was, that anything of consequence was ever found as I've still not heard from them. Unfortunately the published mis-information on Voegele, via M.A. Ricklin, still in current French biographical references, seems destined to remain in circulation as previously published, perhaps forever, and will most likely never be retracted.

*Now that we at last have the **facts**, the only remaining mystery is why this fictitious tale was ever created in the first place? What* *possible purpose was its creation back in 1972? That, we doubt we shall ever know.*

The details of this expose were published (in German only) in January 2012 in the **Marine Nachrichten Blatt,** which is also accessible via their website *www.seekrieg14-18.de* on the back issues page. The English version was first published on our website, *www.lusitania.net* at the same time, in the hope of finally dispelling the Charles Voegele myth, once and for all, both in English and in German.

In April of 2012, Bernd Langensiepen of the *Marine Nachrichten Blatt* managed to obtain the relevant official crew list of *U20* for the patrol which sank the *Lusitania*. It was found in the "War Crimes" documents where it had been filed under the heading "Droescher" (Droescher was in fact *U20*'s first Captain) in the Military Archive section of the German Federal Archives.

There is, unsurprisingly of course, **nobody** by the name of Voegele listed as a crew member.

Appendix VI

Results of the Computer Simulation of *U20*'s attack
on the *Lusitania*.

(Simulation performed by Herr Ralf Bartzke in Germany, with additional working information kindly supplied by Tom at *www.uboataces.com*).

Ralf Bartzke is a highly accomplished student of U-Boat tactics in Germany, who has spent a long time researching *U20*'s attack on the *Lusitania* in order to put all the necessary data into a specially designed computer simulator. The essential attack data was taken from Schwieger's War Diary and witness testimonies and depositions. It was also supplemented with other known torpedo data and U-Boat operational procedures for that time. What follows now is the culmination of that research, plus the simulated attack.

When Schwieger planned his opportunist attack on the passing *Lusitania*, it was, of necessity, a case of rapid response planning. He hadn't time to thoroughly study her movements, as he would perhaps have wanted to. Once *U20*'s pilot, Lanz, had positively identified the target as being one of the two Cunard sisters, Schwieger knew that his target was capable of at least 26 knots, that was no secret, but his experienced eye told him that she was not moving as fast as that.

The first stage of his attack planning involved the systematic assimilation of the information gleaned about the intended target (in this case, by Schwieger) at the attack periscope. This system was called UZO (*U-Boot Ziel, Optik* or U-boat targeting, optics). As Schwieger peered into the precision optics of his attack periscope, he had to estimate the target's speed then work out her heading, distance, and bearing to the U-boat's bow. He estimated her speed as being 22 knots, which was an educated guess on his part. Target speed was usually down to an inspired estimate, but again, data

174

such as that gleaned by positive target identification could help enormously. Then he saw her change course, noting in the boat's War Diary that *"the ship turns to starboard and takes a course to Queenstown."* By following his coded wireless instructions from Vice-Admiral Coke, to divert *Lusitania* into Queenstown, Captain Turner was now unknowingly and unwittingly shortening the range between his ship and the lurking *U20*.

To be sure his torpedo found its mark on such a fast target, Schwieger planned to hit the ship in a fairly centralised location, anywhere between her first and fourth funnels and preferably around the second funnel area. Various instruments aboard the U-Boat were used to assist in this. There was a range finding device in the attack periscope itself, called a Stadimeter, which was essentially a split-prism range-finder. Using a double-image of the target ship, it gave a pretty accurate range calculation up to a maximum range of 6,000 meters. (Though at the 6, 000 meter extremity of its range, the stadimeter's accuracy was subject to a 10% error factor). If certain other geometric information such as a known masthead height or funnel height for the target could also be factored in, even more accuracy could be obtained. Fortunately for Schwieger, *Lusitania*'s specifications were well known, thanks to the wealth of material that had been published about her since her completion, particularly publications such as *The Shipbuilder*. (For example, *Lusitania*'s masthead was 165 feet above her waterline). Contrary to popular belief, there was no cross-wire type of target sight in a U Boat's periscope.

On the outside of the periscope's control column was the Target Bearing Ring, which was usually read by an officer standing next to whoever was using the periscope in the close confines of the base of the U-boat's tower. The Target Bearing Ring gave the compass bearing, measured in degrees, of the intended target in relation to the U-Boat's bow.

All the UZO data was then quickly processed manually, using a slide rule and pre-determined tables to rapidly calculate a firing solution. The torpedoes travelled at different speeds, depths, and bearing to bow - all these factors were manually programmed into the torpedo itself. When the torpedo was ready for firing, a light showed up in the U-Boat's control room for the loaded tube containing the now fully primed torpedo. The final firing solution as predicted by Schwieger's calculations is as follows:

Target's speed estimated at 22 knots. Shot distance; 700 metres. G6 Torpedo, optimal speed; 35 knots = 18.01 m/s (meters per second.) Torpedo running depth; 3 meters. Time to Target after firing= 700 meters @ 18.01 m/s = 38,9 seconds. Angle of intersection; near 90 degrees.

Having run submerged at high speed, following the calculated firing plan, *U20* arrived at the plan's pre-disposed firing point. With the boat's speed then reduced, *U20* was turned to port, into its firing position and the designated torpedo was fired ahead of the target. Schwieger then relied on a stopwatch and further periscope observations to check the accuracy of his attack calculations.

Ninety-seven years later, with **the same data** fed into the simulator, the computer simulator projected that the impact point would have been between *Lusitania*'s second and third funnels, (around Frames 161-164) therefore amidships and pretty much where Schwieger was aiming to hit her.

However, as Schwieger observed his torpedo hitting the *Lusitania* through his periscope, the first thing he noticed was that the hit was much further **forward** of where he'd planned. He immediately realised that he'd *over-estimated* the speed of the *Lusitania*. (The ship was in fact making just 18 knots at the time, not his originally estimated 22). Then he saw and noted the almost immediate second, larger explosion. He was at a loss to explain this, putting it down in his War Diary to possibly *"Boilers, coal or powder?"* Schwieger was not to know that by a combination of chance and mis-calculation, his shot had in fact just hit the ship in the one place that **would** render fatal damage to her: the forward cargo hold. This is where the computer simulator now truly comes into its own. As Ralf states:

Let's take the target's speed difference; estimated speed 22 knots – actual speed 18 knots=4 knot difference. 4 knots = 2.06 meters per second. Hit shift therefore = 2.06 mps for 38.9 seconds = 80.1 meters = 262.5 feet FORWARD of the **original** *projected impact point.*

The control system of the G6 torpedo should have had a maximum rate of 1% possible deviation at a range of 700 metres. Maximum possible deviation was thus 7 meters (23 feet).

Allowing for this possible deviation in the calculation gives us a range of the hit being the original 262.5 feet forward of the first simulated impact point +/- another possible 23 feet either way. Allowing for this possible deviation gives a final range of the hit being between 239.5 to 285.5 feet further forward of the original computer projected impact point. Those measurements, (including the allowance for the full scope of the possible torpedo deviation) when transferred to the ship's deck plans, put the impact range anywhere between Frame 247 and possibly as far forward as, Frame 269. The mid-point of this total range is around Frame 258. These frames are all located within the Lusitania's forward cargo hold.

Given that all relevant witness statements put the torpedo's impact behind the foremast, and that there were no survivors from the Baggage Room, (which was immediately above the aft end of the projected impact area) the impact range is effectively narrowed to being anywhere from Frame 247 forward to Frame 257, three meters below the waterline.

This computer simulation has thus confirmed the likelihood of the correctness of our original findings: that Schwieger's torpedo did indeed hit the ship in the aft end of her forward cargo hold, in the vicinity of her foremast, between frames 247 and 257 (we originally said between frames 251 and 256) and certainly three meters below her waterline. It was also where 5,000 live 3-inch artillery shells from the Bethlehem Steel Corporation were stacked, in simple unprotected wooden crates.

A further note on the type of torpedo that was used against the *Lusitania*.

In the chapter **What Sank the Lusitania**, we originally took Schwieger's word for the type of torpedo he'd used. *U20*'s War Diary clearly states that he fired *"one G-Type torpedo"*. This is true, but as Ralf Bartzke discovered, it is also slightly misleading. *U20*'s torpedo tubes, as originally fitted in 1913, were too small in diameter to take a G-Type. The first conversion work was done in 1914 to enable her and her sisters, *U19* and *U21*, to start using the then new, larger G6 torpedo, which was 500mm in diameter and 6 metres long. The G6 was the *first* of the G-Type torpedoes. Later, an updated, slightly faster and more reliable version of the G6, (thereafter uniformly called the "G-Type"), was made available. It quickly became the *Kaiserliche Marine*'s standard torpedo and it was this *later* "G-Type" that travelled at 38 knots, as originally given in the text of this book. After the *Lusitania* was sunk, *U20*'s tubes were subsequently fully and finally converted to be able to use the latest G-Type, which also gave her a re-profiled bow section. However, the torpedo Schwieger fired with such a devastating result at the *Lusitania* was in fact a 35 knot G6. It was only three knots slower but its effects were exactly as we originally described.

A further note on the ship's sinking.

In the chapter *The sinking of the Lusitania*, there is mention of Captain Turner realising that the ship's bows must have struck the bottom, as her noticeable forward momentum suddenly ceased. After having recently tried to plot this with a scaled paper cut-out of the ship and a simple two-line representation (to the same scale as the ship) of the depth of water she went down in, it was realised that this was not in fact the moment the liner's bow hit the bottom. Having then done some further crude projections with a scaled cut-out model of the ship made from light card, it seems probable that her forward momentum ceased when her bow was in fact about 150 feet off the seabed and her stern was out of the water, though by no means perpendicular.

As the cut-out model was rolled over to starboard against a protractor and inclined down at the head, it seemed likely that the front end of the ship would probably quite literally have "dug into" the water, upon encountering the considerable braking effect from the water's natural resistance. The ship was then in all likelihood held back by the still buoyant stern, so arresting the ship's forward motion. The stern would then have settled back a little, in much the same way a car does after heavy braking. With the ship thus momentarily suspended but still rolling to starboard, the mid-ships section would have started to fill with water, with the speed of the sinking greatly increasing as the water entered through the first two funnels. It was at this point that the cut-out model's bow hit the "seabed"; whilst at surface level, the visible part of the ship was approaching the point of rolling onto its beam ends.

Though by no means a proper, thorough, controlled experiment, (it took quite a bit of trial and error just to get the whole model to behave itself!) it does perhaps offer a slightly better understanding of the ship's sinking, but it is certainly true that she hit the bottom starboard bow first, before her stern disappeared from view. Captain Turner couldn't have seen that scenario as he'd thought, because the Bridge would have been completely submerged at the point when the ship's bow actually touched the bottom and he'd have already been in the water.

Appendix VII

Room 40's involvement in the *Lusitania* disaster.

Room 40 at Admiralty House, London, was the hub of British Naval Intelligence. The tracking of German Navy units was one of the main tasks for the staff of Room 40 and a large amount of the Wireless Telegraphy (W/T) traffic from, to and between U-Boats in the North Sea and the Atlantic Ocean was in fact regularly intercepted and deciphered by them. Once decoded, this type of intelligence was passed directly to the upper echelons of the Admiralty; namely: First Sea Lord Jacky Fisher, First Lord Winston Churchill and Admiral Oliver.

Those three men needed to be fully aware of the very latest intelligence updates, particularly updates on the positions of German U-boats. These were not solely obtained from Room 40's wireless intercepts, but also from sighting reports and from the reports of sinkings. Ultimately, it was those three men who made the operational decisions.

During the first week in May of 1915, one particular German U-boat, *U20*, under the command of Kapitan-Leutnant Schwieger, was causing concern to those in the higher rooms of Admiralty House. She was known to be on her way toward Fastnet. Ever since she'd left her base, *U20* had been giving her position to the German Admiralty by Wireless Telegraphy *every 4 hours*. Unbeknownst to her commander, *U20*'s messages were being intercepted and deciphered immediately by the Room 40 intelligence team. In fact, *U20* had her own ledger at Room 40. That ledger is now in the National Archives at Kew, London. It is part of the **ADM137** series. (The files **ADM137/4152** are the U-boat history sheets compiled by Lt.Cdr. Tiarks). Page 4 of *U20*'s ledger from those files is now featured on our website, *www.lusitania.net* and it clearly shows that the British Admiralty had intercepted and decoded EVERY message and sinking report from *U20*, right up to the sinking of the *Lusitania*. (In fact page 5 follows *U20*'s voyage home afterwards, via her intercepted messages). It also clearly proves that those in charge at the Admiralty were indeed **fully** informed of *U20*'s activities, throughout her patrol.

The whole ledger can now be viewed online at:

http://germannavalwarfare.info/02subm/02/U20.html

Appendix VIII

Is it true that....? Lusitania Myths.

As with almost any lost ship, there is always a certain amount of posthumous mythology that lingers long after the event. What follows now is the sort of accepted truths we are often asked to address via our website. *Is it true that.....?*

The *Lusitania* was carrying a fortune in Gold Bullion when she was sunk. No, she wasn't. This myth seems to have come about due to the fact that in common with other British liners, she often carried British Gold to America, a fact that was always reported in *The New York Times* and other American Newspapers. The US Government however, wasn't sending Gold to England, they were supplying war materials. When the *Lusitania* did carry a cargo such as Gold Bullion, it was on her westbound trips, to pay for the war materials, rather than on her homeward trips. The Americans were selling, not buying.

The Germans knew what she was carrying and they deliberately planned to sink her. They did indeed know about the American made munitions that were regularly being shipped across the Atlantic on British, French and Dutch ships. In fact, on June 3rd 1915, *The New York Times* ran a front page story reporting a visit by the German Ambassador, Count Bernstorff, to President Wilson. On page two, there is a bye-line; **SHELLS ON THE LUSI-TANIA.** Bernstorff had laid a copy of the ship's 27-page supplementary manifest in front of Wilson and he then quoted directly from a copy of Bethlehem Steel's shipping note, telling Wilson that "the consignment of 1,250 cases of shrapnel was in fact 5,000 shrapnel shells, filled; and that the total weight of this consignment was 103, 828 lbs". Bernstorff left a memo of these and other figures with Wilson as proof and called Wilson's attention to the "deliberately incorrect marking" of this consignment as "Non-Explosive Shrapnel", when it was known and proven to have been live shrapnel shells. Count Bernstorff seems to have been remarkably accurately informed, but the specific sinking of the *Lusitania* by *U20* was not pre-planned, it was quite clearly a chance encounter. If *U20* really was lying in wait specifically to sink the *Lusitania*, it is doubtful that Schwieger would have wasted precious torpedoes on small fry such as the *Cayo Romano, Arabic, Candidate* and *Centurion*. He would only get one chance at a target such as the *Lusitania* and he'd have had to make it count. If the *Lusitania* was his absolute priority target, he would hardly have advertised his presence by attacking other smaller ships and he certainly would not have taken such a gamble as to hope that a **single** torpedo would prove to be fatal to 45,000 ton ship. After all, he'd had to use a torpedo AND gunfire just to sink the 6,000 ton *Candidate*.

The cargo holds of liners such as the *Lusitania* were too small to carry a worthwhile munitions cargo. Although smaller than the hold areas of a sizeable freighter, the hold of a transatlantic liner was still quite large enough to make it worthwhile. It must also be recalled that the Admiralty had somewhat modified the *Lusitania*'s interior at the front end so as to utilise some of the space on the upper decks to carry their "freight". The liners were used because they were all faster than freighters and in theory, were less likely to be targeted by U-Boats. If proof of such is needed: On December 10th, 1915, just seven months after the *Lusitania* was sunk, *The New York Times* announced that the White Star Liner *Adriatic* had left New York carrying **"18,000 tons of war munitions"** for the Allies. The *Adriatic* was the same age as the *Lusitania*, though somewhat smaller. She was 729 feet long, 75 feet in the beam and was 24,541 Gross Registered Tons. The *Adriatic*'s munitions cargo was valued at **$10,000,000.** *Not a worthwhile load?!* Less than a year later, in August of 1916, *The New York Times* again reported the sailing of another White Star Liner, one of *Adriatic*'s sisters, the *Baltic*, carrying **"18,500 tons of war munitions"** for the Allies. Such reports usually appeared in the New York papers about three to five days after the ship had left and only after their supplementary manifests had been filed with US Customs. This gives a good idea of the sheer scale of the munitions trade. There was **Twenty Million Dollars** worth of exported munitions on just those two ships alone, and on just one voyage each. Ultimately, **well over $1 billion** worth of munitions were exported in this way to Britain from America before the US entry into World War One. Given that the American Press reported both the sailings and the cargoes of these ships so freely, both as front page stories and business page features, (we have a good selection of such articles on our website), the illegal transporting of American-made munitions aboard transatlantic passenger liners, has to have been the worst kept secret of the First World War.

Lusitania's **funnels were painted black to disguise her identity.** The ship's funnels were indeed painted black on her final voyage, but this was not done as some sort of half-baked attempt at a disguise. There could be no realistic hope of disguising a ship with a profile as distinctive as hers merely with paint. Imagine painting a Concorde or a Space Shuttle black, so that nobody would be certain of their identity! The reason is actually very simple. The funnels of *every* ship sailing under British Admiralty charter, even Churchill's Q-Ships, were *always* painted black, to denote such.

The sinking of the *Lusitania* brought America into the war. The *Lusitania* was sunk in 1915. America entered the war in 1917. The sinking was undoubtedly a catalyst, but it was not the causal factor. The straw that broke the camel's back in this respect was the infamous "Zimmermann Telegram".

Kapitan-Leutnant Schwieger and his crew were decorated by the Kaiser for sinking the *Lusitania*. Not so. The medal so often supposed to have been specially awarded to *U20*'s crew was in fact the famous/infamous satirical medal struck by Karl Goetz. The British seized on this piece and stamped out thousands of copies as propaganda. If many at the time believed it had been awarded by the Kaiser to the crew of *U20*, it could only have served to further the original propaganda purposes of the British. Schwieger was awarded the *"Pour Le Merite"* medal, (more famously known as the *Blue Max*) in 1917 purely in recognition of his success as a U-Boat commander. He was sixth in the league table of the top U-Boat Captains, but the citation for his award made no mention of the *Lusitania*.

Captain Turner disobeyed a specific Admiralty instruction to steer a mid-channel course. Let us be quite clear about this. Captain Turner was *not* navigating his ship through a channel. The **Atlantic Ocean**, off the Old Head of Kinsale (or if you prefer, the **Celtic Sea**), is patently NOT a channel. Trying to re-designate that area (as the Admiralty have ceaselessly tried to do) by constantly referring to it as *The Irish Channel* doesn't change the simple geographical fact that the next piece of land due south of The Old Head of Kinsale is a little over SEVENTY MILES away, and the simple oceano-graphical fact that the wreck of the *Lusitania* lies in water that is 93 metres, that's 50 Fathoms, deep. The English Channel is only 50 *metres* deep on average, or roughly 25 Fathoms if you prefer. The Bristol Channel averages a depth of 14.2 metres, or 8.3 Fathoms approximately. One could go on!

Captain Turner sailed too close to shore. Captain Turner did nothing of the sort. He was told to maintain at least ten miles between his ship and the Irish coastline. The *Lusitania* was four-teen miles offshore when she was hit. The wreck sits on the seabed eleven and a quarter miles offshore, with her bows orientated roughly north-east, toward land. (Turner put the helm toward land to try to beach her after the torpedo struck). Even as she was sinking, she never crossed the Admiralty imposed ten-mile limit. Despite such geographical certainties, the Admiralty have **always** maintained (to this day) that Turner was *deliberately* sailing *perilously* close, to quote Captain Webb in his infamous memo-randum: *"some eight miles off the Irish coast, maintaining what appears to have been his usual peacetime route"*. As a point of interest, *Lusitania*'s "usual peacetime route" was only *three* miles off the Southern Irish coast and only ships coming closer than *five* miles to shore were reported, for the offence of breaching their war risks insurance.

Captain Turner steered a straight, undeviating course, disobeying standing Admiralty orders to Zig-Zag. NO such Admiralty orders were in force till *after* the *Lusitania* disaster. The specific order to Zig-Zag was *draft dated* April 16th 1915 but its actual circulation outside of Admiralty House didn't start till May 2nd, by which time Turner and the *Lusitania* were already on the open ocean, heading home. The *general* circulation of that specific order was achieved about a week or so after that, which is the point in time that it officially became a "standing order", once every British ship's master had a printed copy of it in his possession. Certainly, nobody at the Admiralty ever relayed such an order by wireless to the *Lusitania*. The very first time Captain Turner saw that order was when it was used against him at the Mersey inquiry in June. There was an *advice note* dated February 10th 1915 which Turner *did* have, but that note only *"recommended"* steering *"a* *serpentine course"* if a submarine was actually *"sighted"*. In any case, Turner *had* to steer a straight, undeviating course. He needed to get an *accurate* fix on his position, so as to plot a safe course through the mine-free channel into Queenstown, as per the *direct* wireless order from Vice Admiral Coke, to bring his ship in.

The second explosion was about 15-30 seconds after the torpedo explosion. It is not unlike reading several different witness statements to the same car crash. Everyone means well, but each person has a different perspective on the event. In writing this book, we gave our preference to statements from people who were trained observers, rather than just those of innocent bystanders, but that is not to say that all passenger statements were inaccurate. More than a few of the passenger statements put the second explosion as being *"almost instantaneous"*, *"on the heels of the first explosion"*, *"immediately after the first explosion"*, or more telling; that both explosions were *"like a short **boom**, followed straightaway by a much larger, rumbling sort of **bang**"*. (Anyone who has ever heard ammunition being professionally detonated for the purpose of its disposal will recognise *that* sound description!).

The people who made such statements tended to be near to the *Lusitania*'s Bridge, Forward Well Deck, or Foremast areas. It is most important to remember that their statements were deliberately *NOT* used at the Public Inquiry into the disaster. The further aft people were located at the time of the torpedo strike, the more the perspectives differed in their statements; even down to those people who honestly swore that they had actually seen a second torpedo hit the ship aft or amidships, whilst there were others who sincerely stated that there was a second submarine that put another torpedo into the *Lusitania*'s PORT side. It is equally important to remember that these are the statements that *were, deliberately* used at the Public Inquiry.

One hundred years after the *Lusitania* went to the bottom of the Atlantic Ocean, (or Celtic Sea!) the myths are now slowly dying out. Sadly however, every now and again, some of these "Old Chestnuts" resurface, (usually in scantily researched television documentaries or on the internet). They get repeated, even though they really do not stand up to competent scrutiny. Whenever they do get repeated, they seem to be awarded the status of truth, at least for a time. Until they die out again.

Appendix IX

The *Lusitania*, ongoing.

The indefatigable 86 year-old Gregg Bemis continues his earnest quest for the final answer both on and off the wreck. The 2011 dives however revealed that after nearly a century on the bottom and having been used for naval target practice, (there are still **many** unexploded World War 2 "Hedgehog" depth charges scattered amongst the ship's debris field), the wreck of the *Lusitania* is now deteriorating at an alarming rate. The collapse of the hull has well and truly begun and its total collapse cannot now be far away.

During the 2011 season's dives, which were hampered by bad weather and some equipment problems, they were able to get a small ROV called *Video-ray* inside the forward hold, through a breach in the Port side of the hull caused by the wreck's natural deterioration. Penetrating about twenty five feet or so into the devastated cargo hold, they found and filmed stacks and stacks of upturned copper ingot bars and huge quantities of .303 rifle ammunition, as well as clear evidence of severe damage that was not characteristic of the natural partial collapse of the wreck. However, the crucial area to be examined lies underneath all that devastation, against the sea floor, buried under another twenty or so feet of heavy and probably very unstable wreckage. To get to it, all the debris on top would have to be moved, which given the wreck's condition, could possibly cause the Port side hull plating to collapse on top of it all anyway, unless it were cut away first.

Off the wreck, Gregg had extensive testing done in 2011 at California's Lawrence Livermore Laboratory, a US Government establishment set up specifically to engineer and test explosions. Gregg was looking at the more popular theories as to the probable cause of the fatal, second explosion. As a result of their testing, a coal dust explosion was most definitely ruled out, as were

187

Aluminium fine powder, Gun Cotton and an explosion of the ship's boilers.

Although the coal dust produced something of a fireball, which in its own dense atmosphere didn't last very long; there was no actual, powerful explosion. Likewise, the Aluminium fine powder produced an extremely bright flash and some dazzling burning, but again no powerful explosion was produced and no eyewitness statements described such a brilliant flash. The Gun Cotton however, produced a fiery explosion which did cause some damage, but again, nothing like the catastrophic type required to sink the ship. The last test, boiler explosion, was certainly noisy; but the largest part of that explosion's force was found to have been vented straight up the relevant funnel. Flying fragments of metal would undoubtedly have killed anyone working in the vicinity of a boiler that exploded, but would certainly not have caused catastrophic damage to the hull. So though all four explosions were spectacular in their own different ways, none proved destructive enough to have caused any great damage, and certainly not the kind of fatal structural damage to the ship, that would have caused her to sink in a mere eighteen minutes. As Gregg himself publicly stated:

> *"A munitions explosion* (in the cargo hold) *would have been in the right place to create the devastation we have seen,* (in that area of the wreck) *as well as to create a significant additional inflow of water to make the sinking of the bow take place in such a record time. The bottom line for me, I think, is that the second explosion **had** to be on a par with, or greater than, the torpedo explosion, to result in the ship vanishing beneath the waves in only 18 minutes. That is a record time..."*

And that's it in a nutshell, because the extensive testing has proved beyond any doubt, that not one of the four explosions tried at the laboratory was capable of producing anything like the force of the torpedo explosion. So if nothing else, the thorough California laboratory testing has at least soundly laid four more *Lusitania* myths to rest.

In April of 2013, Gregg had a successful meeting with the Irish Heritage Minister. They finally agreed to Gregg's further detailed underwater examination of the wreck, with a view to possibly gaining the necessary access to the hold area. The projected diving operations to be concluded hopefully in time for 2015, the Centenary of the disaster.

It is of course, still entirely possible that the *Lusitania* will indeed keep her final secret. If the inevitable deterioration of the wreck causes her Port side to finally and fully collapse onto her fatally damaged Starboard side, before Gregg can complete his detailed underwater work, then the Admiralty may yet achieve the physical obfuscation they've sought for a century. But as time marches relentlessly on and more new data is gleaned, it so far only seems to support our initial work; this: *The Lusitania Story.*

Bibliography

Ballard, Dr Robert & Dunmore Spencer, *Exploring the Lusitania* Weidenfeld & Nicholson, 1995

Beesley, Patrick, *Room 40. British Naval Intelligence 1914–1918*, Hamish Hamilton, 1982

Churchill, Winston, *The World Crisis*, MacMillan, 1941

Hoehling, A.A. & M., *The Last Voyage of the Lusitania*, Pan Books, 1959

Jenkins, Roy, *Asquith*, Collins, 1964

Judd, Dennis, *Empire*, HarperCollins, 1996

Keegan, John, *The First World War*, Hutchinson, 1998

Lord, Walter, *A Night to Remember*, Penguin Books, 1978

MacDougall, Phillip, *Mysteries on the High Seas*, Book Club Associates, 1984

Massie, Robert K., *Dreadnought*, Johnathan Cape, 1992

Nowell-Smith, Simon, ed., *Edwardian England*, Oxford University Press, 1965

Papen, Franz von, *Memoirs*, Andre Deutsch, 1952

Peeke, Mitch & Walsh-Johnson Kevin, *Lusitania and Beyond: The Life of Commodore William Thomas Turner*, Avid Publications, 2001

Priestley, J.B., *The Edwardians*, Heineman, 1970

Simpson, Colin, *Lusitania*, Longman, 1972

Reports
– *British Vessels Lost at Sea 1914–1918*, HMSO
– *Board of Trade Report into the Loss of the SS Lusitania*, HMSO
– *British Army's 1915 Treatise on Ammunition*, The Royal Artillery Historical Trust

Other Sources

<u>Videotape</u>
Murder on the Atlantic, The History Channel
Secrets of the Deep, episode entitled *The Mystery of the Lusitania*, Channel 4
The Sinking of the Lusitania, National Geographic

<u>CD Rom</u>
Eyewitness, (interview with Margaret Haig, the second Countess Rhondda, *Lusitania* survivor. Recorded 15 October 1950), BBC History Magazine

<u>Unpublished Papers</u>
Garstin, David, Chief Engineer RN (Retired), *Turbine Propulsion in Ships* –
—— *Notes on Propeller Vibration*

Index